TERMINAL
DEGREES

TERMINAL DEGREES

The Job Crisis in Higher Education

Emily K. Abel

Library of Congress Cataloging in Publication Data

Abel, Emily K.
  Terminal degrees.

  Includes index.
  1. College teachers—United States—Supply and demand.
2. College teachers—Tenure—United States.   3. Graduate
students—Employment—United States.   4. College teachers,
Part-time—United States.   5. Women college teachers—
United States.   I. Title.
LB2335.3.A24   1984   331.7′6137812′0973   83-26876
ISBN 0-03-068917-1 (alk. paper)

Portions of Chapter 3 were reprinted from "Teachers and Students on The Slow
Track: Inequality in Higher Education," *Socialist Review* (November-December,
1981).

Portions of Chapter 7 were reprinted from "Collective Protest and the Meritocracy," *Feminist Studies* Volume 7, Number 3 (Fall 1981): 505–538, by permission
of the publisher, *Feminist Studies, Inc.,* c/o Women's Studies Program, University
of Maryland, College Park, Maryland 20742.

Published in 1984 by Praeger Publishers
CBS Educational and Professional Publishing
a Division of CBS Inc.
521 Fifth Avenue, New York, NY 10175 USA

© 1984 by Emily K. Abel

456789 052 987654321

Printed in the United States of America
on acid-free paper

To
Rick, Laura, Sarah, and Heather

FOREWORD by Stanley Aronowitz

There have been at least two versions of the American dream in this century. The first is the more familiar one: work hard and with a little luck and help from the bank you might open a business and prosper. This is not the "get rich dream" which, for working people at least, only came with winning the lottery. It was the rank and file version of the Protestant ethic, the ideology that held America to be a land of opportunity. In this version of the dream, a small business was the pinnacle, but there were grades of success. In the consumerist variant, diligence and responsibility could also yield a secure and happy life with all its amenities — a single family home, a fairly late model car, some savings to cushion against the inevitable misfortunes that are part of the game. Even if one did not enter the middle class of small shopkeepers, driver/owners of trucks or independent mechanics, "making it" signified working for a powerful large employer, the government, or belonging to a strong union able to win substantial concessions from management at the bargaining table.

The second bite at the dream was professional mobility. Only in America could a poor kid become a doctor or a lawyer — providing he put the old shoulder to the wheel, got good grades, did a little extra work at school, and, equally vital, stayed on the right side of teachers and school administrators. Except for the very few for whom medicine and the law were "callings" in the classical religious meaning of the term, professional achievement was a question of status and economic security; the *content* of the particular field was far less important than its instrumental and social value for the individual.

Emily Abel's *Terminal Degrees* is about the collapse of the second version of the American dream in the 1970s and 1980s. Abel has not only documented the fact of the rapid disappearance of the number of professional jobs in comparison with the capacity of colleges and universities to produce qualified candidates, she has let those who have been cast off by the system that promised them access to the dream speak for themselves. The result is a remarkable book that is unique in the literature concerning the decline of the American century, studies of con-

vii

temporary higher education and employment, and occupational studies. Abel combines a thorough and incisive analysis of the dominant trends in academic employment with a subtle and sympathetic treatment of the psychological dispositions of the victims. Her study focuses on academic employment among those holding advanced degrees in the humanities and social sciences. These categories were once considered anomalous in an otherwise growing demand for qualified professionals. Yet, her study is increasingly relevant for the "hard sciences" and engineering and law, which are beginning to experience labor surpluses. The stagnation in the growth of institutions of post-secondary education in the past fifteen years, combined with the enormous increase in qualified professionals because of the expansion in the previous twenty years owing to virtually continuous economic and demographic expansion, has produced a crisis in academic employment that appears structurally unrelated to temporary changes in the overall performance of the economy. Structural academic unemployment is an endemic feature of the labor market, and it has wrought havoc in the lives of a substantial proportion of two recent generations for whom success meant a secure academic appointment, even when the pay was lower than that enjoyed by similarly trained professionals in the private business sectors.

As long as the American economy expanded, and with it the public educational institutions, the historic Anglo-American doctrine according to which individual achievement was the path to various levels of personal and social success confronted no obstacles. America was a place where white persons of humble origins could enter the status elites when they were effectively barred from places of economic and political power. For the professional, status constituted the equivalent of "crude material success" but it was no less invidious. During the past fifteen years, the traditional assumption that individual achievement is the key to success has suffered significant erosion. As Abel demonstrates, the overproduction of academics with credentials has resulted in rapid expansion of a migrant, part-time labor force in many colleges and universities. Lacking job security, health and pension benefits, or even, in most cases, the rudiments of participation in departmental and disciplinary life, this new academic proletariat, although essential for the maintenance of the shrinking fund-starved public institutions, is almost bereft of rights even as its responsibilities within the academy expand.

In many cases, given the still pervasive ideology of individualism, the degraded professionals frequently blame themselves for their failure to find a permanent, tenure-track job even though they know well the essential facts of the academic economy. Since the labor market conditions oblige them to fend for their individual selves, they either leave their chosen field and enter an entirely unrelated occupation, or remain hopeful in a hopeless world of part-time employment that one day their ship will come in bearing a full-time dignified position.

Although Abel paints a grim portrait, she has not confined her work to analysis and description. She provides prescription as well, one that relies on the ability of the academic proletariat to recognize that its collective fate requires collective organization, chiefly trade unionism. At the same time, she is critical of the existing unions for their almost exclusive concern with the full-time tenured faculty and their refusal to organize among the part-timers.

Here Abel's argument strikes to the heart of the issue. Unless the part-timers recognize that they are destined, for the foreseeable future at any rate, to remain without much hope of getting a full-time job, they will remain at the margins of the academic labor market. Only when they organize as part-timers and win rights on the basis of their collective strength, can they hope to establish some kind of security and dignity. But it is definitely not the American dream. Rather, it resembles what teachers began to understand in the late fifties and early sixties: they were not going "up" in the professional ladder of recognition and success. Their real task was to reject mobility aspirations and win commonly held gains. As history has proved, this changed perspective took nearly a half-century to become part of the collective perceptions of the teachers, but when it was consolidated, they formed two of America's most powerful unions, the American Federation of Teachers and the National Education Association.

This is an important book for those who have with bitterness or bewilderment watched the steady deterioration of the economic and social position of a large fraction of American technical and traditional intellectuals. I am sure that Abel's book will become a kind of reference book, a handbook, a beacon for the academic underclass itself. But more broadly, it is a paradigm for what is happening to America in this era of planned and unplanned shrinkage, a case study in historical and far-reaching change.

ACKNOWLEDGMENTS

I wish to thank Cara Anderson, Edna Bonacich, Alice Clement, Sherna Gluck, Carrie Menkel-Meadow, Margaret K. Nelson, Deborah Rosenfelt, Mary Aickin Rothschild, Sarah Stage, and Julia Wrigley who read and commented on individual chapters. The United Professors of California provided funding for the survey of temporary faculty in the California State University and College system. Above all, I am grateful to the 43 displaced academics who generously shared their experiences with me.

CONTENTS

INTRODUCTION

As the economy continues to contract, increasing numbers of Americans are discovering that they cannot achieve their aspirations. Young people who came of age during a period of abundance and expected to enjoy lives of plenty now are urged to lower their sights. The diminishing value of academic credentials symbolizes this narrowing of opportunities. For over a century, the American dream of success has been based on the premise that economic and social advancement automatically follows scholastic achievement. Moreover, the massive expansion of higher education during the 1960s seemed to fulfill the promise of providing equal educational opportunities for all citizens. However, as the job market for both high school and college graduates deteriorates, it becomes increasingly clear that schools are not the magical path to the good life. Some social analysts argue that graduates who realize their newly minted degrees do not guarantee high occupational status become frustrated, disillusioned, and politically restive.[1] But others contend that schools defuse the potential for radical political activity by convincing students to internalize failure: they are taught to transform occupational defeat into self-directed blame.[2]

Ph.D. candidates and recipients have placed even greater faith in education than other Americans. Most have a long history of academic achievement and excellence. Moreover, their talents

1

and performances have been rewarded with high grades, admission to elite universities, and scholarships. Confident that advanced degrees would entitle them to work that was both meaningful and socially recognized, they remained in school longer than their contemporaries. However, since the early seventies, a growing proportion of doctorates and doctoral candidates in the humanities and social sciences either have failed to find any academic jobs or have obtained only marginal, part-time employment. This book examines these displaced academics at the juncture when they confront the possibility that they may be unable to convert academic credentials into career success.

Many displaced academics entered graduate school during the late sixties and early seventies, when it was widely believed that the golden age of higher education would last forever. The graduate student body more than tripled between 1960 and 1975, growing from 314,000 to 1,054,000.[3] In 1970 alone, almost 30,000 Ph.D.s were awarded and, by 1976, annual production had risen to 34,000. By contrast, fewer than 10,000 people received doctorates in 1960.[4] The growth in the number of Ph.D.s was particularly striking in the humanities.[5] Over 25 percent of all humanities doctorates ever awarded in the United States were conferred during the 1960s and over 44 percent during the following decade.[6]

This rise in the number of doctorates was partly a result of the burgeoning undergraduate enrollment. Between 1960 and 1970, the number of college students jumped from 3.8 million to 9.2 million.[7] In 1960, 11 percent of all people between the ages of 25 and 29 had attended four or more years of college; in 1975, the proportion was 22 percent.[8] This extraordinary enrollment growth can be explained partly by the coming of age of the baby boom. By the mid-sixties, the unusually large crop of babies born during the postwar years began to reach college age. But increased access to higher education during the 1960s and early 1970s also was a response both to changes in the occupational structure and to the demands of working-class and minority groups for equal educational opportunity. Between 1950 and 1970, the proportion of technical and professional workers in the labor force doubled, growing from 7.1 percent to 14.5 percent.[9] Universal access to postsecondary institutions was a key issue for many minority groups involved in the social protests of the sixties. It was also the demand to which state officials may have preferred to respond, for they could create the illusion of upward mobility through education far more readily than they could effect fundamental social and economic changes. Low-tuition, open-admission colleges were established rapidly throughout the country during the 1960s. Women, working-class students, and members of minority groups thronged to these institutions, lured by the belief that a college degree would enable them to cross the great divide separating manual from mental work.

Thus, the pool of students eligible to enroll in graduate school increased greatly. Furthermore, an unprecedented number of college teachers were required to cope with the influx of undergraduates. A study conducted under the auspices of the American Historical Association and published in 1962 warned that a serious shortage of Ph.D.s in history would begin by 1964![10] Students were attracted to graduate school by a number of factors. In those halcyon days of higher education, faculty salaries were high, research support abundant, and class size low. Moreover, students who had been influenced by the political movements of the sixties tended to shun employment in the corporate sector. Although universities were hardly immune to the criticisms of student radicals, academic careers appeared to be more compatible with progressive morality. Graduating seniors assumed that doctorates would enable them to perform meaningful work while obtaining substantial material rewards. The appeal of graduate school was heightened by the ease with which Ph.D. recipients were finding employment. Between 1960 and 1970, the number of faculty in four-year institutions expanded 138 percent, and many new doctorates could choose among several attractive job offers.[11] William G. Bowen, president of Princeton University, has recalled, "At meetings of many professional associations in the fifties and sixties, department chairmen literally stood in line to interview job candidates."[12] Beginning graduate students had little reason to doubt they also would be successful. Most were ignorant of the fact that a high proportion of new doctorates historically have failed to receive academic appointments. As early as 1966, Allan Cartter did predict that the number of college students would begin to decline in the 1970s and that the sellers' market for Ph.D.s would disappear.[13] Nevertheless, as one observer put it, he was a "voice crying in the wilderness."[14] Just as most Americans confidently assumed that their country's affluence and world dominance would last indefinitely, so academics blithely looked forward to the uninterrupted expansion of higher education.

However, by the early 1970s, it became clear that there were limits to growth, even in higher education. The first intimations of dwindling opportunities for Ph.D.s were reports that graduates of some of the most prestigious institutions experienced difficulty finding employment. For example, of the 55 graduates and doctoral candidates from the English Department at the University of California, Berkeley who applied for college teaching jobs in 1973, only 24 found them.[15] By the late 1970s, such incidents had become widespread. Statistics garnered by Lewis C. Solmon clearly demonstrate that doctorates in the 1970s were competing for a diminishing supply of jobs. Only 16 percent of all humanities Ph.D.s in 1969 were still seeking employment at the time they received their degrees, whereas a third of the 1979 cohort had not found work by graduation.[16]

Furthermore, success in obtaining an initial appointment no longer was a guarantee of permanent academic employment. A growing proportion of faculty positions were nonladder, temporary jobs, which terminated automatically after one to three years.[17] And tenure became increasingly difficult to attain. The requirements for tenure and promotion were raised; one or even two books were demanded by schools where previously a few articles had sufficed. Moreover, an increasing number of colleges and universities instituted tenure quotas.[18] Thus, some junior faculty fulfilled all the requirements but still were denied tenure. In the late seventies, the Modern Language Association warned that only a small fraction of all recent Ph.D.s in English and foreign languages could expect to make lifelong careers of college teaching.[19]

Long-term projections of the academic job market are even more sobering. Although predicting social phenomena is an inexact art, at best, most forecasters have been convinced that, throughout the eighties, teaching jobs will be obtained by only a tiny proportion of the scholars who seek them.[20] One of the gloomiest projections is offered by Bowen, who anticipates that between 1980 and 1995 there will be 100,000 openings for new faculty in all disciplines, the same number as were filled during the three peak years of 1965-67. During these fifteen years, about 450,000 new Ph.D.s will be awarded.[21]

Explanations of the current employment situation for Ph.D.s and projections for the future generally rely heavily on demographic and enrollment trends. Undergraduate enrollment growth peaked in 1972.[22] Moreover, by 1997, the number of youth between 18 and 24 will be 23 percent lower than it was in 1981.[23] Because the people who will constitute this cohort already are born, this figure can be calculated with some degree of accuracy. Its significance, however, has been debated widely. Since the early 1970s, the traditional college-age population has represented a dwindling proportion of undergraduate enrollment. Between 1972 and 1978, the fraction of college students over the age of 24 grew from 29 to 35 percent.[24] Although a few forecasters assume the continued rise in the number of "nontraditional" students will offset the decline in the college-age population, most are less sanguine. Older students generally enroll in college on a part-time basis,[25] and they tend to be concentrated in institutions that typically have refrained from employing Ph.D.s.[26] The Carnegie Council on Policy Studies in Higher Education estimates that, by 1997, undergraduate enrollment will be 5 to 15 percent lower than the 1978 level.[27]

This projected enrollment dip will coincide with a drop in the number of vacancies in faculty positions. Because a disproportionate number of all university and college professors were hired during the sixties, the mean age of the faculty is relatively low. In 1978, 60 percent of all faculty were under the age of 45, and just 15 percent were 55 and older.[28] Hence, an unusually small percentage of teachers can be expected either to retire or die during the next fifteen years.[29]

Doctorates in the humanities and social sciences are in a particularly vulnerable position. The primary employment of Ph.D. recipients in these fields traditionally has been college teaching. Although over half of the Ph.D.s in the physical and life sciences entered nonacademic employment in 1974, 70 percent of the doctorates in the social sciences and 85 to 90 percent of those in the humanities obtained academic positions.[30] Most Ph.D. candidates in the latter fields still focus their expectations exclusively on college teaching.[31] Moreover, these disciplines already have suffered from dramatic shifts in student interest.[32] The proportion of all undergraduates majoring in vocational and professional programs grew from 38 to 58 percent between 1969 and 1976; by contrast, the percentage majoring in the humanities plunged from 9 to 5 percent, and in the social sciences from 12 to 8 percent.[33] The surveys of college freshmen conducted annually by Alexander Astin indicate that these disciplines will not recoup their losses in the near future. Six percent of the students entering college in the fall of 1980 expected to concentrate in accounting, 8 percent in business, and 9 percent in engineering. However, just .9 percent believed they would major in English, .6 percent in history, .4 percent in sociology and a mere .1 percent in anthropology.[34]

The one cause for optimism is the recent decline in the number of Ph.D.s awarded.[35] Just as undergraduates are seeking to make themselves market proof by selecting vocational majors, so college graduates who previously might have sought advanced training in the humanities and social sciences are flocking to professional schools.[36] Between 1973 and 1979, the number of doctorates conferred in the humanities decreased 33 percent.[37] Nevertheless, this decline only minimally can alleviate the job crisis. The number of doctorates awarded annually is still greater than the number conferred in 1967, the year when faculty positions were most plentiful.[38] In addition, unsuccessful applicants from previous years swell the ranks of the job seekers. Thus, the demand for college teaching positions continues to exceed the supply.

But changes in demography and enrollment alone cannot explain the collapse of the job market in higher education. By the early 1980s, all social services were under attack by political conservatives. Campaigning against the "excesses" of the public sector, the New Right successfully organized tax revolts to reduce state and local government budgets. Reagan interpreted his election as a mandate to reverse the growth of social entitlements, and he proceeded to accelerate the pace of military spending while cutting welfare and public services.

The consequences of this shift in priorities have been profound throughout higher education. Shortly after coming to office, the Reagan administration announced its intention to reduce research funding for universities and to revise both the eligibility criteria and the scope of financial aid programs. Even before the details of the new schemes were divulged, many middle-class students relinquished their dreams of attending private colleges and settled for state universities or local community colleges. Uncertainty about grants and loans deterred large numbers of poorer students from applying even to public institutions.[39] Although financial aid programs were not cut to the extent originally feared, far less money was available for students.[40] The overall budget for higher education grew from $11.7 billion in 1980 to $11.9 billion in 1983; this represented a drop in real terms of 15 percent.[41] State appropriations for higher education also continued to rise, but almost nowhere did they keep pace with inflation.[42] In 1982-83, the increase in state allocations was the smallest in over twenty years, and two states appropriated less money for colleges and universities than they had in 1980-81.[43] The worst victim was Oregon, whose eight-campus system of higher education suffered an 18 percent loss in purchasing power between 1980 and 1982.[44] Throughout the country, administrators of public institutions, who previously had spoken fearfully of the projected enrollment plunge, sought deliberately to reduce the size of their entering classes by imposing or increasing tuition and raising the standards for admission.[45]

These cutbacks in government spending occurred at a time when higher education already was facing serious financial problems. The impact of inflation on colleges and universities was particularly severe because, as labor-intensive institutions, they could not adopt the usual methods of cutting costs.[46] Between 1970 and 1976, the annual cost per student in higher education rose 44 percent, from $2,450 to $3,580.[47]

Cuts in governmental aid to higher education disproportionately affected public colleges and universities, prompting some observers to argue that academic policy makers deliberately favored the private sector.[48] Nevertheless, private institutions were not immune. Most rely heavily on the federal government for support; moreover, they faced rising competition from public institutions for private sources of funding.[49] During the 1970s, 141 private colleges closed their doors.[50] Others raised their tuition far beyond the reach of the vast majority of prospective students.[51]

Although all human services are under siege, higher education may be especially vulnerable. By the mid-seventies, it had become clear that increased access to higher education had not defused social discontent. In fact, government officials, educators, and members of high-level commissions began to speak with anxiety about the "over-educated workforce."[52] Labor unrest, absenteeism, and high turnover rates were attributed to the dissatisfactions of educated workers whose expectations of meaningful and well-paid jobs outstripped the opportunities offered by the job market. The potential dangers attributed to workers with college degrees were of special concern. Although low-tuition, nonselective colleges promised social mobility, students qualified for jobs that were no less repetitive and routinized than those of their less-educated parents. Moreover, the jobs obtained by most college graduates during this period did not reflect their educational attainment. According to a report prepared by H.E.W. in 1972, a very large proportion of the recipients of B.A.s were forced to accept jobs that previously had been held by people with lesser credentials.[53] The following year, the Carnegie Commission on Higher Education warned that the United States could face "a political crisis because of the substantial number of disenchanted and underemployed or even unemployed college graduates."[54] Policy makers who shared such fears were not eager to promote equal educational opportunities for all citizens.

By the early 1980s, criticism of education took a new turn. Americans suddenly discovered that their youth were grossly uneducated. They rarely read, took few science and mathematics courses, spent little time in the classroom, and did almost no homework. In the spring of 1983, a number of prestigious commissions issued calls for a vast reform of the entire system of education. "Our nation is at risk," declared the National Commission on Excellence in Education, appointed by Reagan to examine the state of the country's schools.[55] This warning soon was echoed by two other groups of prominent business people and educators who alerted the public to the dangers emanating from the educational deficiencies of American youth.[56]

But, though educational reform has been placed at the forefront of the national agenda, it is doubtful that the new concern about the quality of American schooling will stimulate demand for the services of unemployed Ph.D.s in the humanities and social sciences. Because the prevailing view is that education must be made more responsive to the needs of capital, educators are seeking to intensify the shift in emphasis from liberal arts to technical subjects. The current campaign for educational reform has two major focuses, each directed toward a different segment of the work force. Reformers claim first that national survival is dependent on the production of highly skilled scientists and engineers. Just as the launching of Sputnik in 1957 impelled the government to demand an increased flow of scientists and engineers from the nation's universities, so educators now are urged to respond to the challenge presented by Japanese business. Although the competition has altered, the prescription remains the same: the mastery of technical subjects is heralded as the solution to the nation's problems.

The other component of the campaign for educational reform is directed toward lower-level employees. The economy is stagnant, we are told, not only because industry lacks highly trained scientists, but also because the typical worker can neither perform simple calculations nor write a well-constructed paragraph. If we want to restore America's prosperity, we must arrest this decline in basic skills. The "back to basics" movement has created new jobs for English Ph.D.s willing to staff the composition courses that have burgeoned on campuses throughout the country. But, in general, the movement disparages the knowledge and values that the humanities and social sciences traditionally have sought to impart. It champions discipline, uniform testing, and rudimentary arithmetic and writing skills, not imaginative thought or intellectual independence.[57]

The new sense of urgency about the quality of education also is unlikely to stimulate either enrollment or public expenditures. Conservatives unite in blaming the educational reforms of the 1960s for the failures of schools of the 1980s, and they point to lax admissions policies as one of the chief culprits. Although one means of reversing the decline in test scores might be to encourage students to remain in school longer, reformers stress the need to raise the entrance barriers to colleges and universities. Their watchwords are "standards" and "excellence," not "equal opportunity" or "broadened access." Public concern about the state of education may stem the tide of cutbacks, but it will not spur a new infusion of government funds into colleges and universities. The report of the launching of Sputnik could inaugurate a period of unprecedented growth in public expenditures for education because it occurred during a time of unusual prosperity. Coming during an era of fiscal conservatism, accounts of Japan's economic superiority will not evoke a similar response.

In short, it is doubtful that the academic job crisis is simply a temporary phenomenon. One reason to study displaced academics is that a substantial proportion of new Ph.D. recipients in the humanities and social sciences can expect to be dislodged from their career paths. In addition, their plight reverberates throughout the profession. For example, the specter of unemployment has altered the graduate school experience. Not only are college seniors deterred from applying to graduate school, but many Ph.D. candidates either delay the completion of their degrees or drop out entirely. Those who persevere in the face of grim warnings tend to be sustained by unrealistic expectations. Junior faculty also are threatened by the increasing number of unemployed academics and haunted by fears of descending into the ranks of the marginally employed. Anecdotal evidence suggests that they are less willing to take controversial positions, join labor unions, or challenge their superiors. Although senior faculty are shielded from the immediate impact of the unemployment crisis, they are affected indirectly in many ways. Many are concerned that research in their fields may suffer if younger scholars continue to be forced out of academia. Moreover, because their own prestige and power are dependent on the successful placement of graduate students at well-known institutions, their stature is diminished when their most promising protégés cannot find jobs, even at institutions formerly beneath their condescension.

An examination of displaced academics also serves to illuminate a number of interrelated themes. The first is the nature of work. Although work is the primary means of self-expression and of achieving autonomy in our society, only a minute proportion of the population are able to realize their full potential in their jobs.[58] Academics who are prevented from utilizing their skills and training thus face a problem that is endemic among the work force. Second, this study can help to advance our understanding of the meaning of professionalism in the lives of individuals. Displaced academics share with all workers the threat of unemployment and underemployment, but their responses are shaped by their expectations of obtaining the rewards and privileges of professional status. Most believe that their education and expertise give them a legitimate claim to work that commands high salaries, orderly promotions, and social recognition. Finally, their attitudes shed light on the experience of success and failure. Displaced academics are people long accustomed to winning who suddenly are confronted with the possibility of failure. Their responses reveal the ways in which conceptions of personal worth often become enmeshed in both academic achievement and occupational success.

This book relies heavily on interviews with displaced academics because I want to discuss aspects of their lives that cannot easily be quantified. For example, how do they cope with the disparity between the expectations generated by their training and the reality of their work lives? How have their self-images as competent and worthy people been shaped by their failure to achieve their aspirations? To what extent do they begin to question the concept of the meritocracy and notions of professional privilege? The interviews were conducted with 43 academics who either had failed to secure ladder appointments or had been fired from tenure-track positions after pretenure or tenure reviews. (A more detailed description of the methodology appears in the appendix.) At the time of the interviews, 10 of the respondents were out of work, 13 were teaching part-time, and 7 held full-time, temporary appointments. Seven still were completing their dissertations, and 17 already had made decisions to leave academia.[59]

Twenty-three, or slightly more than half the interviewees, were women, as are about half of all displaced academics. Although women as a percentage of Ph.D.s soared during the 1970s, their share of faculty positions did not grow commensurately. Women alone were responsible for the increase in doctoral degrees awarded during the 1970s. The number of men receiving Ph.D.s fell from 25,890 in 1970 to 23,658 in 1978. By contrast, the number of women Ph.D. recipients more than doubled, growing from 3,976 to 8,473.[60] The percentage of women among new doctorates in the humanities rose from 20 percent in 1967 to 39 percent in 1979.[61] However, just as women bear the brunt of unemployment and underemployment in the work force generally, so women academics are affected disproportionately by the job crisis in higher education. In 1979, women doctorates were two to five times as likely as their male counterparts to be unemployed, and they were five times as likely to be employed part-time.[62] The fraction of women Ph.D.s who held terminal, nonladder appointments was almost twice as high as the proportion of men.[63] Finally, women who do secure tenure-track jobs are far less likely than their male colleagues to attain tenure.[64]

The job crisis also falls heavily on minority Ph.D.s. However, I did not make an effort to obtain a proportional sample of minority displaced academics. For one thing, their numbers still are too small. True, the number of minority Ph.D. recipients grew more rapidly than that of whites during the seventies. Sixty-three percent of all U.S.-born minority doctorates in the humanities received their degrees during this decade, compared to 55 percent of all U.S.-born whites.[65] Nevertheless, minorities constituted only 6 percent of all doctorates awarded in the humanities.[66] Furthermore, their problems are sufficiently distinct that a full understanding would require a study directed specifically at them.

Although interviews form the basis for much of the book, three topics are examined through the use of data obtained from other sources. The first is part-time faculty employment. A significant proportion of displaced academics teach on a part-time basis at institutions of higher education. Despite the rapid growth of part-timers during the 1970s, this sector of the teaching faculty has not been studied adequately. Thus, before discussing the response of displaced academics to this type of work, I will analyze the conditions of part-time academic employment, the role that adjuncts play in colleges and universities, and the composition of the part-time academic labor force. Second, I will describe the solutions to the job crisis proposed by the various professional associations. Their recommendations provide a context for understanding the options most displaced academics believe are available. Finally, I will discuss two ways in which displaced academics have fought back. The quiescence of the unemployed typically is explained by their sense of despair, their adherence to an individualistic ideology, and the fragmentation of their lives.[67] However, it also is important to investigate the possibilities that exist for taking effective action. People are more likely to place their faith in private solutions if they believe that their chances of effecting social change are remote. Two possible vehicles for protest by displaced academics are lawsuits and unionization. Because sex discrimination suits are the most common form of grievances filed by women academics against institutions of higher education, I will focus on that activity.[68] I also will assess the extent to which part-time faculty have been successful in improving their working conditions through unionization.

NOTES

1. See, for example, Russell Bellico, "Higher Education: Crisis of Expectations," *Educational Record* 60 (Winter 1979):93-98.
2. See Samuel Bowles and Herbert Gintis, *Schooling in Capitalist America: Educational Reform and the Contradiction of Economic Life* (New York: Basic Books, 1976).
3. National Center for Education Statistics, *Digest of Education Statistics* (Washington, D.C.: Government Printing Office, 1979), p. 96.
4. Ibid., p. 123.
5. Following the National Research Council, I have categorized history as one of the humanities fields.
6. National Research Council, *Employment of Humanities Ph.D.s: A Departure from Traditional Jobs* (Washington, D.C.: National Academy of Sciences, 1980), p. 7.
7. National Center for Education Statistics, *The Condition of Education* (Washington, D.C.: Government Printing Office, 1978), p. 102.
8. *Digest of Education*, p. 16.
9. Jerome Karabel, "Community Colleges and Social Stratification," in *The Educational Establishment*, ed. Elizabeth L. Useem and Michael Useem (Englewood Cliffs, N.J.: Prentice-Hall, 1974), pp. 117-18.
10. Dexter Perkins and John L. Snell, *The Education of Historians in the United States* (New York: McGraw-Hill, 1962), pp. 1-35.
11. Luis Fernandez, *U.S. Doctorate Faculty after the Boom: Demographic Predictions to 2000*, Carnegie Council on Policy Studies in Higher Education, Technical Report No. 4, April 1978, p. 1.
12. William G. Bowen, *Graduate Education in the Arts and Sciences: Prospects for the Future*, Report of the President (Princeton University, 1981), p. 10.
13. Allan Cartter, "The Supply and Demand for College Teachers," *Journal of Human Resources* 1 (Summer 1966):22-38.
14. Paul Blumberg, "Lockouts, Layoffs, and the New Academic Proletariat," in *The Hidden Professoriate: Credentialism, Professionalism and the Tenure Process*, ed. Arthur S. Wilke (Westport, Conn.: Greenwood Press, 1979), p. 45.

15. Richard B. Freeman, *The Over-Educated American* (New York: Academic Press, 1976), p. 28.

16. Lewis C. Solmon, Laura Kent, Nancy L. Ochsner, and Margo-Lea Hurwicz, *Underemployed Ph.D.'s* (Lexington, Mass.: Lexington, 1981), p. 20.

17. See Chapter Three of this book. The Modern Language Association reported that in 1978 only about 40 percent of Ph.D.s in English and foreign languages secured positions that officially were tenure track. ("A Statement on the Academic Job Market in Language and Literature," [n.d.].)

18. Charlotte V. Kuh, *Market Conditions and Tenure for Ph.D.s in U.S. Higher Education*, Carnegie Council on Policy Studies in Higher Education, Technical Report No. 3, July 1977; Roy Radner and Charlotte V. Kuh, *Market Conditions and Tenure in U.S. Higher Education: 1955-1973*, Carnegie Council on Policy Studies in Higher Education, Technical Report No. 2, July 1977; Roy Radner and Charlotte V. Kuh, *Preserving a Lost Generation: Policies to Assure a Steady Flow of Young Scholars until the Year 2000*, Carnegie Council on Policy Studies in Higher Education, Report, October 1978, p. 2.

19. MLA, "Statement on the Academic Job Market."

20. Allan M. Cartter, *Ph.D.'s and the Academic Labor Market* (New York: McGraw-Hill, 1973); R. G. D'Andrade, E. A. Hammel, D. L. Adkins, C. K. McDaniel, "Academic Opportunity in Anthropology, 1974-90," *American Anthropologist* 77 (December 1975): 753-73; Stephen Dresch, "Educational Saturation: A Demographic-Economic Model," *AAUP Bulletin* 60 (October 1975): 236-46; Fernandez, *Doctorate Faculty*; Freeman, *Over-Educated*, pp. 81-110; Solmon, Kent, Ochsner, and Hurwicz, *Underemployed Ph.D.'s*, p. 1.

21. Bowen, *Graduate Education*, pp. 19-20.

22. *Condition of Education* (1978), p. 102.

23. *Three Thousand Futures*, Report of the Carnegie Council on Policy Studies in Higher Education (San Francisco: Jossey-Bass, 1980), pp. 37, 153.

24. National Center for Education Statistics, *Condition of Education* (Washington, D.C.: Government Printing Office, 1980), p. 96.

25. *Condition of Education* (1980), p. 97. For budget purposes, the federal government assumes that three part-time students are equivalent to one full-time student. (Fernandez, *Doctorate Faculty*, p. 8.)

26. Just under 10 percent of all new full-time faculty hired by community colleges in 1977-78 held doctorates. (Milton L. Smith, "The Two-Year College and the Ph.D. Surplus," *Academe*, November 1979, p. 430.) See also Gertrude S. Fujii, "Those 'Undertrained' Ph.D.'s in English," *Chronicle of Higher Education*, 23 February 1981, p. 25.

27. *Three Thousand Futures*, p. 152.

28. Joan Huber and Edna Bonacich, "Ad Hoc Committee Report on Un- and Underemployment," American Sociological Association (1983), p. 3.

29. Huber and Bonacich, "Committee Report," pp. 305-6; Fernandez, *Doctorate Faculty*, p. 89. According to a study sponsored by the American Council on Education, the raising of the mandatory age will reduce by another two-thirds the number of faculty openings between 1983 and 1990. (Thomas Corwin and Paula Knepper, "Finance and Employment Implications of Raising the Mandatory Retirement Age for Faculty," [Washington, D.C.: American Council on Education, 1978].) Many colleges and universities have offered incentives to professors to retire early, but these have not been very successful. (See Robert M. Soldofsky, "Few Professors Will Retire Early Without a Guarantee of Security," *Chronicle of Higher Education*, 20 January 1982, p. 27.) If the real income of professors continues to decline, some may choose to enter more remunerative fields in business or government. However, so far, relatively few professors have left higher education. Turnover also will be restricted by the unusually high proportion of tenured faculty: between 1969 and 1978, the percentage of faculty with tenure grew from 50 to 64 percent. (*Three Thousand Futures*, p. 311.)

30. Allan M. Cartter, "The Academic Labor Market," in *Higher Education and the Labor Market*, ed. Margaret S. Gordon (New York: McGraw-Hill, 1974), p. 301.

31. Lewis C. Solmon, Nancy L. Ochsner, and Margo-Lea Hurwicz, *Alternative Careers for Humanities Ph.D.s* (New York: Praeger, 1979), p. 54.

32. According to the American Historical Association, the total number of college teachers in history fell from 12,900 in 1975 to 10,875 in 1980, a drop of 16 percent. (Ernest R. May and Dorothy G. Blaney, *Careers for Humanists* [New York: Academic Press, 1981], p. 2.)

33. Verne Stadtman, *Academic Adaptations: Higher Education Prepares for the 1980s and 1990s* (San Francisco: Jossey-Bass, 1980), p. 3.

34. *Chronicle of Higher Education*, 28 January 1980, pp. 4-5. These figures are particularly disturbing because faculty hiring generally is tied more closely to the number of majors than to course enrollments. (May and Blaney, *Careers*, p. 25.)

35. This drop is a source of concern to some academics, who fear universities will lack qualified faculty members in the 1990s. (Malcolm G. Scully, "Possible Faculty Shortage in 1990s Worries Today's Academic Leaders," *Chronicle of Higher Education*, 6 October 1982, p. 1.)

36. The decline in the amount of financial aid available also may have influenced their choices. Although the cost of graduate education

escalated during the 1970s, the Danforth, Ford, and Wilson fellowship programs were phased out, and the number of National Science Fellowships awarded fell from 1,198 in 1970 to 450 in 1981. (Huber and Bonacich, "Ad Hoc Committee Report," p. 4.)

37. Solmon, Kent, Ochsner, and Hurwicz, *Underemployed Ph.D.'s*, p. 11. The proportion of Swarthmore College graduates going directly to graduate school fell from 75 percent in 1965 to 29 percent in 1979. (*Swarthmore College Bulletin*, February 1980, p. 14.)

38. Solmon, Kent, Ochsner, and Hurwicz, *Underemployed Ph.D.'s*, p. 11.

39. Edward P. Fiske, "Higher Education's New Economics," *New York Times Magazine*, 1 May 1983, pp. 46, 48, 50, 52, 54, 57-58.

40. Janet Hook, "Student Loans Drop 35 Pct. in Latest Quarter," *Chronicle of Higher Education*, 14 July 1982, p. 1.

41. *On Campus*, February 1983, p. 13.

42. Janet Hook and Kim McDonald, "First Effects of U.S. Budget Cuts Beginning to Hit Many Colleges," *Chronicle of Higher Education*, 2 December 1981, p. 1; Jack Magarrell, "Serious Financial Problems Facing States Portend a Lean Year for Public Colleges," *Chronicle of Higher Education*, 17 February 1981, p. 1; Jack Magarrell, "Falling State Revenues, Cuts in Payrolls Bring Hard Times to Public Institutions," *Chronicle of Higher Education*, 10 February 1982, p. 1; Jack Magarrell, "Public Colleges in Michigan and Ohio Troubled by Further Efforts to Reduce State Spending," *Chronicle of Higher Education*, 7 April 1982, p. 8.

43. Jack Magarrell, "Recession Hits State Support for Colleges," *Chronicle of Higher Education*, 20 October 1982, p. 1.

44. Barry Mitzman, "On Oregon's Campuses, the Refrain Is 'We Can't Cut Anything More,'" *Chronicle of Higher Education*, 1 December 1982, p. 6.

45. *Chronicle of Higher Education*, 24 February 1982, p. 2; *Chronicle of Higher Education*, 17 March 1982, p. 2; *Chronicle of Higher Education*, 4 October 1982, p. 1; Anne C. Roark, "End of Free Colleges for All Possible," *Los Angeles Times*, 19 March 1982, p. 3; Malcolm Scully, "Entrance Rules Tightened at Some Public Institutions," *Chronicle of Higher Education*, 9 September 1981, p. 1.

46. See May and Blaney, *Careers*, p. 19.

47. Stadtman, *Academic Adaptations*, p. 120.

48. See, in particular, Barbara Ann Scott, *Crisis Management in American Higher Education* (New York: Praeger, 1983), pp. 149-65; Sherry Gorelick, "Boom and Bust in Higher Education: Economic and Social Causes of the Current Crisis," *Insurgent Sociologist*, Spring 1983, pp. 77-90.

49. *Chronicle of Higher Education*, 13 January 1982, p. 13; Jack Magarrell, "Federal Cuts May Prove Especially Painful for Private Institutions," *Chronicle of Higher Education*, 24 February 1982, p. 9.

50. Scott, *Crisis Management*, pp. 139-40.

51. Between 1979-80 and 1981-82, the percentage of students from families with incomes between $6,000 and $24,000 at private colleges fell 39 percent. (Jack Magarrell, "Number of Lower-Income Students Drops 39 Pct. at Private Colleges," *Chronicle of Higher Education*, 1 September 1982, p. 1.)

52. See *Work in America*, Report of a Social Task Force to the Secretary of Health, Education and Welfare (Cambridge, Mass.: MIT Press, 1973), pp. 134-38.

53. Ibid., p. 135.

54. Carnegie Commission on Higher Education, *College Graduates and Jobs* (New York: McGraw-Hill, 1973), p. 5.

55. "Report of the National Commission on Excellence in Education," reprinted in *Chronicle of Higher Education*, 4 May 1983, p. 1.

56. See *Chronicle of Higher Education*, 11 May 1983, pp. 5, 10; see also Norm Fruchter, "Quality of Education Reports Attack the Wrong Problems," *In These Times*, 27 July-9 August 1983, p. 17.

57. See Robert Rosen, "Back to Basics," *The Radical Teacher* no. 20 (n.d.), pp. 1-4.

58. See Alvin Gouldner, "The Unemployed Self," in *Work*, vol. 2, ed. Ronald Fraser (Harmondsworth, Eng.: Penguin, 1969), pp. 346-65.

59. These categories are not mutually exclusive.

60. National Center for Education Statistics, *Digest of Education Statistics* (Washington, D.C.: Government Printing Office, 1980), p. 102.

61. Solmon, Kent, Ochsner, and Hurwicz, *Underemployed Ph.D.'s*, p. 127.

62. National Research Council, *Career Outcomes in a Matched Sample of Men and Women Ph.D.s* (Washington, D.C.: National Academy Press, 1981), p. 8.

63. Ibid., p. 46.

64. Ibid., p. xvii.

65. National Research Council, *Employment of Minority Ph.D.s: Changes Over Time* (Washington, D.C.: National Academy Press, 1981), p. 10.

66. National Research Council, *Minority Ph.D.s*, p. 12.

67. See Kay Lehman Schlozman and Sidney Verba, *Injury to Insult: Unemployment Class and Political Response,* Cambridge, Mass.: Harvard University Press, 1979).

68. *NEA Advocate*, May 1981, p. 1.

Chapter 1
OUT OF WORK

I became an academic because I graduated from a small elite college in 1966 when all my professors assumed that if you were bright and good, then you went directly to graduate school. I thought it would be easy to have the very nice, comfortable life they all had. But the whole year I wasn't working, I had the image of myself as someone in the middle of a swimming pool and just kicking to keep my head above water, and not really being anywhere.

—*A woman who was unemployed for a year after being denied tenure at a liberal arts college in 1974.*

Sociologists first studied the personal injuries inflicted by unemployment during the Depression. Their reports illustrate the dramatic shift in attitudes that had occurred since the late nineteenth century. Victorian social reformers examined the "underside" of society in order to confirm their preconception that the unemployed were deficient. Looking for evidence of moral failure, they proceeded to describe the jobless as ignorant, lazy, and shiftless[1]. However, by 1930, a number of influential experts had challenged prevailing assumptions. Additionally, the staggering incidence of social distress weakened the contention that unemployment resulted from personal inadequacy. Sociologists thus sought to comprehend the human damage wrought by the catastrophe, not to assign individual blame.

The pioneering studies were conducted by E. Wright Bakke, who first investigated jobless workers in London as early as 1931.[2] After returning to the United States, he embarked on a systematic examination of the lives of the unemployed in New Haven. His findings, published in 1939, revealed that idled workers postponed essential trips to doctors, missed mortgage payments, sold household belongings, and ate less nutritious meals. The emotional costs were equally devastating. Unemployment eroded self-confidence and undermined relationships with family and friends.[3]

During the subsequent forty years, few sociologists continued this line of research. Although the numbers out of work in the United States remained high,[4] most investigators regarded joblessness as a minor concern, and the literature on unemployment produced during these decades was remarkably small.[5] However, the upward spiral of unemployment during the seventies and early eighties revived interest in the questions that had animated Depression-era commentators. Because increasing numbers of people have become resigned to the prospect of the workless being ever with us, sociologists and journalists have turned their attention to the impact of unemployment on the lives of its victims.

Their studies reveal that the world of the unemployed closely resembles that of the jobless fifty years ago.[6] Unemployment compensation and supplementary benefits have helped to mitigate the worst consequences of unemployment, but the emotional and economic costs remain profound. Moreover, joblessness falls disproportionately on workers who already are disadvantaged by virtue of class, race, sex, and age, and who cannot afford to lose income.[7] Because professionals are more likely than other workers to have access to financial resources during periods without work, unemployment places a smaller burden on them. Nevertheless, professional status cannot insulate one completely from the ravages of unemployment. Although very few professionals experience actual deprivation, most are forced to lower their standard of living, and they suffer both physical and emotional distress.[8]

The academics I interviewed enjoyed still greater advantages than other unemployed professionals. Because most were dislodged from their career paths at an early stage in their lives, the consequences were muted. Some had to defer their dreams of obtaining middle-class life-styles, but very few experienced the shock of downward mobility. When they sought work in other fields, their youth was a vital asset.[9] More significantly, their primary complaint was not unemployment itself but failure to find the particular job on which their dreams were fixed; most did not doubt they could find some type of work. In fact, a few displaced academics interpreted their defeats as blessings in disguise. They had opportunities to reevaluate their original career choices, reassess the place of scholarship in their lives, and explore other career options. However, most of the academics in this study complained that repeated rejections had weakened the fabric of their lives. Moreover, the distinctions between their reactions to career failure and those of most idled workers were differences of degree, not of kind; their responses followed similar patterns.

For example, a number of displaced academics discussed the psychological costs of their failure to find appropriate employment. A few had consulted therapists to help them cope with the emotional problems that resulted. When one man realized his chance of finding a tenure-track job was slim, he went "through a great psychological crash." Although he subsequently improved emotionally, he still felt as if he had "been killed in a car accident" and was "just coming back as a ghost." One woman described her year of joblessness this way:

> The whole time I was unemployed I felt incredibly shaky and everything that happened was so threatening. If I called a friend and left a message and she didn't call me back I was convinced she didn't like me anymore. Just any of the good, resilient, sensible things you have about yourself if you're more or less sane in your thirties just totally went by the board.

Having experienced the loss of cherished careers, many people found themselves more cautious, less willing to take risks. One man commented, "There's this sense of constriction, I have to be careful a lot, to hold on to what I have." A woman lamented the "absence of spontaneity" in her life.

Career failure also exacted a toll on close personal relationships. The two divorced men in the sample attributed the dissolution of their marriages to their inability to find academic appointments. Many others reported that diminished self-confidence had undermined ongoing relationships. Because their sense of themselves was intertwined with occupational success, they believed they were unworthy of love. One woman recalled a period of joblessness:

> Not having a job caused a lot of strains in the relationship between Jim and me. It amazes me that we didn't break up. I had no center, no sense of myself, and when Jim criticized me and said things about me that clearly had nothing to do with who I was, I didn't feel like I could summon enough of who I was to answer that.

Although some of the academics spoke gratefully of the encouragement and reinforcement they had received from their partners, many others complained that, when they were most in need of affirmation, only limited support had been forthcoming. But they also acknowledged that their own misdirected hostility had caused frictions and tensions; they vented at home the anger and frustration they prudently refrained from expressing elsewhere.

Three of the interviewees lived with partners who also were disenfranchised academics. Although anxieties doubled, they claimed they had grown closer as couples as a result of their shared ordeals. Together they tried to eke out a living from a number of part-time jobs, surveyed the employment prospects each October, and submitted themselves to the judgments of hiring committees during the late fall and winter. However, most of the married academics had partners whose job situations were superior to their own.[10] Sociologists during the 1930s paid particular attention to the destructive effects on men of losing their roles as breadwinners. Writing at a time when the division of labor between the sexes was unquestioned, they reported that failure to support families invariably weakened men's morale and that their status within the family plummeted.[11] Nine of the twelve married men in this sample had relied on their wives' earnings at some point. Their attitudes testify to the dramatic change in the relations between men and women during recent years. Most of these men claimed to be liberated from traditional beliefs and to view their reversal of roles as socially desirable. Several took pleasure in their wives' accomplishments, and three boasted of having assumed primary child-care responsibilities. Nevertheless, some men did acknowledge that traditional societal expectations still had force. A few men worried that their wives no longer looked up to them: "To respect another person, you have to respect his vocation also, and to feel that that person is capable and doing well in some ways," one man explained. Others felt guilty about having "cheated" their wives by not providing the status and income they had anticipated.

Women typically had to contend not only with the higher earning power but also the far greater professional success of their husbands. Only four of the married men had wives with occupations in the managerial or professional levels, but nine of the eleven married women had husbands in established professional careers; in fact, seven of these husbands had obtained the type of academic appointments their wives coveted. Although these women shared in some of the privileges of their husbands' status, daily contact with tenure-track professors highlighted their sense of relative deprivation. One woman discussed the pain of watching her husband do the work for which she also was qualified and gain the recognition and honors to which she considered herself entitled:

> I have felt very resentful of the benefits of Tim's career—the conferences, the being on circuits where he gets known and then being invited to more conferences. Also he has office support and departmental support and collegial support. And it's hard that he has ongoing students who will go out in the world as his students. I have found these things very difficult to accept, very painful, and they have put a tremendous strain on the relationship. I consider myself equally intelligent, equally well prepared, and equally competent, but there's this other person gaining these rewards with whom I'm in constant contact. It's not like the Joneses.

Another woman, married to an associate professor in the same field as herself, felt diminished when she contrasted her own truncated career with her husband's expanding opportunities:

I feel doubly discounted because not only am I not achieving my goals but I measure myself against my husband and I really lag behind.

In addition, these women often moved in circles where one's position in the academic hierarchy is a criterion of personal worth.

Because the academics had sought to prove their value to parents and siblings by compiling impressive records of academic achievement, they feared that job failure would undermine that accomplishment. True, displaced academics who were the first in their families to attend college remained confident of securing their families' esteem:

Whatever I do, I'm a wild success. Finishing my Ph.D. was an enormous thing in my family: I'm the star.

There is a certain aura about having one's doctorate. There has never been one in my family, never, never, never.

But the academics from families in which a high level of academic achievement was commonplace reported that a Ph.D. alone did not provide a solid basis for asserting worth. When these academics compared themselves to siblings, they tended to come up short. One woman, with a recent Ph.D. in anthropology, noted the special sting of being surpassed by the one sister to whom she had always felt superior:

Even my poor younger sister, who never did anything, recently got a job. I was really happy for her, but it was also really depressing. I thought, even Joan now has a halfway decent job. So I see everyone passing me by.

Others expressed guilt about disappointing their parents. Granting parents the right to take reflected glory in the achievements of their children, these academics stressed the discrepancy between their parents' high aspirations for them and their actual accomplishments. There were also tensions with parents fearful of downward mobility:

My parents look at us and say, "You're thirty-five years old, you don't own a house, you have no job security, where are you? When we were twenty-five we were paying mortgage payments, we had a car, we had jobs," and it's a real difficult thing to answer them.

Still another consequence of unemployment was that social lives became more circumscribed. A sense of loneliness was a pervasive theme in several of the interviews. One woman articulated the thoughts of many:

When you're employed you become a member of a group, you gain acceptance. One reason I chose anthropology was that the people were congenial to me. But then when you can't get a job, it's like your whole reference group has thrown you out, it isn't there. I constantly feel that I'm not a member of the group any more; I feel more isolated than any time in my whole life.

But these academics also acted in ways that accentuated their isolation. For example, like many unemployed workers, they withdrew from social situations.[12] A combination of shame and envy motivated one unemployed man and his wife to sever ties with former friends:

We've cut ourselves off from some of our older friends because they're middle management now or they're rising up to become partners in law firms or maybe tenured faculty at major universities. They're all ten years ahead in their lives. We're at a different stage, our lives have been kind of arrested. We're still waiting to do what most of our contemporaries did years ago, such as having children and buying a house. You always wonder just how much they can really understand.

Because this man was not on a career track, he had a sense of marking time, of being out of stride with his contemporaries; he had been left behind when everyone else was moving on. A woman commented, "I envy people, even close friends, if they're doing things I want. I don't like to be around them, so everything is affected." Another remarked, "The only person I'm glad to see is the one person who's worse off than me."

In addition, these academics typically shunned former colleagues. Several believed that, as one man put it, they had "lost face with that crowd." Thus, they removed themselves from networks that might have helped them obtain employment. Despite keen interests in new developments in their disciplines, many ceased attending professional meetings. A man who had been unable to find a tenure-track position after a two-year job search saw himself as having been marked by failure:

> I can't go to a conference and have them say, "there's poor Ross who doesn't have a job." I turned down an all-expenses paid conference in Europe although I've never been to Europe before. The next year I was invited to a conference at Harvard. My grandmother lives there and I wanted to visit her and again all the expenses were paid for, but I turned it down because I couldn't bear to face my colleagues when I was out of work.

Jealousy of more successful academics prevented a woman fired from a tenure-track position from participating in conferences closer to home:

> I couldn't go to those meetings. They made me feel too bad. Here were people doing this work and I was still on the outside.

The interviewees also exhibited little solidarity with other displaced academics. The few who continued to attend professional meetings did not reach out to other job seekers. Although they felt estranged from more successful contemporaries, they made no attempt to form an alternative community, to substitute their own reference group for the one that appeared to have excluded them. One reason was a fear that close contact with other unemployed academics would aggravate their own sense of hopelessness. Moreover, clinging to the value system that defined unemployed and underemployed academics as deficient, they wanted to remain apart from the people they viewed as losers. Both a man who attended a program to retrain Ph.D.s for business careers and a woman who joined a self-help group for unemployed doctorates spoke of the other participants as "failures" and noted their discomfort at associating with them.

Even casual acquaintances frequently were avoided. A woman who recently had lost her job at a university did not want to encounter people in her community because "they knew me by what my status was"; she was convinced she would be devalued in the eyes of others if she no longer could display the title of an appropriate occupation. Like many jobless, these academics also sought to withhold information about their employment situation.[13] One historian, married to a man who had been out of work for two years, floundered for a proper response to inquiries about her husband:

> When Bob was first unemployed, we both found it difficult to know how to explain it. Simply what form of words do you use when people ask what do you do, or what's Bob doing this year. So I always used to work out all kinds of ways of talking around the fact, like saying, "He's between jobs," or "he's retraining," not actually using the word "unemployed."

For some, the sense of being unemployed lingered after they found jobs. One man commented, "It took me two years to stop feeling unemployed after I started working again. It took that long to really feel secure." A woman had a similar experience:

> I started to work and I immediately went on a diet and lost five pounds and then faltered and then promptly gained back eight. Because I had had this feeling, "O.K., now I have this job, I am going to get my life back together," and it was much less easy than that. For nine months a lot of my bad feelings were still with me.

But, this woman continued, her life did improve dramatically:

> This past fall I really began to feel like my prefired self and Gary is amazed because I was fired when he met me, he never knew me in my earlier state and he says he's fallen in love with me all over again, but I'm even nicer

than he knew. You know, I'm much funnier than I was, I'm much more relaxed, I'm much thinner than I was. And I feel good because I feel like my soul has come back to inhabit my body.

ASSIGNING BLAME

A key issue in the studies conducted during the 1930s was the extent to which the unemployed held themselves responsible for their plight. There was some variation by place and date. For example, the jobless in the United States were more likely than the British to regard unemployment as the mark of personal failure.[14] Workers who were dismissed toward the end of the Depression, when joblessness was endemic, tended to blame themselves less than did those who lost their jobs during the early years of the thirties.[15] Nevertheless, having absorbed the ideology that glorifies individual success, the great majority of the unemployed assumed at least some responsibility for their failure. Even when distress reached calamitous proportions, many attributed their misfortune to personal deficiencies.[16] As Studs Terkel recalled, "True, there were hunger marches and protestations to City Hall and Washington, but the millions experienced a private kind of shame when the pink slip came. No matter that others suffered the same fate, the inner voice whispered, 'I'm a failure.'"[17]

Contemporary studies also have documented the contradictory attitudes of the unemployed. According to Harry Maurer, "Unemployed people feel they have been robbed of something, yet on a deeper level they feel it was their fault."[18] Richard Sennett and Jonathan Cobb, who have studied the process by which the disadvantaged learn to internalize failure, speak of the "split" existing in many adults between "conscious belief and inner conviction." A working-class man often "feels ashamed for who he is" although he may insist that "it isn't right society should think of him as a 'nobody'...because he never had a chance to be anything else."[19] Similarly, the vast majority of jobless workers believe that society is grossly unfair, that layoffs hit even the most diligent and competent workers, and that jobs are distributed in an irrational manner. Nevertheless, they continue to find fault with themselves.[20]

When asked to account for their own lack of success, most displaced academics began by discussing systemic factors. All had at their command the latest figures about the dearth of academic jobs. In addition, they were well informed about the causes of unemployment in society at large and accustomed to interpreting social phenomena. The social scientists rested their claims to professional status on their superior understanding of social and economic forces. One man asserted, "Being a historian, I have a perspective. I'm an economic historian and I realize there are social trends and themes and patterns that no individual has any control over. I'm just a casualty of that." Moreover, a number of the women identified closely with the women's movement, which they credited with demonstrating how individual lives fit into larger patterns.

Nevertheless, even the man who insisted most strongly that his problems were rooted in social conditions admitted that feelings of inadequacy "seep through." As we have seen, this response is common in a society that stresses individual achievement and propagates the dream of universally attainable upward mobility. But the attitudes of the interviewees also were shaped by their particular experiences and expectations as academics. All had spent an unusually long period of time in schools, which are primary disseminators of the ideology of individualism. Students are taught to believe there is a close correlation between reward and merit. The relatively recent experience of these academics with career failure could not extinguish their faith in the efficacy of hard work. Furthermore, they had a stake in believing the best and the brightest rise naturally to the top because their own sense of self was heavily dependent on academic achievements. Any suggestion that their present failure was caused by systemic forces cast doubt on the validity of past successes and the possibility of future triumphs.

Many of the interviewees gave specific reasons why they should blame themselves. The "big mistake" of a woman with a Ph.D. in Slavic languages was not spending a year in Russia. A woman anthropologist regretted her decision to conduct her field work in the United States rather than in Southeast Asia. Conversely, an Italian historian berated himself for having spent two years doing research in Italy; because he had completed his doctorate two years later than his classmates, he gave the appearance of being a slow worker, and he had entered the job market after the boom. A French historian was certain he would have been "ensconced in a good university," had he returned from France two years earlier. Others also placed the onus on their lack of foresight. One woman "found it difficult to cope" with the knowledge that she had chosen advanced training in medieval history when she might just as easily have entered business school. Still others rued their former naiveté: they had selected a graduate school without investigating its placement record or ignored the significance of studying with "big names."

But it is important to recognize the difference between holding oneself responsible for specific mistakes and viewing oneself as unworthy generally. In fact, these academics may have focused on errors of judgment or on miscalculations in order to stave off feelings of inadequacy. They could place the burden of failure on themselves without focusing on their deficiencies as scholars or teachers. Although they did not free themselves entirely from feelings of shame, they may well have reduced the injury to personal dignity.

In addition, they were able to present themselves as active agents, not simply as passive victims of social and economic forces. Kay Lehman Schlozman and Sidney Verba reported that, although a high proportion of all jobless workers berate themselves for past mistakes, unemployed professionals are especially likely to speak regretfully of personal choices. In part, they are realistic. As Schlozman and Verba pointed out, professionals typically have had greater freedom than other workers to plan their own lives.[21] However, by viewing themselves as masters of their fates, they also can counteract feelings of helplessness and hold out the possibility of taking effective control over their work lives in the future.

ON THE DOLE

One experience these academics shared with most jobless workers was applying for unemployment compensation. Although a relatively small percentage were jobless at the time of their interviews, slightly over half had been eligible for unemployment at some point.[22] Previous studies of the unemployed have noted the wide variation in their attitudes toward collecting benefits. Some file claims routinely, but many have scruples about accepting government money. Linking unemployment compensation with need, they conclude that only material deprivation justifies applying for it. Still others regard unemployment benefits as synonymous with charity and moral weakness; self-respect demanded that they remain self-sufficient.[23]

A similar diversity characterized the responses of displaced academics. At one extreme were those who, though eligible for unemployment, refused to apply. Two rejected unemployment as a matter of principle: "There is plenty of work for those who really want it," one proclaimed. Another saw reliance on the government as a disgrace:

> Although I spent last year looking for jobs, I insisted on making enough money to live on. I was adamant about not going on welfare or unemployment. That was too repugnant to contemplate.

At the other extreme were a few academics who needed the money, considered themselves entitled to it, and accepted it without question; they were surprised to be asked if they had any qualms about filing claims. Most, however, fell somewhere between these two extremes. They collected benefits but felt uneasy about doing so.

For some members of this intermediate group, unemployment raised moral issues. Like other jobless workers, they worried about applying because they were not in desperate need; in other words, they fell short of their own self-imposed definitions of "deserving." A few also expressed discomfort about their activities while receiving weekly checks. Government regulations stipulate that recipients must actively be looking for work, but they had devoted their time to research and writing, viewing the benefits as a type of grant. Although they had enhanced their own marketability, they confessed they had produced fraudulent evidence of having conducted daily job searches.

Several others considered collecting unemployment as a personal indignity. They eventually did file claims, but pride compelled them to postpone their first trips to the center. One part-timer reported:

The first two years I had the feeling that I shouldn't be collecting unemployment. I didn't go and get all the money I was entitled to, because I just couldn't go. That was when you had to go and pick up the checks at a certain day and a certain hour. I just wouldn't go one week, two weeks, because I felt so guilty. I just felt guilty because if I wasn't working, there must be something wrong with me.

Now I realize that in another age I would have a job.... But I've changed a lot in the last couple of years.

Experiences at the unemployment office reinforced feelings of humiliation. The long lines, the bleak decor, and the intrusive questions informed the academics that they had entered the ranks of the unwanted. The procedures often seemed needlessly complicated:

At first I breezed through it, but one of the things that happened ... as I began to work part time was that I had to be on line B instead of on line A or something, you had to fill out a form every week that you worked part time, and so being there, instead of taking half an hour, would take two hours and two and a half hours. I was just going through the most ridiculous procedures week after week, and it just got more and more impossible.

An equally persistent complaint was the attitude of the officials they encountered:

One woman last year kept my form on her desk for months. She kept wanting more verification. She was very mean to me, trying to put me down in interviews. They feel superior because they're working.

The more time went on, I could stand less and less the kind of arrogance of the people who worked there. I kept thinking and would occasionally say this to people on line, that if I had been as incompetent I would have gotten fired long ago. And their sort of attitude that because they had a job they were better than you was very difficult.

It's really hard to go to that damn unemployment office. The people who work there are real nasty. They're overwhelmed with people and very insensitive. They see the dregs of society and categorize you as just one of them. They don't treat you with respect. It's really a humiliating experience.

Although displaced academics are not alone in complaining about the harshness and insensitivity of state personnel in unemployment offices, they may have been particularly disposed to view their treatment as a personal affront. Most were accustomed to regarding themselves as special people, and they had expected to secure jobs that granted them responsibility for sorting and judging others.[24] Subjecting themselves to the scrutiny of people they had viewed as their social inferiors was an almost unbearable degradation. A trip to an unemployment office was also a levelling experience: impressive credentials and exceptional competence failed to distinguish academics from others in line. A number of the scientists and engineers interviewed by Paula G. Leventman donned suits in order to differentiate themselves from the people they met at the center.[25] Similarly, a few academics sought to distance themselves from the "typical" unemployed. For example, an anthropologist pretended she was conducting a field project about the mores of an unemployment office. Another woman reported that "the endless sitting around didn't seem quite as peculiar as it might" because her center catered to a large number of unemployed actors and public school teachers.

TAKING REFUGE IN PROFESSIONAL STATUS

Although a sense of professional pride may have exacerbated the problems of collecting unemployment compensation, it may also have mitigated some of the strains of unemployment. Schlozman and Verba have argued:

The unemployed professional retains a sense of his professional identity. A number of them—for example, the Broadway-show musician—actually continue to practice their professions in one way or another. The unemployed assembly-line worker or the jobless typist is less likely to have derived a sense of self-esteem from his profession in the first place; rather, he is more likely to have gained a sense of self-worth from his ability to hold a steady job and to act as a responsible breadwinner. Under these circumstances unemployment would seem to be peculiarly threatening: deprived of being a good provider, the unemployed nonprofessional has no other identity to fall back on.[26]

One unemployed historian was convinced that his degree did grant him an ineradicable mark of distinction:

Having a Ph.D. represents a level of academic achievement that gives me a lot of satisfaction. It means that no one in the country is considered better educated or smarter than I am, that I have some degree of self-confidence to carry off a project, to apply myself to work. It means that I can achieve what you can achieve....They can't take that away.

Most of the interviewees, however, were not so confident. They wanted external validation that their credentials had conferred some kind of superiority. A woman who had received her degree just a month prior to her interview described her search for evidence that she had a claim to professional status:

After I received my Ph.D., I went away for the weekend and kept trying to think of a way to communicate to other people that I had my Ph.D. This seemed especially important because I am not employed. I kept thinking, the only thing I have is this degree....

Then I enrolled in a programming course and snuck it in when I registered. I also asked a lot of questions because my level of understanding was much higher than what most students require. When students asked, condescendingly, if I had taken algebra, I felt like saying in response, "I have a Ph.D., you little stupid...what I want to understand is more than what you want to understand, you just take it on the surface level." Nobody cared whether or not I could make connections to developments in the social sciences.

I was very aware throughout the course how important it was to me to be above other people. It is very hard to think of yourself as just one of the masses. I kept looking around and saying, "I have this Ph.D., what does it mean? Can I do anything better than Joe Schmoe next to me?" and I didn't see anything.

One man was more successful in obtaining the reassurance he craved:

A few months ago I spent a day with my old graduate school department. I was really gratified by their reception....I was invited to lunch with a distinguished member of the field. When I said that the others should go alone, the chairman said, "nonsense, you're a musicologist and you'll always be." That was very nice.

To others, the trappings of professionalism were important. Uncertain that they deserved the label "professional," they looked to the symbols of professional status to certify their worth. One woman was delighted to be introduced as "doctor" when she gave a talk at her daughter's high school. Two men spent time abroad, where their expertise commanded the deference to which they felt entitled. One, a European historian, commented:

One reason I have a strong attachment to Italy is that people relate to me as if I'm a professional. I am someone studying a particular area that they think is important. I am treated the way that I always thought was at the end of the rainbow for me, but somehow never has been in this country.

The other, a specialist in Latin America, echoed this theme: "I like Latin America because I'm called 'doctor' there; I'm like a god."

PERISH BUT PUBLISH

As Schlozman and Verba suggest, the primary means of retaining a professional identity is continuing to practice a craft.

Time is a burden for most unemployed workers, who rarely find sufficient pastimes to occupy themselves.[27] Because of the radical separation of work and recreation in our society, leisure activities often lose their meaning when they no longer are circumscribed by the demands of a job. However, when academics are unemployed, they are not necessarily out of work. Their skills reside in themselves, rather than in the institutions that employ them.[28] Although scientists and engineers cannot conduct research without institutional affiliations, most scholars in liberal arts fields do not need university appointments in order to read, think about ideas, and publish. Furthermore, most humanists and social scientists view their work as "callings," and they remain attached to their fields of study even when unemployed. As one of the women interviewed for this study observed:

> Very often there is some resonance in a topic an academic picks, in a personal sense. People get interested in topics as a kind of key to their own lives, or to some problem they've dealt with or are dealing with. In a very real sense, the topics I've been interested in have been critical areas throughout my life.

Others spoke of the pleasure derived from the process of research. One woman was "fired up by finding material that no one had ever seen before"; another considered scholarship "a real stimulation, a real joy."

Nevertheless, academics typically engage in research for extrinsic rewards as well as for intrinsic gratifications. All have performed very well according to the rules of school systems that stress the utilitarian value of knowledge. Students typically learn to master a variety of techniques for pleasing teachers; they do not necessarily pursue subjects that excite their curiosity or stir their imaginations. Moreover, publishing is the primary way university faculty gain recognition and advancement. Thus, once the link between effort and reward is broken, scholarship may lose its appeal.

Twenty-six displaced academics had completed their degrees but had not changed careers.[29] Of these, nine no longer engaged in any form of scholarship. One claimed that he never had enjoyed research and was happy to drop it. Two others asserted that their interests had changed, and their former disciplines no longer had the same meaning for them. Still others attributed their lack of scholarly activity to low self-esteem, as the following comment reveals:

> When I was unemployed, people would sometimes say to me, "you should write a book, you should look on this as a fellowship," but I couldn't because I felt so rotten, just so unutterably rotten and low. As the time went on, I spent whole days just walking around the city. But as I look back on it now, and think about having had all that time, and about all the things I could have done, of all the reading and writing I could have done, and how little I actually did, I find it appalling.

But the most common rationale was that, as two academics put it, research no longer seemed "productive of anything." Disenchanted with the reward structure in academia, they refused to make further investments in scholarship. One woman explained why she did not complete a book for which she had received a contract with a prestigious university press:

> The question is, does one continue to pound one's head against the wall? I guess I'm very disaffected right now. I just had a phone call from this woman asking about publishing her article. She wants to get back into the academic world. I gave her nothing but discouragement. I told her it was a waste of time. It's very hard to publish an article these days...and what good is it going to do anyway if it is published? I told her to use all that energy and effort to bettering herself in the real world.

Some, in fact, feared that additional publications would damage their chances in the job market. Convinced that search committees sought the cheapest candidates, they believed they risked pricing themselves out of jobs. In addition, they might be eliminated from serious consideration simply because they would no longer fit into any recognized job categories. An extensive publications record would qualify them for positions as associate professors, but they lacked the teaching experience required for appointments at this rank.

Seventeen others had continued to engage in some form of scholarship. Although some had simply revised dissertations to prepare them for publication, written articles that were related closely to previous work, or prepared bibliographic materials, nine had embarked on totally new projects. These displaced academics reported a mixture of motives for pursuing research. The majority confessed to residual hopes that better publication records would significantly enhance their employment prospects. Although jobs had eluded them in the past, they still placed their faith in hard work. Publishing also provided an alternative means of demonstrating competence, as one woman remarked:

> I like the challenge it represents to get articles put in journals where they're in competition for space with people who have all the status and prestige and resources of an institutional job. It is very ego gratifying to get my research in *their* journals. It says to me that I'm still functioning as an academic.

In addition, these academics were sustained by the satisfactions derived from their work and by their conviction of its significance. One man, who no longer considered himself an active contestant for academic jobs, remarked that, should he not be able to pursue scholarship, a "really important part" of his life "would drain away." A woman with few illusions about obtaining a tenure-track position explained her determination to complete her book: "I want to finish it because of the reason I wanted to write it. It's a story I want to tell, it has a lot of good research in it, it's a part of my life."

But these academics also discussed the difficulties of sustaining creative work. A few lacked access to research libraries. Several were convinced that publishers and journal editors were prejudiced against authors with no institutional affiliations.[30] Research was also expensive. After calculating the money spent on duplicating, typing, books, travel, and computer time, one woman concluded she was "subsidizing the profession." Many were painfully aware of the opportunity cost of research; their time in the library or at the typewriter could have been devoted to more remunerative pursuits. An additional disadvantage was that their work held meaning only when embedded in a particular social context. One historian lamented:

> There are times when it seems quite futile to be sitting in California writing about English local history with the sense that no one here cares much about what I do or knows much about it professionally.

Individuals and organizations have attempted to solve these problems in a variety of ways. Professional associations are beginning to extend their services to members of their disciplines without university appointments.[31] Many colleges and universities grant library privileges to researchers in their communities, and a few have awarded them status as unpaid affiliates.[32] In order to provide recognition to the scholarship produced by displaced academics, the Rockefeller Foundation announced in 1982 that it would fund awards made by three professional associations for the work of researchers lacking faculty jobs.[33]

Displaced academics themselves have worked to create the conditions that make possible autonomous and creative research. Adopting the proud title of "independent scholars," they have organized research institutes in several cities. The model is the Institute for Research in History, founded in New York in 1975, by a group of historians looking for a practical response to the academic job crisis. All members are required to participate in at least one of the constituted study groups, and the Institute staff facilitates grant writing for foundation support. Similar groups have been established in Cambridge, Los Angeles, New Haven, and San Francisco.[34] The three displaced academics in this study who helped to create independent institutes testified to the encouragement and stimulation they received. Several women also relied for positive reinforcement on the network of friends they had found through the women's movement. Nevertheless, though successful in establishing supportive milieux, all complained that they continued to be isolated from the normal channels of communication and exchange within the profession.

Graduate students confronted still other difficulties. Seven of the academics I interviewed had not yet completed their theses, and eight others had obtained degrees within the past three years.

Some responded to grim job warnings by finishing their work as rapidly as possible. In the absence of definite promises of jobs, they wanted at least one tangible accomplishment. Furthermore, they hoped that completed dissertations would increase their chances of selection by hiring committees. But many others intentionally prolonged their work. For one thing, they wanted to retain the advantages of graduate student status, such as eligibility for university housing and positions as teaching assistants. In addition, they sought to forestall the tensions and problems of unemployment.[35] One woman spent over five years writing her dissertation because "the thought of finishing and having nothing to do was just too overwhelming."

COPING

In short, the sense of professional identity of many of these academics was shaky at best. Several doubted they deserved to define themselves as professionals. Although many did sustain some types of scholarly activities, they also emphasized the problems of publishing without institutional affiliations, public recognition, or the assurance of secure futures as university faculty. How, then did they cope with the strains of unemployment? Bakke claimed that the workers he studied during the Depression found resources within themselves to deal with their joblessness. They bowed to the inevitable and gradually modified their objectives in line with actual possibilities.[36] Writing from a sociological tradition that emphasized the virtues of adjustment rather than social change, Bakke placed a positive moral value on these strategies of adaptation. Unemployed workers who accommodated themselves to their reduced circumstances were not likely to challenge basic social institutions.[37] But the process of adjustment can be viewed from another perspective; it is still one more price paid by the victims of unemployment. In denying or rationalizing their loss, the jobless learned to live with a diminished sense of self.

The academics in this study similarly employed a variety of stratagems for coping with their situations. Some placed additional weight on alternative sources of self-esteem. One man, out of work for two years, acknowledged:

> I find that other accomplishments, whether it's having something accepted for publication or becoming president of the condominium association, which is a very minor accomplishment, begin to seem extremely important.

A woman who supported herself by working in a printing office commented:

> I'm a great success as a typesetter. I went from three dollars to nine dollars an hour. I make more than anyone there. It's probably one of my few links to sanity: here's one place where my competence is clearly shown.

Such achievements alone could not form a solid basis for a sense of self-worth, but they did help slightly to restore pride. The displaced academics also capitalized on whatever opportunities were available for asserting control over some aspect of their lives. Although their major plans had gone awry, they wanted at least the illusion of being masters of their fate.[38] One woman established her own company to publish the books she had written:

> I decided I didn't want to hassle editors. What I wanted was total control because for so many years I had no control over my own destiny. It's very nice to be in charge of a whole process.

Another woman also sought a sense of personal empowerment through the traditional American dream of self-employment. When her job prospects seemed particularly bleak, she began to formulate plans to open a dress shop in order to "have control over my own life." In addition, the academics focused on the misfortunes of others. Those who had held teaching positions pointed to classmates who never had a chance to utilize their training. Others also stressed their own relative advantages: their marriages had remained intact, they had no responsibilities for supporting children, or they had not had to move. In this way they differentiated themselves from friends and colleagues who were "really" unfortunate.

But the primary way in which these academics reconciled themselves to their circumstances was by redefining their goals. As will be discussed later, over half of the respondents had decided to change fields. Furthermore, the majority claimed that academia no longer seemed a highly desirable career choice. A need to disparage faculty jobs was common even among those still striving to obtain one. A few explained that they had entered graduate school during the late sixties and had participated actively in social movements. In contrast to the many radicals who had rejected graduate school as irrelevant to the pressing issues of the times, they had viewed academic work as an outgrowth of their involvement in political movements. Explicitly rejecting the detached mode of intellectuals, they believed that active engagement with social and political issues heightened the significance of their work. "My graduate education was in a very, very political context," noted one woman who had studied the history of the Communist Party. "As that context has fallen away, my interest in history has waned." Others had molded their visions of academic careers on the lives of the university faculty they had known at elite institutions. When they realized most professors taught at less prestigious institutions, where class loads were larger, the student body less educated, and the administration more intrusive, their interest in the profession evaporated.

Some displaced academics also contended that the worth of academic careers had diminished as a result of changes within colleges and universities during the seventies. After cataloguing in great detail the deteriorating conditions of the faculty at a state college where he taught part-time, one man concluded, "It's a dying way of life; I don't want to go down with it." Indeed, throughout higher education, faculty have witnessed the decline of their real incomes, their autonomy, and their research support. Nevertheless, it is possible that the harshness of the critique of displaced academics stemmed from a need to depreciate the value of what they had lost.

Although these academics sought to defuse discontent, they did express anger. Some railed against the system of tenure, which they viewed as the means by which university faculty warded off competition from younger scholars, not as the essential bulwark of academic freedom. One man, for example, charged:

Many professors have exploited the privilege of tenure, not allowing young, bright people to move in, sucking the blood out of the system. This enrages me. It's bad enough that there are no jobs, but to have dead wood in the positions that could be available—that's just outrageous.

Graduate school advisers were also the objects of special attack. Some displaced academics accused their professors of callousness or indifference: ensconced in secure positions themselves, they had exhibited little understanding of the difficulties encountered by younger scholars.[39] The misdeeds of the advisers of other interviewees had been sins of omission: they had neglected to inform their students of the grim job prospects or had failed to furnish information about alternative careers. One historian set forth a peculiarly paternalistic model of appropriate faculty behavior:

My professors would wring their hands and say how horrible the job market was, but they never had the lunch with me that they should have, when they put an arm around me and said, "Son...."

But their anger generally remained restricted to these two targets. Frances Fox Piven and Richard A. Cloward have asserted:

People experience deprivation and oppression within a concrete setting, not as the end product of large and abstract processes and it is the concrete experience that molds their discontent into specific grievances against specific targets.... No small wonder, therefore, that when the poor rebel they so often rebel against the overseer of the poor, or the slumlord, or the middling merchant, and not against the banks or the governing elites to whom the overseer, the slumlord, and the merchant also defer.[40]

The attitudes of displaced academics serve to validate this point. They carefully analyzed broad social and economic patterns, but they displayed little hostility toward either "the system" or toward the legislators, regents, and trustees who defined the institutional realities within which senior professors operated. Intergenerational conflict may also have been a factor in focusing their wrath. Graduate school fosters a sense of dependence, and relationships between professors and graduate students often resemble those between parents and children. As the above quotation by a historian indicates, some students looked to their advisers not just for intellectual direction but for personal guidance as well. Disappointed in their expectations, they turned their fury on their mentors and on the system of tenure that protects them.

The anger of the respondents was not only narrow in focus; it was also diluted by feelings of guilt and inadequacy. Doubting themselves, some displaced academics feared that their professors may have been justified in overlooking them. In addition, they worried that they had disappointed their advisers. By remaining unemployed, they not only had failed to fulfill their promise but had withheld an important reward from professors, who gain prestige and power from the successful placement of students. The comment of a woman who had continued to live near her former graduate school reflected thoughts that were widespread:

> I felt very uncomfortable when I ran into one of my old professors. I was apologetic, although they didn't do a thing to help me. None lifted a finger to help me get a job, but I worried that I was an embarrassment to them because you're supposed to find a job and go away.

Western society periodically has been haunted by the specter of an unemployed intelligentsia growing increasingly disaffected and becoming drawn into revolutionary activity. The displaced academics in this study, however, exhibited little potential for collective action. Most were unwilling to challenge the academic structures that had rewarded them in the past. In addition, they accepted without question a market analysis of the job crisis: if the number of teaching positions was declining, then some people inevitably must be out of work. Their adherence to the concept of a career also shaped their response to unemployment. For many years, these academics had organized their behavior around the belief that success was a personal victory, failure a personal defeat. To form alliances among themselves would threaten well-established attitudes and patterns of action.

Graduate training also had discouraged them from developing a sense of solidarity. Graduate schools are ranked in prestige, and graduates from institutions at opposite ends of the hierarchy assume they share neither scholarly interests nor career prospects. Within schools, knowledge is fragmented into separate and often competing disciplines, and students in different departments rarely interact. The emphasis on specialization further segregates students. Because successful academic careers depend on the mastery of a narrow body of information, students try to become specialists in an esoteric field, and they select research topics that are exceedingly narrow in scope. Seeking a monopoly of expertise, they jealously guard their work from others. Even if they share similar interests, students find themselves isolated. Because they are evaluated on the basis of their individual achievements, collaboration is discouraged. Moreover, students within the same subspecialty are forced to vie for the favor of their chosen mentor. Writing a dissertation thus may be an especially lonely process. Many academics enter the job market immediately after having spent one or two years in solitude, enjoying only fleeting interactions with colleagues. Finally, the experience of unemployment itself accentuates a sense of estrangement from others. Like all jobless workers, the displaced academics in this study held themselves aloof from those who found themselves in the same predicament. Thus, they had little opportunity to share grievances, which might have led to the development of a group consciousness. Although they insisted that their misfortune was caused by social and economic forces beyond their control, they simultaneously believed that job failure resulted from serious personal flaws, and they turned their anger back on themselves. Career loss was, in their view, primarily a personal problem, requiring individual solutions.

NOTES

1. See Emily K. Abel, "Middle-Class Culture for the Urban Poor: The Educational Thought of Samuel Barnett," *Social Service Review* 53 (December 1978):596-620.

2. E. Wright Bakke, *The Unemployed Man* (New York: Dutton, 1935).

3. Bakke, *Citizens Without Work: A Study of the Effects of Unemployment Upon the Workers' Social Relations and Practices* (New Haven: Yale University Press, 1940); Bakke, *The Unemployed Worker: A Study of the Task of Making a Living Without a Job* (New Haven: Yale University Press, 1940).

4. Richard B. DuBoff, "Unemployment in the United States: An Historical Summary," *Monthly Review*, November 1977, pp. 10-24; Eli Ginzberg, *Good Jobs, Bad Jobs, No Jobs* (Cambridge, Mass.: Harvard University Press, 1979), p. 35.

5. Works published during this period include Eva Mueller and Jay Schmiedeskamp, *Persistent Unemployment, 1957-61* (Kalamazoo, Mich.: Upjohn Institute for Employment Research, 1962); Harold L. Sheppard, Louis A. Ferman, and Seymour Faber, *Too Old to Work—Too Young to Retire: A Case Study of a Permanent Plant Shutdown* (Washington, D.C.: Government Printing Office, 1962).

6. Paula Goldman Leventman, *Professionals Out of Work* (New York: Free Press, 1981); Harry Maurer, *Not Working: An Oral History of the Unemployed* (New York: Holt, Rinehart and Winston, 1979); Kay Lehman Schlozman and Sidney Verba, *Injury to Insult: Unemployment, Class and Political Response* (Cambridge, Mass.: Harvard University Press, 1979). For a comparison of the effects of unemployment during these two eras, see Marie Jahoda, *Employment and Unemployment: A Social-Psychological Analysis* (Cambridge: Cambridge University Press, 1982).

7. Schlozman and Verba, *Injury to Insult*, p. 2; Maurer, *Not Working*, p. 3.

8. Leventman, *Professionals Out of Work*.

9. Leventman found that the younger men (aged 34-39) in her sample adjusted more easily to unemployment than did older ones. (*Professionals Out of Work*, p. 147.) Similarly, during the Depression, younger workers fared better than older ones.

10. For the sake of simplicity, I am differentiating only between married and unmarried interviewees and am not discussing diverse household patterns.

11. Bakke, *Citizens*; Bakke, *Unemployed Worker*; Mirra Komarovsky, *The Unemployed Man and His Family* (New York: Dryden Press, 1940).

12. Bakke, *Citizens*, p. 7; Marie Jahoda, Paul Lazarsfield, and Hans Zeisel, *Marienthal* (Chicago: Aldine-Atherton, 1933); Maurer, *Not Working*, p. 60.

13. Bakke, *Citizens*, p. 113; Katharine H. Briar, *The Effect of Long-Term Unemployment on Workers and Their Families*, unpublished manuscript (San Francisco: 1978), p. 48; Leventman, *Professionals Out of Work*, p. 150; Maurer, *Not Working*, p. 91.

14. See Schlozman and Verba, *Injury to Insult*, p. 191n.

15. Frances Fox Piven and Richard A. Cloward, *Regulating the Poor: The Functions of Public Welfare* (New York: Vintage, 1971), p. 61.

16. John A. Garraty, *Unemployment in History: Economic Thought and Public Policy* (New York: Harper & Row, 1979), pp. 177-87.

17. Studs Terkel, *Hard Times: An Oral History of the Great Depression* (New York: Pocket Books, 1970), p. 19.

18. Maurer, *Not Working*, p. 5.

19. Richard Sennett and Jonathan Cobb, *The Hidden Injuries of Class* (New York: Vintage, 1972), p. 97.

20. Leventman, *Professionals Out of Work*, pp. 154-55; but see Schlozman and Verba, *Injury to Insult*, pp. 191-98.

21. Schlozman and Verba, *Injury to Insult*, pp. 193-94.

22. Eligibility depended partly on the laws of the states in which these academics lived. In some states, part-time faculty can collect unemployment during intersessions and summer vacations; in others, they can file claims only when dismissed. Significantly, some part-timers had not even inquired about whether or not they were eligible to collect benefits.

23. Leventman, *Professionals Out of Work*, p. 119; Maurer, *Not Working*, pp. 40, 49, 62, 112, 130, 158; Schlozman and Verba, *Injury to Insult*, p. 199.

24. See Magali Sarfatti Larson, *The Rise of Professionalism: A Sociological Analysis* (Berkeley: University of California Press, 1977), p. 241; Sennett and Cobb, *Hidden Injuries*, p. 227.

25. Leventman, *Professionals Out of Work*, p. 119.

26. Schlozman and Verba, *Injury to Insult*, p. 65.

27. Irving Bernstein, *The Lean Years* (Boston: Houghton Mifflin, 1960), p. 332; Jahoda, *Employment and Unemployment*, pp. 22-24; Komarovsky, *Unemployed Man*, p. 80; Maurer, *Not Working*, pp. 42, 44-45, 99, 226, 233, 245-46; Schlozman and Verba, *Injury to Insult*, p. 58. During the Depression, some unemployed workers became so disoriented that they lost their sense of time and allowed small chores to take hours. (Jahoda, Lazarsfield, and Zeisel, *Marienthal*, chap. 7.)

28. Larson, *Professionalism*, p. 215.

29. The problems particular to academics who change careers will be discussed in Chapter 6.

30. A study conducted by two psychologists lends credence to their fears. Douglas P. Peters and Stephen J. Ceci resubmitted twelve articles already published by investigators from prestigious universities, disguising the authors' names and changing their affiliations to such institutions as the "Tri-Valley Center for Human Potential." Three of the resubmissions were detected by reviewers. Eight of the other nine were

rejected. (See Angus Paul, "Scholars Propose Methods of Improving the Peer Review of Journal Articles," *Chronicle of Higher Education*, 11 June 1982, p. 19.) We can assume that the papers of scholars without any institutional affiliations would be judged at least as harshly as those of researchers at low-status institutions.

31. Ronald Gross, "Independent Scholarship: Passion and Pitfalls," *Chronicle of Higher Education*, 8 June 1981, p. 64.

32. "Independent Scholarship Newsletter," no. 6, July 1983, p. 3.

33. Malcolm G. Scully, ' "Independent' Scholars Backed at Conference," *Chronicle of Higher Education*, 17 November 1983, p. 3.

34. Scully, ' "Independent Scholars Find There Is Life Beyond the University," *Chronicle of Higher Education*, 29 October 1979, p. 11; *Time*, 28 July 1980, p. 48.

35. See also Lewis C. Solmon, Laura Kent, Nancy L. Ochsner, and Margo-Lea Hurwicz, *Underemployed Ph.D.'s* (Lexington, Mass.: Lexington, 1981), p. 11.

36. Piven and Cloward have challenged Bakke's account of the thirties. They describe the large-scale demonstrations that, they claim, were responsible for the inauguration of governmental relief programs. (*Poor People's Movements: Why They Succeed, How They Fail* [New York: Vintage, 1979], chap. 2; see also Bernard Sternsher, "Victims of the Great Depression: Self-Blame/Non-Self-Blame, Radicalism, and Pre-1929 Experiences," *Social Science History* 1 [Winter 1977]:137-77.)

37. Bakke, *Citizens*; Bakke, *Unemployed Worker.*

38. See also Leventman, *Professionals Out of Work*, p. 5.

39. See Paul Blumberg, "Lockouts, Layoffs and the New Academic Proletariat," in *The Hidden Professoriate: Credentialism, Professionalism and the Tenure Process*, ed. Arthur S. Wilke (Westport, Conn.: Greenwood, 1979), p. 45.

40. Piven and Cloward, *Poor People's Movements*, p. 20.

Chapter 2
ENTRANCES AND EXITS

Like most other unemployed workers, many displaced academics have experienced both the despair of fruitless job hunting and the trauma of dismissal. The first section of this chapter will examine the process of looking for academic jobs. The second will discuss academics who were dismissed from tenure-track positions at the stage of tenure or pretenure reviews.

LOOKING FOR WORK

During this period of serious imbalance between supply and demand in the job market, prospective job seekers should be aware above all...that the search may well be one of the most difficult endeavors they have ever undertaken.
>   —*Modern Language Association, "A Guide for Job Candidates and Department Chairmen in English and Foreign Languages," 1978.*

The possibility of failure is the most uncomfortable phenomenon in American life.
>   —*Richard Sennett and Jonathan Cobb, The Hidden Injuries of Class, 1973*

In academia, the search for work assumes a prescribed form. Job hunting follows the seasons of the academic year, beginning in early autumn, when the first job openings are advertised, and ending in late spring, when all but a few temporary positions are filled. Throughout the fall, unemployed academics answer advertisements, prepare their dossiers, and wait for requests for letters of recommendation and samples of their written work. Their primary hopes center on the annual conventions held by many disciplines in December, when colleges and universities interview about twenty-five of the leading contenders for each position. The next step is to receive a summons for a day-long, on-campus interview, a prize awarded only to the top two or three candidates. The final selection is announced several weeks later.

All the academics interviewed for this study had applied for jobs at some point in their careers, and many had searched unsuccessfully for several years in succession. They explained their tenacity in several ways. One woman, interviewed while attending the convention of the Modern Language Association (MLA) for the fifth time, remarked, "An industrial worker or someone on an assembly line is never going to fulfill himself through a job, but that's what I want. I'm playing for very high stakes. I know the odds are small, but if I win, I win a great deal." Thus, she described herself as a "bulldog" who "was just going to hang in there until something breaks; it absolutely has to." Another long-term job seeker viewed an academic position as "not just a job, not just what you do from nine to five, but as salvation." One academic, who had never seriously investigated alternative careers, assumed there was "an enormous chasm" between college teaching and every other type of work. In order to utilize his skills and training, it was essential to obtain a tenure-track appointment.

An equally compelling motivation was to gain recognition for hard work. One man, who had enrolled in film school even before finishing his Ph.D. dissertation and had decided that to be "locked into an academic career" would be a "nightmare," nevertheless looked for jobs as diligently as any of his classmates:

I wanted to receive a stamp of approval after putting all those years into getting a Ph.D. When I went to the MLA convention, I wanted them to put a gold star on my forehead and say, "Look, you're good, you've done it, and now we want to hire you." That would have made me feel really good.

A woman entered the job market hoping to find "confirmation that I'm charming and that my dissertation is good and original research."

Moreover, graduate students frequently oriented their efforts toward success in the marketplace. Many displaced academics acknowledged that they had chosen courses that would impress prospective employers, dissertations that could be converted easily into books, and advisers who were reputed to have the best records for placing protégés. Although several also criticized the commodification of academic work—the displacement of scholarly mastery by marked competitiveness—they realized that a refusal to enter the race, or a concession of failure after only one or two unsuccessful attempts, would render years of effort meaningless.

Finally, despite their awareness of the grim job market, many academics convinced themselves that their own prospects were excellent. In their study of humanities doctoral students, Lewis C. Solmon, Nancy L. Ochsner, and Margo-Lea Hurwicz noted the unrealistically high expectations they held. Even students who knew that only one job would be available for every ten new doctorates assumed they would be the lucky ones.[1] Similarly, a woman I interviewed, who had been looking for jobs for the past seven years, stated: "I really do start every year with hope, with genuine optimism, with a sense that this is going to be the year that it all pays off." A second woman explained the source of such confidence: "We've been the ones to get the fellowships and the scholarships and the TAs [teaching assistantships]. Without recognizing it, when we hear that the job market is bad, we remember that some people get jobs and we think, 'Well, I will, too.'" One example demonstrates that displaced academics occasionally interpreted statistics to justify choices made for other reasons. The same figures that convinced one recent graduate of the utter futility of persevering in the job search provided his classmate with a glimmer of hope. The first explained his determination to enroll in business school by the fact that only six out of twelve classmates had found teaching jobs. But, like the proverbial cup that can be either half-full or half-empty, this placement record was viewed hopefully by the other. He planned to continue looking for academic positions because six people did obtain jobs.

When asked to describe the application process, several academics began by discussing the professional conferences they had attended in search of work. They used the conventional metaphors to refer to these meetings—"slave auction" and "cattle market." Although candidates expected to demonstrate their special merits as individuals, they found themselves subjected to an "assembly-line interview system." Occasionally job seekers recalled the joy of performing well in an interview for a particularly desirable position. A more typical experience was chronicled by a woman shortly after her first trip to the convention of the Modern Language Association:

> The MLA was beyond my wildest dreams. The main hotels were just so mobbed with miserable graduate students. In order to get to your interview in the hotel, you had to get to the people you were looking for on the phone. In the most crowded of the hotels, there were huge lines on the house phones, and the operators were so swamped that you would just stand there while minutes of your interview ticked away.

One of her interviews forced her to question both her own capabilities and the meaning of academia:

> I was interviewed by five people and my feeling was that they wanted to expose my ignorance. It became just like a Ph.D. exam. I felt terribly humiliated and lay awake that night and heard it and heard it and heard it. Throughout the rest of the convention, as I was listening to the papers, a name would come up and, instead of thinking oh yes, there's such and such whom I still want to read, I would feel panicked. It was a terrible ordeal that distorted what I thought academia was supposed to be about.

Another woman, who had attended the same convention five times in succession, focused on the relationships between the candidates:

> There's a very predatory atmosphere. There's just incredible tension. Everybody's eyeing everyone else and checking out their credentials and asking, "and how many publications do you have?" It's just terrible.

Because every peer was a potential competitor, the candidates could not provide consolation to each other.

Others emphasized the time and money invested in the application process. A woman who eked out a marginal existence by piecing together a number of part-time teaching jobs estimated that she annually spent about $1,000 on postage, telephone calls, air fare to conventions, and hotel accommodation. A man who had been applying for jobs for eight years lamented the time he had wasted:

> One of the many serious and severe inequities of being in this position is that one spends, over a period of years, months and months and months of working time in all the various phases of job hunting. Yet this does not show up on a curriculum vite. You get no credit. All that simply disappears, it goes down the drain.

As he was well aware, academic reputations must be made early, and the worth of a publication often varies inversely with the age of its author.[2] Thus, he feared that his value was diminishing steadily because the process of job hunting prevented him from adding as many entries to his resumé as he thought he should.

Job candidates also worried about losing control over their lives. Failure to reap the rewards they anticipated flowing from their talents and achievements had jeopardized their assumptions about how the world operated, and they came to doubt their ability to take effective action on their own behalf. Familiar methods of improving their rank in the academic hierarchy—publishing another article or delivering a paper at a prestigious conference—now seemed pointless. In addition, they rapidly became convinced of the futility of personal initiative in the job search itself. As one man put it:

> One of the most difficult things is that you can't seem to make a move that makes any difference to what's happen-

ing to you. You can say, "O.K., I'm going to write a letter to every college and junior college in California and one of them is bound to hit the mark, somebody's going to see it somewhere," but that doesn't happen.

One woman initially pursued what she described as "an aggressive approach," contacting everyone who might be privy to new information about job openings and seeking out acquaintances who knew members of various search committees. But she abandoned such activities when her efforts came to naught.

In addition, candidates were acutely aware that their futures were dependent on the decisions of others. One historian explained:

Because of the job situation, my wife and I are not going to be able to choose a lot of aspects of our lives that normally we'd assume that we'd be able to choose—the kind of life that we live, the kind of place that we'd live in. In the field of history you can't rely on saying we'll go someplace for three years and then we'll move on to a better job because there are no better jobs and, even if there were, a hundred other people would be applying for them. That increases the importance of any one particular job. It may mean that for the rest of your life you're going to live in Oklahoma, or it may mean that you'll live in some cosmopolitan city. But somebody else is doing all the deciding and you're simply sitting there and waiting for your life to be decided for you.

A woman recalled the ephemeral feeling of control she enjoyed at the moment when she believed she was on the verge of receiving two desirable job offers:

I felt so powerful. I really thought, this is a big decision. I am this whole human being and I have choices, I have something to offer and I don't have to go somewhere just because they tell me to. Those feelings that I had control and that I had some choices over my life were so wonderful.

This woman's image of a "whole human being" was a professional —someone whose unique competence freed him or her from dependence on others. The sharpest blow to displaced academics was the discovery that their expertise no longer guaranteed them autonomy in their work lives.

When academics did have options, they tended to be exceedingly narrow. For example, one woman historian was offered a tenure-track position at a church-related college in a small town in Missouri. She saw herself faced with two equally unacceptable alternatives—to spend the rest of her life in a town "consisting of Baptist churches and bars" or to drop out of academia, "turning my back on everything I had prepared for." Ultimately, she did reject the job offer and enter a new field of work, but she had no sense of having determined her own destiny.

In sum, despite the terms "job hunt" and "job seeker," many candidates felt themselves to be passive participants in the recruitment process. Although they had initiated numerous applications, they experienced the rest of the job search as something that happened to them. One woman compared herself to a "marionette" because "other people pulled the strings." For several other women the process evoked memories of teenage dating: "It was like high school, waiting for the phone to ring," one stated.

People who entered the job market year after year also noted that this quest tended to pervade their lives. The wife of one veteran job seeker explained how the rhythms of the year came to be shaped by the dynamic of expectation and frustration:

> Job hunting starts out in September and October. You're feeling pretty good because the first job notices come out in October and there are a few jobs there and at that time you don't fear getting your mail and when the phone rings you don't think it's going to be a job so you can be fairly relaxed. The big goal is to get interviews at the AHA [the annual history professional conference] in December. Bob's been to every AHA for ten years.
>
> Then in January and February you begin to wait to be notified about on-campus interviews. When you don't hear from a job for about two months, you begin to assume, well, that one's gone. And then in our lives what

seems to happen every year is that late, about April, some job comes up and Bob gets really close to it. Each time we go through a sort of cycle. I kind of try to adjust myself to living in this particular place, find out a bit about it, think of all the good things, and think about what I could do there. Quite often Bob's been to the particular place and comes back with an armful of booklets and maps and pictures and he tells me all about it and about the people and everything and we get really involved....They invariably take longer than they said they would to make the decision and then they also take a very long time to notify you that you've been unsuccessful. It usually ends up with Bob phoning them. We set a date usually: if we haven't heard by such and such a date, Bob will phone. So he phones, and so far, every year, the job has gone to somebody else. I've now written a succession of letters to my parents. It's beginning to be almost a ritual. I start out, "here's my annual letter that we didn't get this year's job" and we go through a few days of depression. We throw out all the literature that Bob brought back, we gradually tell our friends and then we sort of psychologically adjust to spending another year here and start the whole cycle all over again. And all that energy and planning and thinking and hoping has been absolutely wasted.

As this quotation indicates, near misses tended to be doubly devastating. For one thing, the more seriously applicants were considered, the more thoroughly their credentials were sifted and weighed by the search committee. Rejection of candidates at a preliminary stage could imply that they were not even minimally qualified; but it also could indicate that their fields of study were inappropriate. By the time candidates' names appeared on short lists of finalists, they had submitted resumés and writing samples and been interviewed briefly at the convention. At the next stage, scrutiny was even more exhaustive. During on-campus interviews, candidates presented formal talks and met with every member of the department. After they left, their files again were rigorously examined. Thus, rejected finalists tended to feel that they had failed major inspections. Moreover, because they had made personal contacts with members of the search committees and begun to perceive them as potential colleagues, they were particularly vulnerable to adverse judgments. There was no prize for second place. Some runners-up proudly recited the names of the institutions to which they had been invited for interviews, but all were aware that in this race the winner takes all. Rejected aspirants had to resume the search process anew. Finally, applicants often cultivated strong attachments to the institutions at which they considered themselves serious contenders for jobs. One woman explained that she indulged in fantasies about each prospect partly as a means of convincing herself that she "really did want to live in X or Lubbock, Texas." The closer she came to any particular job, the more elaborate her fantasies grew. When a job in New Jersey seemed particularly promising, "I literally had to force myself to stop thinking about the kind of house I would buy and my cousin in Patterson, New Jersey, who's married to a school teacher whose hobby is fixing old VWs." After a day-long interview at another university the following year, she began to make mental lists of the members of the department she would invite to each dinner party. When she received a letter of rejection, "it felt like when a lover leaves."

All of the academics interviewed for this study had to contend with the damage to their self-confidence. One man saw himself as having been scarred by continual rejections:

> You tell yourself that you're really competent, really good, and there's just a lot of stiff competition out there, so the fact that you send out all these letters and can't get hired shouldn't mean anything. But it does. It gets to you—rejection notice after rejection notice, form letter after form letter.

Applicants employed a variety of stratagems to deal with the repeated rebuffs. Some tried to disassociate themselves from the whole process. One woman claimed that she was able to be "a little bit more detached" than some of her male counterparts: "As a woman, it's slightly easier to present myself as sort of dabbling in my own time." Although she was seriously committed to the field of history, she could save face by pretending that scholarship was peripheral to her life. Another woman distanced herself by asking friends to type her application letters. Two job seekers forced themselves to forget the names of the institutions to which they had applied, and they claimed to throw away rejection notices without reading them. Still others made games out of their accumulation of form letters. One woman set herself the goal of receiving a letter from every state in the Union; a second used his pile of rejection letters to wallpaper his breakfast room; and a third prided himself on being a "connoisseur of 'no' letters." Finally, a woman described the tactics she used to cope with the suspense of waiting when she was a finalist:

> I find myself making two sets of plans all the time: the things I would do immediately should I be offered the job, people I would have to notify and various things I would have to do right away. I also have a sort of reserve list that I'll do if I don't get it. Like I have some plans of things I'll plant in the garden. In the week after I heard that I hadn't got the job, I'd go out and I'd spend some money on the garden and I'd plant things and that would be my way of telling myself, "O.K., I'm going to be here for a while." You learn little dodges like that.

Displaced academics also sought to defend themselves by stressing the size and quality of the competition and by focusing on the irrationality of the entire recruitment process. In some cases, they claimed, decisions were made long before jobs were advertised, the criteria announced in official notices were disregarded routinely, and search committees cursorily reviewed the records of candidates. Cynicism about the capabilities of those doing the hiring also was shared widely; several job seekers contended that, because the qualifications of applicants have escalated, the credentials of the interviewers tended to be inferior to those of the candidates they were evaluating. Furthermore, they charged, the skills most valued by hiring committees were not necessarily the ones that produced inspiring teachers or creative scholars. One discouraged job seeker explained the source of her difficulties as follows:

> I really do feel that I am being judged a great deal on personality and that is not one area in which I shine. I

have now a body of written work that they can go to, but I think they assume I can't teach because I'm shy, basically...In fact, I do a first rate job in my teaching and for them to decide that because I'm reticent in an interview I can't teach is absurd. I have all these teaching evaluations that should indicate otherwise.

Finally, academics raised the issue of sex and race discrimination. Although this is illegal, the law is widely flouted and, in any case, leaves ample room for favoritism.[3] Surprisingly, however, it was white men more than any other group who dwelt on this topic. Although most of the women assumed that bias was built into the appointment process, they rarely complained of individual instances. Similarly, when asked about racism in the job market, a black man explained that he neglected to mention discriminatory practices "because they go without saying." By contrast, several white men expressed outrage at what they perceived to be the prevalence of reverse discrimination, and about half of the white male interviewees stated unequivocally that, had they been women or minorities, they would be employed in tenure-track jobs.[4]

Nevertheless, all of the job seekers wanted to believe that the academic selection process correctly identifies the worthy. Their long experience of academic success had given them a stake in the meritocracy. Thus, most of the displaced academics acknowledged the legitimacy of search committees and continued to look to them for recognition of scholarly promise. Even some of the most cynical interviewees confessed to a residual belief in the close correlation between ability and success in the job market.

Nor could statistical evidence fully assuage feelings of unworthiness. Most candidates were aware that a single advertised opening could elicit over four hundred applications.[5] But, as one man observed, "I have a terrible feeling of failure because even if there's just one job in the United States and a thousand applicants, somebody's getting it and if you don't, you fail." Richard Sennett and Jonathan Cobb have argued, "In this society...the consciousness of human worth is a consciousness of self as individual, standing out from a mass who seem pretty much the same."[6] It is particularly important to be a "star" in higher education, as in sports and entertainment. Terms such as "the very best," "the truly outstanding," and "the ablest" are used repeatedly in academic discourse; academics seek to convince themselves that they belong in their fields because they possess extraordinary talent, not just competence. Failure to obtain any job thus forces them to confront the possibility that someone else might be better.

Some displaced academics claimed that rejection in the job market was particularly painful to them because they were not accustomed to losing academic competitions. One woman explained that she had come to depend on success in school as the basis of her social identity:

> When I was growing up, the largest source of praise for me was that I was such a good student and I became so ego-involved in that that it remains the strongest source of my self worth. Getting praise for being bright compensates in a lot of ways for other areas of my life where I don't feel quite so positively about myself. So to be failing in that one area, which is my area of success, has been quite destructive.

But reliance on academic achievement as the source of self-esteem could be viewed from a different perspective. Intellectual ability is not simply one among a number of undifferentiated qualities that an individual can possess. In our society, skill at performing the tasks set by teachers is accorded the highest value. It also plays a significant role in determining class position. Like several of the interviewees, the woman quoted above had been able to transcend a working-class background through outstanding success within the educational system. Thus, it is possible that academics are better able than most to withstand rejection. From an early age they have been recognized as special, and this has endowed them with a self-image that may continue to sustain and support them. Failure in the job market may jeopardize this sense of superiority, but it cannot erase it entirely.

When do people become discouraged and drop out of the race? Many were unwilling to relinquish their attempts to find teaching jobs as long as they could preserve any hope. One historian observed, "You give up, but you don't give up, that's the trouble. There's an ambivalence that's just tremendous. I hung in for about five years, hoping beyond hope, believing but not believing, taking other jobs and still hoping." During the Depression, the unemployed continued to pound the pavement long after they knew there was no possibility of finding work.[7] Similarly, even a few displaced academics who already had enrolled in retraining programs continued to reply to job notices because, in the words of one, "there's always that long last chance."

Nevertheless, several people had ceased to apply for teaching jobs by the time I interviewed them. Some had found rewarding careers in other fields. Others formed part of the large category of "discouraged job seekers." A few doubted that they could continue to present themselves as convincing candidates because they had so little self-confidence. A number gave up when they realized that each passing year lessened the likelihood of eventual success.

But the hope of obtaining an academic position dies hard. Even formal renunciation of the competition did not erase the secret dream of success. Long after one woman had put job hunting behind her, she continued to bring her resumé to conferences "just in case something turned up." Another confessed to a lingering fantasy that "if I do something really sterling, some university will call me up and *insist* that I come and work for them." Still another woman continued "to publish like mad" so that people "won't be able to overlook me. I think I'm counting on there being some sort of merit system in the sky."

LOSING A JOB

> It was the worst blow I ever had. I've been divorced. My father died a few months before I got fired. Both constitutionally and by event I've been through a lot of emotional upheaval in my life, and I've never been through anything like getting fired. Never.
> —*Thirty-year-old woman interviewed by Harry Maurer, Not Working, 1979.*

During the sixties and early seventies, academics who succeeded in obtaining tenure-track jobs justly could be confident of being promoted up through the ranks. Tenure was granted frequently, and faculty members could move easily from one institution to another.[8] However, in this era of retrenchment, the careers of an increasing number of junior faculty are truncated prematurely. Although the promise of regular promotions and tenure may have been implicit in their original appointments, many realize there is no longer any room for them at the top.

Seven of the academics interviewed for this study had been fired from tenure-track positions. Unlike most displaced academics, who only gradually became aware that they could not achieve their original aspirations, this group experienced abrupt and traumatic losses. As a result, their responses resembled those of people who have recently lost intimate and essential relationships.[9] Even faculty members who had anticipated adverse decisions were shocked when they finally occurred. Two became physically ill, a characteristic reaction of the bereaved.[10] One was a woman who had been denied tenure at a major research institution:

> The immediate thing that happened to me was that I got violently ill for the first time in years. I got bronchial pneumonia which I think was my body's response to the whole thing.... It just simply collapsed.

The other was a man who failed to pass a pretenure review at a small New England college:

> I spent a lot of time with a doctor last year because I thought I had an ulcer and I'm not the ulcer type. And yet I really started having stomach pains.... I went scuba diving in the Keys during a week off—felt great—came back Monday morning, went to the office and by Monday lunch I had to go back and see the doctor.

Others tried to deny that dismissal affected them. One woman claimed to feel more liberated than bereft; she "breathed a huge sigh of relief" when informed that she would not be retained by her college although she desperately wanted to pursue her career. Two other women spent the summers following negative pretenure reviews pretending that nothing had happened. One saw friends, drank a lot, and tried to forget the institution at which she had taught for three years. The other traveled throughout the West, at one point sending a friend a postcard boasting that she was "as happy as I have ever been in my life." In retrospect, she realized that her refusal to acknowledge her loss caused her to feel detached from everything around her. She regained a sense of connectedness only when she decided to stop "hiding" and "face reality."

Even after the shock wore off, a number of academics remained severely depressed. One woman spoke of her "real slough of despond," and of her "inability to act because of the emotional sense of helplessness." Another remarked:

> I had to deal with lots of wild, conflicting emotions. It took me about six months before I could really go out into society without suddenly bursting into tears at strange moments. I would have to watch whom I was with.

How can we account for such strong reactions? The loss of a tenure-track job often signals the end of one's academic career. One woman noted that the "intellectual life had fitted me supremely well, and to be thrown out of that into the cold hostile world was very hard to cope with." Some of these academics staunchly refused to apply for subsequent academic positions. Having discovered that a career as a college teacher was less secure than they had believed, they wanted to find a completely different type of work. "I couldn't afford another failure," one man explained. A woman interpreted her determination to leave higher education as sour grapes: "One of the things I was saying to my college was, 'na, na, if you don't want me, I don't want you either.'" But the displaced academics who did enter the job market rapidly discovered that their prospects of moving to other institutions were exceedingly slim. During the years that had elapsed since they first applied for jobs, the number of openings had plunged. Furthermore, the drop in the available jobs at the senior ranks had been particularly steep.[11] The few colleges and universities that advertised such positions sought luminaries, not the "rejects" of other institutions. Thus, as these academics applied for jobs, they gradually became aware that they had suffered irreplaceable losses.

The grant of tenure is the only significant means by which institutions of higher education acknowledge the services and achievements of their junior faculty. One woman found herself constantly "reflecting on all my wasted energy and what did I have to show for it?" The curt letter of dismissal received by a second woman intensified her belief that her efforts were totally unappreciated:

> The letter I got was from the president. It's funny that I don't remember the words anymore because I would have said two years ago I would never forget those words. It was a form letter, and it was obviously written by a college lawyer so that no one would sue them. There was nothing about the kind of service I had performed, about what a good teacher I was. And that was horrible, just horrible.

In addition, the interviewees had to sever their connections with institutions at which they had spent critical years of their lives. One woman stated:

> When I first went to this university I was able to psychologically disassociate myself from my colleagues and department. But then I got hooked and made a psychological commitment to really make it work. I got to know a lot of people. I went there prepared to leave at any moment but something happened along the way. This identification with the department and the university made the rejection all the worse.

Another woman expressed an even deeper sense of loss:

> I was incredibly invested in that place. I had really loved it and I had really felt at home there in a way I had really never felt any place else in my life. It had to do with what age I was and what else was going on in my life but I had finally gotten out of school, I had finally finished my thesis. I had dragged out the dissertation and finishing it had to do with becoming an adult and getting out of that dependent childlike relationship with my adviser. It was a rite of passage. I came to this college as an adult, I wasn't a teaching assistant anymore, I wasn't saying, "Well, here is what Professor Harris wants you to know." It was *my* class and certainly in my classes I really learned more about authority and presence than I had ever known. I also had

a house, the first house I ever had. So it was the place where I had gone from being 26 to 31. Five very, very significant years. One of the things I was afraid about being fired was that I would lose all that.

Just as the bereaved typically discover that they have defined themselves largely in terms of the relationships they have lost,[12] so this woman's sense of herself as a mature person was embedded in her position as a professor at a specific institution; she feared she would lose her entire status as an adult.

The traumatic effects of termination are intensified by the manner in which they occur. Unlike most worker layoffs, these generally are individual, not collective, thereby insinuating that the victims are personally responsible. One woman in this study had been fired along with several other instructors when her college declared financial exigency. But most of the academics lost their jobs after their records had been scrutinized carefully by their institutions. Three had been denied tenure, and three others had failed to pass extensive pretenure reviews conducted after they had taught three or four years. One woman initially internalized the unfavorable report of her department:

I had a feeling of failure, just utter failure. You start to incorporate the judgments of these people. You're handed all this stuff that they have said about you and while you know that they have falsified the record, you believe it....It takes a while for you to realize that that sort of thing does not really define you.

A man similarly had difficulty maintaining an image of himself as a competent and worthy individual:

You go through this tremendous soul searching, bottom-ing out of the ego. You think that personally, as well as professionally, you must not be worthy because these people in a very public, august procedure turn you down in everything you spent ten years of your professional life working for. And, yes, once in a while you can stand up above it all and say, "I know better, I know my credentials, I know my qualifications, I know from people who can judge me correctly and properly because they told me my worth. How can I conceivably let these people tell me that this is not the case?" But that self-encouragement you give yourself is rare—at least in the first year.

Here the academic rituals that serve to validate successful candidates worked in reverse. Because his department voted against him after formal and elaborate proceedings, he concluded he was wholly without merit.

Continuing contact with colleagues tended to reinforce feelings of inadequacy and self-doubt. Because tenure and pretenure decisions typically occur in early spring, academics must continue teaching at their schools during the months immediately following their dismissals. Furthermore, the rules of the American Association of University Professors require member institutions to grant a year's notice, and four of the academics in this study returned to their colleges or universities for final years. One woman described her experience of remaining at an institution after it had rejected her:

That year at X was just unutterably painful, in the constant feeling of being excluded, the constant feeling of a good thing having turned sour. Here I was now living in a place where they said they didn't want me. It was like being at a party and looking at a circle of people laughing together and thinking, "I'm outside that circle."

Other members of her department were preoccupied with finding her replacement; when she learned that a student doubted her ability to assign grades fairly, she realized that "students' relationships to me were being colored by the fact that I had been fired." The responsibilities entrusted to these academics also were affected by their altered status. As one lame-duck professor observed, "When you're on the way out, your teaching load is light and you have no committee assignments, so when you finally leave it's almost as if you haven't been there for the past year." Finally, displaced academics discussed their treatment by colleagues. One woman asked:

Has anyone ever done an analogy between the way they talk about you as a terminal case and about terminal diseases? They start dealing with you personally as many people deal with people who are terminally ill: people won't talk to you in the halls, friends you've known for eight years will avoid you. They really start treating you as if you're one of the living dead. People you've come up with in the system who have made it are the worst. They will have nothing to do with you.

A man who had been fired from a liberal arts college found that he was "a nonperson" when he attended social events in his department: "There was no hostility, just looking right through me, and making me feel like I wasn't there."

But some of the academics also acknowledged that they purposely withdrew from the institutions that had spurned them. Despite her sense of isolation, one woman shunned her former colleagues. She particularly resented solicitous inquiries from her supporters in the department because she didn't "like to be constantly reminded of what [had] happened." In order to avoid others and thus protect herself from feelings of rejection, she began to spend long afternoons at home by herself. Similarly, although pleased and flattered when a group of students wrote a letter to the administration protesting her dismissal, she also wished they had not done so; the students' glowing remarks about her unusual dedication as a teacher renewed her sense of loss and made her feel as if she had been "fired all over again."

She also sought to disassociate herself from teaching. She ceased to lavish her customary care and devotion on her classes:

I had taught most of the courses that I was teaching that year, but usually I would revise the syllabus year after year; I would read new stuff so I would have enthusiasm. That year I didn't. I taught usually at ten in the morning and I had a rule for myself: I would wake up at eight and I would do no more class preparation than I could do between eight-thirty when I finished breakfast and ten when I walked into the room. And I did that all year.

And she spent less time on campus:

> I got involved with Bill and he lived in New York, and that was certainly one of his attractions. I went down to New York and just stayed there. Also he was not an academic and the people he knew were not academics, and I enjoyed that.

As the year wore on, she "disengaged more and more." By the end of the spring semester she was "really spending no time there except when I was actually in the classroom."

Feelings of pain, resentment, and anger did gradually recede. As displaced academics gained distance, they became less sensitive to the judgment of former colleagues. Many found satisfying new careers that provided alternative sources of self-worth. But, although they succeeded in reconstructing their lives, the experience of being fired had left permanent scars.

NOTES

1. Lewis C. Solmon, Nancy L. Ochsner, and Margo-Lea Hurwicz, *Alternative Careers for Humanities Ph.D.'s* (New York: Praeger, 1979), p. 188.

2. See Arlie Russell Hochschild, "Inside the Clockwork of Male Careers," in *Women and the Power to Change*, ed. Florence Howe (New York: McGraw-Hill, 1975), p. 61.

3. See Emily Abel, "The Changing Academic Market," *Teachers College Record* 82 (Winter 1980):357-63.

4. Significantly, many of these men also mentioned that their careers had been aided in the past by personal influence. For example, some had been able to circumvent formal procedures for the allocation of temporary positions because their advisers had known department chairs. It is important to note that exclusion from the "old boy network" is a primary way in which women and minority group members are disadvantaged in the academic job market. After examining the career progression of matched samples of male and female Ph.D.s, the National Research Council reported that it found no evidence of reverse discrimination. (*Career Outcomes in a Matched Sample of Men and Women Ph.D.s: An Analytical Report* [Washington, D.C.: National Academy Press, 1981], pp. xvii, 43.)

5. Modern Language Association of America, "A Guide for Job Candidates and Department Chairmen in English and Foreign Languages" (New York: MLA, 1978), p. 27.

6. Richard Sennett and Jonathan Cobb, *The Hidden Injuries of Class* (New York: Vintage, 1972), p. 65.

7. E. Wright Bakke, *The Unemployed Worker* (New Haven: Yale University Press, 1940), pp. 165-252; Paula Goldman Leventman, *Professionals Out of Work* (New York: The Free Press, 1981), pp. 5-6.

8. See Charlotte V. Kuh, *Market Conditions and Tenure for Ph.D.s in U.S. Higher Education*, Technical Report No. 3 (Berkeley: Carnegie Council on Policy Studies in Higher Education, 1977); Roy Radner and Charlotte V. Kuh, *Market Conditions and Tenure in U.S. Higher Education: 1955-1973*, Technical Report No. 2 (Berkeley: Carnegie Council on Policy Studies in Higher Education, 1977).

9. See Ellis Ragland-Sullivan and Peter Barglow, "Job Loss: Psychological Response of University Faculty," *Journal of Higher Education* 52 (1981):45-66.

10. See Peter Marris, *Loss and Change* (New York: Doubleday, 1975), p. 29.

11. Joan Huber and Edna Bonacich, "Ad Hoc Committee Report on Un- and Underemployment," American Sociological Association (1983), p. 10.

12. See Marris, *Loss and Change*, pp. 36-37.

Chapter 3
THE MARKET FOR PIECEWORK

Many Ph.D.s in the humanities and social sciences who are unable to find tenure-track jobs have accepted appointments as part-time or full-time temporary teachers. In 1972, the Carnegie Commission on Higher Education recommended that colleges and universities employ increasing proportions of nontenure-track faculty to retain "flexibility" during a period of declining or shifting enrollment.[1] The number of teachers on short-term, nonrenewable contracts grew rapidly during the next several years. Known variously as "gypsy scholars," "academic nomads," and "the migrant laborers of academe," such teachers have transformed the shape of the faculty in higher education.[2] The following figures demonstrate both that a growing number of Ph.D.s have obtained marginal faculty positions and that women doctorates are overrepresented. Six percent of the men and 16 percent of the women who received Ph.D.s in the humanities between 1972 and 1974 and who were academically employed in 1977 held nonladder positions. As many as 14 percent of the men and a striking 25 percent of the women in the 1975-76 cohort were employed in temporary jobs in 1977.[3]

The expansion of the part-time sector has been especially dramatic. The number of part-timers in colleges and universities throughout the country began to grow during the 1960s as these institutions sought to cope with soaring enrollment, but the greatest increase of part-time instructors occurred after enrollment had peaked. Between 1972 and 1977, the number of part-time teachers at four-year institutions jumped 73 percent, from 120,000 to 208,000. During the same period, the number of full-time faculty rose by only 18 percent, from 380,000 to 448,000.[4] By 1982, part-timers constituted about a third of all faculty in institutions of higher education.[5] Because the conditions of employment of part-time teachers differ significantly from those of all other faculty, this chapter will focus on them.

THE SECONDARY WORK FORCE

By hiring large numbers of part-time faculty, colleges and universities have adopted employment practices common in the economy at large. The part-time work force in the United States burgeoned during the 1950s and 1960s and continued to grow at a slower, though steady, pace throughout the 1970s. In 1980, part-time workers constituted 23 percent of the total labor force.[6] Most part-time jobs are located in the "competitive sector" of the economy, consisting of small retail and service industries, where conditions of work differ dramatically from those in the "monopoly sector." Whereas employees in monopolistic industries typically enjoy relatively high salaries, job security, and opportunities for advancement, "secondary workers" receive lower pay, lack security of employment, and have no clear channels for promotion.[7] In every respect, part-time faculty positions resemble work in the competitive sector. Although no academic job can be equated with marginal employment in industry, the basic structure of part-time work in colleges and universities is similar to that of jobs in auto repair shops, cleaners, restaurants, and neighborhood grocery stores.

For example, the wages of part-time teachers generally are lower than those of tenure-track faculty.[8] Part-timers are paid between 25 and 35 percent less per course than their full-time colleagues.[9] Furthermore, because adjuncts rarely receive either promotions or increments for inflation, this differential tends to increase over time.[10] Very few part-timers are eligible for fringe benefits. About 50 percent of adjuncts teaching at least half-time receive some retirement coverage, 19 percent are entitled to worker's compensation, and 21 percent are covered by some form of health insurance.[11] But most teach less than 50 percent at any one institution.[12] Just 40 percent of adjuncts working less than half-time have access to retirement coverage, 9 percent to worker's compensation, and a mere 5 percent to medical benefits.[13]

The great majority of part-time faculty also lack job security. Only 15 percent are even eligible for tenure.[14] At most colleges and universities, part-timers are subject to being bumped by full-time faculty, and, at virtually all, their jobs are conditional on enrollment.[15] Like other secondary workers, they are temporary labor. About three-quarters of all part-timers are appointed for only one term at a time; just 5 percent have jobs lasting over a year.[16] Some administrators specifically discourage adjuncts from believing that they have any claim to reappointment. At one institution where I taught, the vice president cautioned department chairs against allowing any part-time faculty to become "entrenched." Ironically, affirmative action procedures also have undermined whatever frail security part-timers have obtained. At many schools, hiring is confined to the part-time ranks, and the administration seeks to demonstrate compliance with federal guidelines by "recycling" adjuncts.

Part-timers also lose their jobs first during retrenchment. Unfortunately, reliable information about the dismissal of adjuncts rarely is available.[17] Because their contracts terminate automatically at the end of each term or year, an administration that wants to reduce the size of its part-time staff can simply refrain from reappointing some of them. Thus, even part-timers who have taught regularly at a particular school for several years may disappear without counting in layoff statistics. One must read between the lines of reports that speak of "cancelling classes," "cutting sections," or "reassigning full-time faculty." Moreover, administrators often do not release information about the number of part-timers they employ.[18]

Nevertheless, an investigating committee of the American Association of University Professors reported that 91 percent of the part-time instructional staff at the City University of New York were fired during the New York City fiscal crisis of 1975 while only 24 percent of the full-time faculty were dismissed.[19] Government officials in California announced that 7,000 part-time community college faculty, or just under one-quarter of all adjuncts in the system, lost their jobs immediately after the passage of Proposition 13; the number of full-time teachers declined only 2 percent.[20] When Boston State College was merged with the University of Massachusetts, Boston, in the fall of 1981, the entire part-time teaching staff of the former was dismissed.[21]

The presumption that adjuncts are short-term, easily replaceable workers explains other aspects of their employment situation. Just as employers in business and industry avoid training their marginal workers, so colleges and universities invest few resources in part-time faculty. Only about 15 percent of all postsecondary institutions provide formal orientations for part-time teachers, and just 20 percent furnish new adjuncts with information about either students or pedagogy.[22] In most cases, faculty handbooks are not available.[23] More seriously, part-timers lack access to research support; very few are reimbursed for travel to professional meetings, and virtually none is eligible for paid research leaves.[24]

Moreover, part-time academic positions are dead-end, not entry-level, jobs. Only a small proportion of part-timers can advance in either rank or salary.[25] Although department chairs occasionally encourage adjuncts to believe they have secured a "foot in the door," the two sectors of the teaching staff are kept distinct; part-timers rarely are promoted to the ranks of the full-time faculty.[26] In fact, teaching part-time at one institution does not increase the likelihood of securing a regular position at any other; a tiny fraction of all part-timers who apply for tenure-track positions obtain them.[27] Like secondary workers in general, adjuncts find themselves consigned to a random series of part-time jobs.

It is true that part-time faculty in higher education hold advanced degrees though most other secondary employees are unskilled workers. Nevertheless, gas station attendants and short-order cooks who do bring specific skills to their jobs find that their talents go unrewarded. Similarly, part-timers often complain that employers routinely discount their achievements and efforts. For example, most are paid a flat fee regardless of academic credentials, publication record, or prior teaching experience. One justification for hiring adjuncts is that they offer specialized skills for which student demand is limited, but, in fact, they typically are discouraged from developing courses in their fields of expertise and very often are relegated to introductory courses.[28] Finally, although their classes frequently are cancelled just prior to the beginning of the semester, or even after a term already has started, they almost never are reimbursed for time spent preparing syllabi or teaching materials.[29]

To some extent, part-time academics can be distinguished from other secondary workers by the way in which they are controlled. Although the latter tend to be administered directly by individual supervisors, formal rules specify the pay scales, duration of employment, and duties of part-time faculty. Nevertheless, adjuncts are subjected to more particularistic forms of control than their full-time colleagues. In fact, a key demand of part-timers is the establishment of regular procedures for hiring, evaluation, and retention. Only a small proportion of all institutions conduct systematic evaluations of the adjuncts they employ.[30] Hiring practices tend to be particularly informal. At many institutions there are no set times for filing applications and no specific criteria governing selection. Thus, the recruitment process often appears completely capricious. One part-timer I interviewed explained how she obtained her job:

> I happened to run into someone who had been my old professor when I was an undergraduate at this college. I just ran into him in the parking lot and he said, "Would you be interested in teaching here?" I had no expectations of teaching here, I'd never even talked to him at all about it, but because he wanted me to, I was in.

A man also emphasized the element of luck:

> I found a job by pure chance. My father is a piano tuner and he was just tuning the piano of someone who taught in one of the state colleges. I talked to this guy and four months later, just before the fall semester began, someone in the department suddenly had to undergo an operation and they needed someone in a week and I happened to be available.

This haphazard manner of recruitment can be viewed as still another means of reducing the security of part-timers; the absence of the elaborate rituals surrounding the appointment of tenure-track faculty serves to underline the point that they are casual laborers and readily expendable.

THE STRATIFICATION OF HIGHER EDUCATION

The transformation of higher education during the 1960s and early 1970s also produced the rapid expansion of part-time faculty. We have seen that enrollment in colleges and universities soared during this period. The changing composition of the student body was equally remarkable. Throughout these years, the proportion of working-class and minority students rose steadily. For example, black students constituted 4.6 percent of the nation's undergraduates in 1966 and 8.6 percent by 1972.[31] Although enrollment growth peaked in 1972, women continued to enter postsecondary institutions in greatly increased numbers. Between 1972 and 1977, the number of men enrolled in higher education grew from 5,239,000 to 5,789,000, an increase of less than 11 percent. During the same period, the number of women students jumped from 3,976,000 to 5,497,000, an increase of 38 percent.[32] By 1979, women represented 50 percent of all undergraduates.[33]

Nevertheless, the critical issue may not be access but the type of education that students obtain after they enroll. As revisionist educational historians have demonstrated, many of the first students to enter public high schools were tracked into dead-end vocational programs.[34] Similarly, most of the "nontraditional" students who swarmed into colleges and universities in the 1960s received a separate and unequal education that did not greatly enhance their occupational status. Although some mobility undoubtedly occurs, most systems of public higher education have served to sort students into predetermined slots in the social hierarchy.

California, the pioneer in extending opportunities to new groups of students, provides the most frequently cited example.[35] The three-tiered system clearly replicates the class structure and racial composition of the state. At the pinnacle is the University of

California (UC), with 15 percent of the full-time enrollment in California public institutions in 1977 and 1 percent of the part-time enrollment.[36] A disproportionately high number of these students are middle class and Anglo, and many UC graduates become high-income professionals and managers.[37] The nineteen campuses of the California State University and Colleges (CSUC) constitute the middle tier. In 1977, these institutions enrolled 30 percent of the state's full-time and 8 percent of the part-time students.[38] A higher proportion of working-class and minority students attend the state colleges rather than the university, and fewer state college graduates enter the most prestigious careers.[39] The community colleges, which prepare students for low-level technical and paraprofessional jobs, have the highest proportion of working-class and minority students enrolled.[40] Community colleges expanded rapidly throughout the country during the 1960s, when their numbers increased 68 percent;[41] during the latter part of the decade, they grew at the phenomenal rate of one a week.[42] However, community colleges are the hallmark of higher education in California in particular. The unusually high rate of college enrollment in this state (21 percent of all adults aged 18 to 45, compared to a nationwide average of 14 percent)[43] is largely the result of the extensive network of 102 community colleges. In 1977, these two-year institutions enrolled 56 percent of all full-time students and 91 percent of all part-time students;[44] 77 percent of all high school graduates who entered a public institution enrolled in a community college.[45]

Not only are community colleges located at the bottom of the academic hierarchy, they also operate their own internal tracking system. The great majority of students who enter community colleges expect to transfer to four-year institutions after obtaining Associate of Arts degrees. However, through such means as individual counseling, orientation classes, and probation notices, all but a fraction of the students gradually are convinced of their personal inadequacies.[46] In California, only 7 percent of the second-year students from community colleges transferred to either a UC or CSUC campus in the fall of 1977.[47] Moreover, throughout the nation, the small corps of community college students who do succeed in completing their education in four-year colleges or universities come disproportionately from middle-class and Anglo backgrounds.[48] The opaqueness of this "cooling out" process protects the meritocratic image of higher education; students blame themselves rather than the institution for the frustration of their ambitions.

Furthermore, most nonelite institutions transmit skills to students without sharpening their imaginative or analytic capacities. As Ira Shor has written:

> The work-world can tolerate neither the economic demands of worker-graduates nor the development of their critical faculties. Career training is a way of keeping workers materially and ideologically in their place....Employers do not want workers who think for themselves or who demand and deserve raises and advancement.[49]

In fact, a vocational orientation frequently infuses the entire curriculum. The highly authoritarian atmosphere of community college classrooms has earned them the derisive appellation, "high schools with ashtrays." Even the liberal arts courses typically demand an unusual amount of rote learning, preparing students for work situations that strictly limit their creativity or individual judgment.[50]

Differential funding reinforces the inequities of the entire state system in California. During the late sixties, such different groups as the Joint Committee on Higher Education of the California legislature and the strikers at San Francisco State criticized the fact that the least amount of money was allocated for students at the lower tiers.[51] Nevertheless, the funding gap at the various types of institutions has remained constant. The per student expenditure currently is $3,900 at the university, $2,200 in CSUC, and $1,400 at community colleges.[52] The relatively small budgets of community colleges and other low-status public universities often are reflected in their physical settings, which reinforce students' self-perceptions that they are second-class citizens. Such inferior facilities curtail even the small amount of interaction that might be possible for students already burdened with jobs and, in many cases, childcare responsibilities. Thus, these "nontraditional" students receive educational experiences that diverge sharply from those of their middle-class counterparts at more selective institutions. Whereas one significant effect of these latter universities is to foster feelings of solidarity among future elites, community colleges and the less prestigious public universities discourage working-class and minority students from developing a sense of community.

The quality of education at nonelite institutions is more profoundly affected by a second money-saving tactic—the hiring of part-time temporary faculty. Although part-timers are employed in all tiers of the academic hierarchy, they are concentrated in the schools established to accommodate groups previously denied access to higher education. Almost half of all adjuncts teach in community colleges.[53] In 1977, part-time teachers constituted 51 percent of the faculty in community colleges but only 24 percent of the staff in four-year colleges and universities.[54] Once again, California can be considered the pacesetter in higher education. The number of part-time faculty in the University of California is growing, but adjuncts are far more prominent in the two lower tiers.[55] By the fall of 1977, part-time teachers represented 38 percent of the faculty in the California State University and Colleges system, and they taught over 40 percent of the classes.[56] During the same semester, 66 percent of the faculty in California community colleges held only part-time positions.[57]

Can we argue that students relegated to second-class and poorly-paid instructors are being denied an equal opportunity? This question cannot be answered conclusively. Most studies of education focus on the issue of structure; we know comparatively little about how knowledge is transmitted or how imaginative and critical thinking are fostered. Moreover, teachers, like other professionals, generally justify their own positions of privilege by appealing to the quality of service they provide their clients. As we have seen, part-timers lack both the security and opportunities for research that many academics consider essential to their success as teachers. However, there is no evidence of a correlation between either tenure or scholarly publication and effective teaching.

Nevertheless, some aspects of part-time employment clearly do affect the quality of instruction adjuncts can provide. Many lack such support services as duplicating and secretarial assistance. Most have to share offices with a number of other part-timers, and a few are not provided with any space in which to meet privately with students. Those who receive assignments just before the beginning of term or even after the semester already has begun have little time to prepare thoughtful or imaginative teaching materials. Some are required to teach according to standardized syllabi or with preselected texts. Although the majority of part-timers are allowed to prepare their own curricula, their relatively greater autonomy entails numerous disadvantages. Because they rarely interact with their full-time colleagues, they lack information about how their classes relate to other course offerings. Furthermore, their departments are unable to devise systematic and cohesive educational programs. The omission of part-timers' names from class schedules creates additional difficulties. Students cannot select their instructors or take consecutive courses from the same teachers. Adjuncts have no opportunity to work closely with students over a period of several semesters and thereby shape their thinking and influence their college careers in a systematic manner.

As many of these examples suggest, the employment of a large corps of part-time teachers may well reinforce those features of nonelite institutions that foster the attitudes and ways of thinking considered appropriate for low-level technicians and paraprofessionals. Although I will argue in the next chapter that many part-timers are especially committed to their jobs, it is possible that their classes may tend to become increasingly rigid and authoritarian over time. Certainly many individual part-time teachers strive to break down hierarchical relationships within their classrooms and to enhance the critical awareness and imaginative powers of their students. However, their working situation is hardly conducive to such efforts. If they are employed at several different institutions, they may lack the time and energy to experiment with teaching methods that involve students actively in the learning process; thus, they may resort to reliance on last year's lecture notes and use quantified exams that can be graded by computer. The precariousness of all part-time faculty also might inhibit them from departing too far from traditional pedagogy. In addition, we will see that the effect of part-time employment on teachers themselves often blunts their enthusiasm for innovative teaching methods.

The point could be made that part-time faculty in community colleges and the large state universities should be compared with teaching assistants (TAs), not with the regular faculty in elite institutions. The major research universities rely heavily on graduate students who perform a function roughly analogous to that of part-timers and are treated in similar ways. In California, the rapid increase of part-timers in the lower two tiers during the 1970s replicated the rise in the number of TAs in the university fifteen years earlier.[58] Freshmen and sophomores at the university currently have more contact with TAs than with regular faculty members, and, in such fields as English and foreign languages, TAs are responsible for the vast majority of courses.[59] The inequities of the employment of TAs have been amply documented. Although paid at a higher rate per course than most part-time teachers, TAs usually share offices, they rarely have access to adequate secretarial assistance, and they lack grievance rights. The similarity of the two types of positions is underlined by the fact that they often are filled by the same people. Occasionally TAs supplement their sparse earnings by picking up extra courses at nearby community colleges. More often, people enter the part-time circuit after their teaching assistantships have expired and they have been unsuccessful in the regular academic job hunt.

But there are important distinctions between TAs and community college part-timers that may well be reflected in the quality of the education they provide. Unlike most part-time faculty, TAs tend to be well integrated into their departments. Because they simultaneously are students and faculty, they generally have extensive knowledge about the institutions in which they work. They also may develop a sense of community among themselves because they meet to discuss teaching methods and course content. Moreover, as apprentices, they are supervised by tenure-track faculty. In the social sciences, their responsibilities typically are restricted to leading discussion groups. Although TAs in such fields as English and the foreign languages may be placed in charge of courses, they enjoy regular contact with faculty members. Thus, even departments employing large numbers of TAs can devise cohesive and well-integrated curricula. Moreover, because their employers' recommendations will be critical to their success in the job market, TAs may well be motivated to devote considerable time and energy to their courses. They also may be less subject to burnout because they retain their positions for a limited number of years and are at an early stage in their careers.

Although the proliferation of part-time faculty intensifies the stratification of higher education and impairs the quality of instruction in the lower tiers, it also provides substantial benefits for administrators. First, they increase their control over their schools. Faculty who lack job security, do not participate in university governance, and acquire almost no information about the educational process as a whole cannot influence either personnel or curricular decisions. Because part-time teachers can be hired and fired so easily, administrators have the power to expand some educational programs and curtail others. As we will see, the widespread use of part-time faculty also undermines the power of faculty unions.

But the primary advantage of part-time faculty for administrators clearly is economic. Colleges and universities are labor-intensive institutions: faculty salaries and fringe benefits represent 45 percent of the operating costs of a typical community college.[60] During the academic year 1975-76, one community college saved a total of $2,467,000 (19 percent of its total budget) as a result of hiring large numbers of part-time faculty who were paid about half as much as their full-time counterparts for teaching one course and received no fringe benefits.[61] Additional money is saved by denying adjuncts access to research funds, sabbatical leaves, promotions, office space, and secretarial assistance.[62]

PROFILE OF TEMPORARY FACULTY

Despite the dramatic expansion of temporary faculty during the past decade, we know little about their qualifications, backgrounds, and expectations. Statistical reports published by administrators generally omit them, and most studies of university and college teachers concentrate on tenure-track professors.[63] Lacking reliable data about short-term teachers, different groups have generated the theories that suit their needs. Displaced academics often consider themselves representative of all temporary faculty. Administrators claim that the teachers in nonladder appointments are less qualified than other professors and well satisfied with their working conditions. In order to test these opposing generalizations, I conducted a survey of both part-time and full-time temporary faculty employed in the California State University and Colleges (CSUC) system in the spring of 1981.[64] The results are reported in the remainder of this chapter. Although the survey does not focus on Ph.D.s in the humanities and social sciences, it provides a statistical framework for discussing displaced academics who hold marginal appointments.

CSUC was selected for the survey because it represents one of the most extensive systems of higher education in the country and employs a higher proportion of short-term faculty than most four-year institutions. The nineteen campuses of CSUC span the state, from the Oregon border to San Diego. Both part-time and full-time nonladder faculty grew rapidly throughout CSUC during the 1970s. In the fall of 1980, 1,123 full-time temporary teachers and 6,621 part-timers were employed in the system. Together they constituted 40 percent of the entire faculty.[65]

Although the term "lecturer" is used to designate both full-time and part-time temporary faculty members in CSUC, there are important distinctions between these two groups. Full-time lecturers typically receive the same salary and fringe benefits as tenure-track faculty, and they are expected to assume departmental duties. Part-timers are paid 20 percent less per course than tenure-track faculty, are not required to counsel students or participate in campus governance, and, in most cases, are denied fringe benefits. I will first discuss part-time faculty as a group, then distinguish among various categories of part-timers, and finally examine the differences between part-time and full-time lecturers.

Who Works Part-time?

Like many employers, administrators of colleges and universities justify their employment practices by pointing to the personal characteristics of their workers.[66] They claim that part-time instructors are unqualified, lack commitments to the institutions at which they teach, and do not need higher salaries. The results of the survey rebut each of these arguments.

The primary criteria for assessing merit in postsecondary institutions are academic credentials, teaching experience, and publications. Table 3-1 shows the highest degrees obtained by the respondents. Part-timers do not hold as many advanced degrees as the tenure-track teachers. Almost 70 percent of the latter have earned Ph.D.s,[67] opposed to just 25 percent of the part-time staff. Nevertheless, the overwhelming majority of the respondents have received an M.A., the minimum degree required for teaching most courses in CSUC. Just 13 percent of the part-timers have only B.A.s, and many of these teach either at rural campuses (which do not have access to many "surplus" academics) or in vocational subjects (for which an advanced degree often is less significant). Moreover, 16 percent of the part-timers indicated that they are working toward Ph.D.s. Although this often is an interminable process, we can assume that some are at an advanced stage. Finally, part-timers are concentrated in lower-level introductory courses, which require less specialized knowledge than upper-level ones.[68]

TABLE 3-1
Highest Degree Obtained

Degree	Number of Respondents	Percentage of Total Respondents
B.A.	117	13
M.A.	439	49
Appropriate terminal M.A. (e.g., M.F.A., M.B.A.)	111	12
Ph.D.	186	21
Other Doctorate	33	4
Degree not stated	5	1
Total	891	100

TABLE 3-2
Years Teaching at the College Level

Years	Number of Respondents	Percentage of Total Respondents
½ to 1½	141	16
2 to 2½	99	11
3 to 5	275	31
6 to 8	154	17
9 and over	219	25
Years not stated	3	—
Total	891	100

Part-timers clearly come to their jobs with relevant experience. Seventy-three percent of the part-timers have taught at least three years at the college level (see Table 3-2). Table 3-3 shows the number of years the respondents have been working at their current campuses. The sizable number of part-timers who have taught less than two years suggests that the turnover rate is high. In fact, institutional policies encourage a high level of attrition. Because part-time faculty rarely receive salary increments for seniority, they have little economic incentive to remain. Furthermore, their contracts terminate automatically at the end of each semester or school year, and university regulations stipulate that searches must be conducted before part-timers can be rehired. Nevertheless, most are not casual employees: over half have taught three years or more at the campuses at which they received the questionnaires.

TABLE 3-3
Years of Teaching at Campus at Which
Questionnaire Was Received

Years	Number of Respondents	Percentage of Total Respondents
½ to 1½	273	31
2 to 2½	147	16
3 to 5	278	31
6 to 8	107	12
9 and over	85	10
Years not stated	1	—
Total	891	100

Because appropriate scholarship assumes varied forms in different disciplines, it is difficult to quantify the outside scholarly activities of the lecturers. The respondents thus were asked to specify the number of hours weekly they devote to scholarship, research, or publishing work. As Table 3-4 indicates, many of these faculty spend a considerable amount of time on such activities.

Although penalized for exhibiting limited commitment to the institutions that hire them, part-timers have few opportunities to demonstrate loyalty to their schools. Part-time employment is structured in such a way that the involvement of part-time faculty in campus life is restricted severely. As noted, part-time faculty are not expected to assume responsibilities for student advising or academic governance, and they never are reimbursed for such activities. Most are not informed of the time and place of department meetings, and many are specifically excluded from them. Thus, it is striking that 17 percent of the part-timers reported they have participated in faculty committees, that 21 percent believed they are expected to attend department meetings, and that 34 percent have served as advisers to students. Moreover, 41 percent of the part-time faculty expressed dissatisfaction with their inability to participate in academic governance. In other words, a substantial group want greater integration in their campuses and more control over both their own working conditions and the educational policies of their schools. Far from shunning extracurricular responsibilities, they appear to feel they have been deprived of an essential aspect of teaching at an educational institution.

TABLE 3-4
Number of Hours Weekly Spent on Scholarship,
Research, or Publishing Work

Hours	Number of Respondents	Percentage of Total Respondents
0	221	25
1-3	144	16
4-6	123	14
7-9	47	5
10-12	72	8
13 and over	173	20
Number of hours not stated	111	12
Total	891	100

More significantly, part-timers invest substantial time in their teaching jobs. Sixty-eight percent devote at least four hours to preparing each class, and 30 percent spend over seven hours. They also are strongly committed to academic careers. Sixty percent of the part-time staff consider themselves primarily educators, and the same proportion would accept tenure-track positions if offered them.[69]

The most common rationale for the low salaries of part-time teachers is that they do not need more money. Just as employers justify women's inferior wages by arguing that they work for self-fulfillment, so administrators claim most part-time faculty are fully employed professionals who teach for the pleasure and prestige of sharing their expertise with students. But most part-timers, like the overwhelming majority of women workers, rely heavily on their earnings. Forty-four percent of the part-time faculty derive the major part of their personal incomes from their teaching jobs in CSUC. Relatively few part-time teachers are "moonlighters." Only 31 percent hold nonteaching, full-time jobs, and just 7 percent teach full-time at other educational institutions.

Not surprisingly, a large proportion of adjuncts do hold additional part-time jobs. Thirty percent of the part-timers teach on a part-time basis at other educational institutions, and 31 percent work part-time in other types of jobs. The average part-time wage per course in CSUC during the fall of 1980 was $1,969, and the administration permits each part-timer to teach no more than three courses each semester. Thus, the maximum annual salary of a part-time faculty member in the fall of 1980 was $11,815. The many part-timers teaching one or two classes each term earned substantially less. Most part-time faculty clearly required additional sources of income.[70]

Concerns

Because self-esteem in our society is so intimately connected to employment, people often are reluctant to admit they are dissatisfied with their work. However, they are more likely to express discontent if asked about specific aspects of their jobs.[71] The questionnaire thus asked the respondents to indicate whether they were "very satisfied," "satisfied," "dissatisfied," or "very dissatisfied" with a number of factors relating to their conditions of employment. Table 3-5 lists these concerns in order of their importance to the respondents.

The prominent place of medical benefits in this list suggests that a high proportion of part-timers lack access to medical insurance. One respondent wrote, "Because of nonexistent medical benefits, I am ignoring a medical problem; I cannot afford to go to the hospital at $300 a day."

The three other major sources of dissatisfacion (security of employment, opportunity for full-time, tenure-track employment, and opportunity for step and rank increases) indicate that it is unacceptable to most lecturers to occupy dead-end, revolving-door positions. They want stable jobs with prospects of advancement and rewards for longevity. Security of employment was not only the paramount concern to the lecturers but also the one that elicited the largest number of written comments. One woman wrote "The work is very alienating because we are all disposable, like Kleenex. No part-timer feels valued or prized without security of employment." Others complained of feelings of "vulnerability" because they lacked job protection and could be dismissed or replaced at any time.

The fifth most serious concern was the brief notification time for teaching. Many respondents spoke of the difficulty of maintaining "high professional standards" when informed of assignments shortly before classes began. One exclaimed, "My main dissatisfaction is the uncertainty and delay in being notified to teach a class. Would you believe *two* days?"

TABLE 3-5*
Job Satisfaction

Concerns	Number of Respondents Who Were "Dissatisfied" or "Very Dissatisfied"	Percentage of Respondents Who Were "Dissatisfied" or "Very Dissatisfied"
Security of employment	667	81
Medical benefits	566	79
Opportunity for full-time tenure-track employment	516	70
Opportunity for step and rank increases	551	70
Notification time for appointment to teach	552	65
Salary	411	47

Opportunity for professional development and/or research	341	45
Participation in departmental or campus governance	307	41
Number of courses taught	263	31
Selection of subject matter	236	28
Respect from tenure-track faculty	204	25

A number of respondents commented on aspects of their employment about which the questionnaire had not specifically inquired. Several, for example, complained that office space was either unavailable or inadequate. A typical statement read:

Part-time faculty members here are relegated to the leftover offices, some of which must accommodate as many as fourteen people. Even those part-timers who teach two to three classes every semester for years really do not have a place to call their own. It makes it difficult to keep organized on campus.

Others noted that the absence of regularized procedures for hiring and retention left ample room for favoritism by department chairs. Although some respondents spoke gratefully about the support they received from sympathetic or benevolent chairs, many resented their dependence on the "whim" of single individuals. Others focused on their inability to control their work lives, for example:

Feast or famine: either too much teaching to do research or too little to survive; they—chancellor, administrators, deans—yank us around as if we were on a string.

Finally, several respondents stated that they were forced to change careers. As one part-timer wrote, "I'm getting burned out

*The percentages in Tables 3-5 through 3-11 express the proportion of respondents who answered the questions.

because of lack of respect, opportunities, and equitable pay. I love to teach but I'm not sure it's worth the struggle."

Can Collective Bargaining Work?

Because most part-timers do not belong to unions, it often is assumed they are indifferent to collective bargaining. However, 54 percent of the part-timers believe that unions could improve their conditions of work, and 61 percent would be willing to vote in a collective bargaining election.[72] The main problem is ignorance, not hostility to unionization. Many respondents wrote that they never had heard of either union on campus, although the questionnaires were distributed at the beginning of a collective bargaining campaign. In addition, they expressed skepticism that any union, controlled by tenure-track faculty, would demonstrate a strong commitment to the concerns of part-timers. As one respondent commented, "The groups have first in mind the well-being of full-time, tenured faculty. I do not blame them for this, but they do not represent my interests, although they claim to."

Itinerant Professors

Thirty percent of the part-timers teach on a part-time basis at more than one institution. Table 3-6 demonstrates the ways in which they differ from other adjuncts. Although 15 percent of these commuters hold full-time jobs in addition to their part-time teaching positions, most are committed firmly to academic careers. Seventy percent consider themselves primarily educators, and 76 percent would accept full-time positions if offered them; 80 percent are dissatisfied with their inability to qualify for tenure.

The bulk of itinerant professors thus appears to constitute part of the new and increasingly large group of academics who depend on their salaries from part-time teaching at two or more schools. Unable to find full-time positions, they have pieced together a number of part-time jobs. Their fragmented work lives often mirror those of the students they teach.

TABLE 3-6*
Itinerant Academics

	Part-time Faculty Teaching Part-time at Other Educational Institutions (268)		Other Part-time Faculty (623)	
Have taught over three years at the college level	83%	(223)	69%	(425)
Discipline:				
Humanities	30%	(78)	14%	(87)
Social sciences	17%	(46)	13%	(77)
Natural sciences and math	14%	(37)	16%	(95)
Other liberal arts	8%	(22)	7%	(40)
Physical education	3%	(8)	2%	(13)
Engineering	3%	(7)	13%	(79)
Education	7%	(19)	10%	(62)
Business/management	8%	(22)	14%	(84)
Other professional or occupational	9%	(24)	11%	(68)
Believe job makes full and proper use of educational background and professional skills	47%	(125)	61%	(377)
Consider selves primarily educators	72%	(192)	55%	(343)
Would accept full-time tenure-track position at college at which received questionnaire	76%	(204)	54%	(335)
Hold full-time nonteaching job	15%	(41)	37%	(213)
Obtain at least 50% of *personal* income from teaching job	52%	(136)	41%	(246)
Obtain at least 50% of *household* income from teaching job	32%	(79)	25%	(144)
Concerns:[a]				
Salary	58%	(149)	43%	(262)
Medical benefits	86%	(203)	75%	(363)

(continued)

Security of employment	89%	(231)	77%	(436)
Opportunity for full-time tenure-track employment	80%	(191)	65%	(325)
Opportunity for step and rank increases	74%	(187)	74%	(364)
Notification time for appointment to teach	71%	(183)	62%	(369)
Selection of subject matter or courses taught	33%	(84)	26%	(152)
Number of courses taught	42%	(107)	26%	(156)
Participation in departmental or campus governance	52%	(123)	36%	(183)
Opportunity for professional development and/or research	55%	(130)	40%	(211)
Believe collective bargaining could help to improve conditions of work	61%	(164)	51%	(315)
Would vote in a collective bargaining election	68%	(183)	59%	(363)

[a]Presented as representing proportion who were "dissatisfied" or "very dissatisfied."

These part-timers are particularly discontent with their working conditions. They also are more likely than other part-timers to believe unionization could improve their employment situation. Finally, a disproportionate number teach in the humanities, the field most severely affected by the academic job crisis.

Sex and Race

In CSUC, as in most of academia, women and minority faculty are clustered in nonladder, revolving-door positions. According to statistics provided by the chancellor's office, racial and ethnic minorities constituted 18 percent of the part-timers, but only 12 percent of the tenure-track faculty in the fall of 1980. The figures for women show even greater discrepancies. Women represented 20 percent of the tenure-track professors in the system and 38 percent of the part-time teachers.[73]

Data from the survey permit us to make a number of distinctions between men and women part-timers (see Table 3-7). Like women faculty throughout higher education, women part-timers remain concentrated in such stereotypical female fields as the humanities and education, and they are less likely than their male counterparts to have earned Ph.D.s. In addition, women tend to make greater investments in the institutions at which they work: more women stated that they are expected to attend department meetings, that they participate in departmental committees, and that they serve as advisers to students.

TABLE 3-7*
Gender Differences

	Men Part-timers (515)		Women Part-timers (376)	
Expected to attend department meetings	17%	(19)	25%	(94)
Have served on departmental committees	13%	(69)	23%	(85)
Have served as adviser to students	30%	(153)	40%	(149)
Consider selves primarily educators	50%	(258)	74%	(277)
Would accept full-time tenure-track position at college at which received questionnaire	56%	(289)	67%	(250)
If a part-time job carried security of employment and pay proportional to that of a full-time job, would prefer it to a full-time job	54%	(278)	67%	(251)
Teaching at another educational institution:				
Part-time	29%	(149)	31%	(117)
Full-time	8%	(40)	5%	(17)

(continued)

Hold nonteaching job:				
Part-time	25%	(127)	38%	(130)
Full-time	43%	(207)	13%	(47)
Highest degree:				
B.A.	15%	(78)	10%	(39)
M.A.	41%	(211)	61%	(228)
Appropriate terminal M.A.	14%	(72)	10%	(39)
Ph.D.	25%	(128)	15%	(58)
Other doctorate	4%	(23)	3%	(10)
Working toward doctorate	13%	(69)	19%	(73)
Obtain at least 50% of *personal* income from teaching job	31%	(162)	58%	(217)
Obtain at least 50% of *household* income from teaching job	24%	(123)	27%	(100)
Discipline:				
Humanities	13%	(68)	26%	(97)
Social sciences	15%	(75)	13%	(48)
Natural sciences and math	16%	(84)	13%	(48)
Other liberal arts	5%	(25)	10%	(37)
Physical education	2%	(8)	4%	(13)
Engineering	16%	(82)	1%	(4)
Education	5%	(27)	14%	(54)
Business/management	17%	(87)	5%	(19)
Other professional or occupational	10%	(51)	11%	(47)
Concerns:[a]				
Salary	42%	(217)	52%	(194)
Medical benefits	62%	(320)	64%	(246)
Security of employment	69%	(355)	83%	(312)
Opportunity for full-time tenure-track employment	53%	(271)	65%	(245)
Opportunity for step and rank increases	58%	(297)	68%	(254)
Notification time for appointment to teach	54%	(295)	68%	(257)
Selection of subject matter or courses taught	25%	(129)	28%	(107)

Number of courses taught	25%	(130)	35%	(133)
Respect from tenure-track faculty	20%	(102)	27%	(102)
Participation in departmental or campus governance	32%	(167)	37%	(140)
Opportunity for professional development and/or research	33%	(168)	46%	(173)

[a]Presented as representing proportion who were "dissatisfied" or "very dissatisfied."

One explanation for women's greater commitment to their jobs is that they have fewer outside professional interests. A significantly higher proportion of the female respondents consider themselves primarily educators. Although women are more likely to work part-time outside CSUC, over three times as many men as women hold full-time nonteaching jobs. As a result, women rely on their salaries from their colleges for a much higher proportion of their personal incomes. Fifty-eight percent of the women obtain over half their personal incomes from their jobs in CSUC, compared to 31 percent of the men.[74]

Although the women part-timers are more discontent with most aspects of their working conditions, more women are satisfied with their teaching loads: 67 percent of the women, compared to 54 percent of the men, would prefer part-time positions if such jobs carried all the privileges and perquisites of tenure-track appointments. Nevertheless, a higher proportion of women would accept full-time tenure-track jobs if offered them.

Part-timers who identified themselves as belonging to an ethnic or racial minority resemble their Anglo counterparts on many counts.[75] Similar proportions of both groups participate in campus governance, consider themselves educators, would accept tenure-track positions, and teach in the various disciplines. Although slightly more minority lecturers are working toward doctorates (21 percent, as opposed to 15 percent of the Anglos), the formal educational attainments of the two groups are virtually identical. Both groups also derive similar proportions of their total income from their teaching jobs. Nevertheless, as Table

3-8 demonstrates, minority faculty are substantially more dissatisfied with most aspects of their employment situation, and more of them favor collective bargaining.

TABLE 3-8*
Racial and Ethnic Minorities

Concerns:[a]	Minority Part-timers (131)		Anglo Part-timers (760)	
Salary	54%	(71)	45%	(336)
Medical benefits	70%	(91)	63%	(469)
Security of employment	72%	(94)	74%	(556)
Opportunity for full-time tenure-track employment	67%	(87)	57%	(425)
Opportunity for step and rank increases	72%	(94)	60%	(451)
Notification time for appointment to teach	61%	(80)	52%	(464)
Selection of subject matter or courses taught	31%	(41)	26%	(192)
Number of courses taught	36%	(43)	29%	(220)
Respect from tenure-track faculty	27%	(35)	22%	(168)
Participation in departmental or campus governance	46%	(60)	33%	(245)
Opportunity for professional development and/or research	49%	(64)	36%	(272)
Believe collective bargaining could help to improve conditions of work	66%	(87)	52%	(389)
Would vote in a collective bargaining election	68%	(89)	60%	(450)

[a]Presented as representing proportion who were "dissatisfied" or "very dissatisfied."

Academic Disciplines

Significant distinctions can be drawn between the part-timers on the basis of teaching area. Table 3-9 demonstrates the differences between part-time faculty in the humanities and those in engineering, which represent the extremes found in the survey.

TABLE 3-9*
Subject Matter Taught

	Part-timers in Humanities (168)		Part-timers in Engineering (87)	
Have taught at least three years at the college level	79%	(133)	67%	(58)
Teach one course	23%	(38)	56%	(49)
Believe job makes full and proper use of educational background and professional skills	38%	(64)	74%	(64)
Expected to attend department meetings	30%	(50)	7%	(6)
Have served on departmental committees	23%	(38)	7%	(6)
Have served as adviser to students	42%	(70)	23%	(20)
Consider selves primarily educators	76%	(127)	23%	(20)
Would accept full-time tenure-track position at campus at which received questionnaire	84%	(141)	26%	(23)
Teach at another educational institution:				
Part-time	46%	(78)	8%	(7)
Full-time	2%	(4)	5%	(4)
Hold nonteaching job:				
Part-time	35%	(59)	11%	(10)
Full-time	5%	(8)	74%	(64)

(continued)

Women	59%	(97)	5%	(4)
Men	41%	(68)	95%	(82)
Obtain at least 50% of *personal* income from teaching job	74%	(124)	11%	(10)
Obtain at least 50% of *household* income from teaching job	42%	(71)	7%	(7)
Concerns:[a]				
Salary	68%	(114)	34%	(30)
Medical benefits	77%	(129)	51%	(44)
Security of employment	93%	(157)	49%	(43)
Opportunity for full-time tenure-track employment	83%	(140)	31%	(27)
Opportunity for step and rank increases	73%	(123)	48%	(42)
Notification time for appointment to teach	73%	(122)	41%	(36)
Selection of subject matter or courses taught	36%	(60)	20%	(17)
Number of courses taught	45%	(75)	17%	(15)
Respect from tenure-track faculty	36%	(60)	16%	(14)
Participation in departmental or campus governance	51%	(86)	19%	(17)
Opportunity for professional development and/or research	56%	(93)	21%	(18)
Believe collective bargaining could help to improve conditions of work	79%	(133)	34%	(30)
Would vote in a collective bargaining election	83%	(139)	40%	(35)

[a]Presented as representing proportion who were "dissatisfied" or "very dissatisfied."

The typical adjunct in engineering is a man who is fully employed outside CSUC, does not consider himself an educator, and would not accept a tenure-track position if offered one. By contrast, the majority of part-time faculty in the humanities are women, and they rely on their salaries from CSUC for substantial portions of their own incomes. They also have made firm commitments to academic careers. If they are employed elsewhere, they tend to hold only marginal teaching positions at other educational institutions; as a group, they have taught longer, teach more courses, are more likely to consider themselves educators, and participate more actively in student advisement and committee work. Furthermore, humanities part-timers are more discontent: they are less likely to believe their jobs make full and proper use of their educational and professional skills, and they are considerably more concerned about their salaries, lack of fringe benefits, and working conditions. Finally, part-time faculty in the humanities are far more likely to believe that collective bargaining could improve their conditions of employment and to be willing to vote in a collective bargaining election.

Ph.D.s in the Humanities and Social Sciences

Part-timers who have earned Ph.D.s and teach in either the humanities or social sciences can be distinguished clearly from other adjunct faculty. Table 3-10 shows that these part-timers tend to be particularly committed to academic careers. Very high percentages consider themselves primarily educators, would accept full-time, tenure-track jobs, teach more than one course, and are looking for regular academic positions at other educational institutions.[76] Relatively few are employed full-time, and over half rely on their incomes from their teaching jobs for the major portion of their livelihoods. Finally, they are substantially more discontent with every aspect of their working conditions and more supportive of collective bargaining than other part-time faculty.

TABLE 3-10*
Doctorates in Humanities and Social Sciences

	Part-timers with Ph.D.s Teaching in Humanities or Social Sciences (94)		Other Part-time Faculty (792)[a]	
Have taught over three years at the college level	87%	(84)	71%	(564)
Teach only one course at campus where received questionnaire	32%	(29)	47%	(362)
Expected to attend department meetings	27%	(25)	20%	(160)
Have served on departmental committees	29%	(27)	16%	(127)
Have served as adviser to students	38%	(35)	33%	(266)
Consider selves *primarily* educators	78%	(73)	60%	(462)
Would accept full-time tenure-track position at campus at which received questionnaire	87%	(76)	58%	(463)
Looking for full-time tenure-track position at any other educational institution	53%	(49)	22%	(173)
Teach at another educational institution:				
Part-time	36%	(34)	30%	(232)
Full-time	5%	(5)	7%	(52)
Hold nonteaching job:				
Part-time	35%	(32)	30%	(225)
Full-time	14%	(13)	33%	(241)
Obtain at least 50% of *personal* income from teaching job	54%	(49)	43%	(330)
Concerns:[b]				
Salary	79%	(74)	43%	(337)
Medical benefits	86%	(75)	78%	(491)

Security of employment	93%	(87)	79%	(580)
Opportunity for full-time tenure-track employment	90%	(79)	68%	(437)
Opportunity for step and rank increases	82%	(72)	69%	(479)
Notification time for appointment to teach	84%	(74)	63%	(478)
Selection of subject matter or courses taught	51%	(46)	25%	(190)
Number of courses taught	48%	(45)	29%	(218)
Respect from tenure-track faculty	34%	(30)	24%	(174)
Participation in departmental or campus governance	58%	(49)	38%	(258)
Opportunity for professional development and/or research	72%	(61)	41%	(280)
Believe collective bargaining could help to improve conditions of work	83%	(75)	51%	(405)
Would vote in a collective bargaining election	88%	(76)	58%	(470)

[a]These two groups of part-timers do not add up to 891 because a few respondents did not indicate both their degrees and the subject matter taught.

[b]Presented as representing proportion who were "dissatisfied" or "very dissatisfied."

Full-time Lecturers

Table 3-11 summarizes the ways in which full-time lecturers differ from their part-time colleagues. As noted, full-time temporary faculty are required to assume responsibility for student advisement and campus governance. Thus, it is hardly surprising that they report far greater participation in school affairs. Because they teach full-time and earn more per course than part-timers, these lecturers are able to rely more heavily on their incomes from their teaching positions in CSUC. In general, full-time temporary faculty also have made greater investments in academic careers.

They are more likely to view themselves as educators, to be willing to accept tenure-track positions, and to be looking elsewhere for tenure-track jobs; furthermore, they express greater dissatisfaction with their inability to qualify for tenure. Nevertheless, they are slightly more content with many other aspects of their working conditions.

TABLE 3-11*
Full-time and Part-time Lecturers

	Part-time Lecturers (891)		Full-time Lecturers (309)	
Believe job makes full and proper use of educational background and professional skills	56%	(502)	68%	(209)
Expected to attend department meetings	21%	(185)	87%	(268)
Have served on departmental committees	17%	(154)	61%	(188)
Have served as adviser to students	34%	(302)	70%	(217)
Have frequent contact with tenure-track faculty meetings	59%	(525)	92%	(284)
Consider selves *primarily* educators	60%	(535)	87%	(268)
Would accept full-time tenure-track position at campus at which received questionnaire	60%	(539)	83%	(258)
If a part-time job carried security of employment and pay proportional to that of full-timers, would prefer it to a full-time job	59%	(529)	37%	(113)
Looking for full-time tenure-track position at any other educational institution	25%	(222)	41%	(127)
Teaching at another educational institution: Part-time	30%	(266)	11%	(32)

Full-time	7%	(57)	1%	(2)
Hold nonteaching job:				
Part-time	31%	(257)	31%	(83)
Full-time	31%	(254)	3%	(6)
Highest degree:				
B.A.	13%	(117)	6%	(20)
M.A.	50%	(439)	42%	(128)
Appropriate terminal M.A.	13%	(111)	13%	(41)
Ph.D.	21%	(186)	34%	(106)
Other doctorate	4%	(33)	4%	(13)
Obtain at least 50% of *personal* income from teaching job	44%	(379)	94%	(282)
Obtain at least 50% of *household* income from teaching job	27%	(223)	79%	(232)
Concerns:[a]				
Medical benefits	79%	(566)	25%	(73)
Opportunity for full-time tenure-track employment	70%	(516)	79%	(221)
Opportunity for step and rank increases	70%	(551)	65%	(187)
Notification time for appointment to teach	65%	(552)	59%	(175)
Participation in departmental or campus governance	41%	(307)	26%	(77)
Believe collective bargaining could help to improve conditions of work	54%	(479)	54%	(166)
Would vote in a collective bargaining election	61%	(546)	71%	(218)

[a]Presented as representing proportion who were "dissatisfied" or "very dissatisfied." These were the only items for which responses of full-time and part-time lecturers diverged.

The thirty-nine full-time lecturers who have earned Ph.D.s in the humanities or social sciences resemble other full-time temporary faculty in most respects. However, considerably more of the

Ph.D.s are looking elsewhere for full-time, tenure-track positions (69 percent, as opposed to 37 percent of other full-time temporary faculty) and are dissatisfied with their opportunities for professional development and research (85 percent, compared to 51 percent). In addition, these lecturers are more likely to believe that collective bargaining could improve their conditions of work (72 percent versus 51 percent) and to be willing to vote in a collective bargaining election (85 percent, contrasted to 69 percent).

CONCLUSION

The survey demonstrates that the majority of lecturers in CSUC are qualified, steady, and committed employees who have ongoing interests in the affairs of their institutions. Similarly, most invest a considerable amount of time in class preparation, engage in some form of scholarly activities, and want regular tenure-track positions. Although a significant proportion of the part-timers do hold outside jobs, most rely heavily on their salaries from CSUC. The primary difference between a large proportion of lecturers and tenure-track faculty may simply be this: the former entered the job market too late to obtain the positions the tenure-track teachers already were holding.

Nevertheless, lecturers are not a homogeneous group. Sharp distinctions can be drawn between the temporary faculty in terms of workload, gender, ethnicity, and teaching area. It is particularly important to note that, although part-timers with Ph.D.s in the social sciences and humanities share many of the goals, needs, expectations, and motivations of other marginal academics, they cannot be considered representative of temporary faculty in general.

NOTES

1. Carnegie Commission on Higher Education, *The More Effective Use of Resources: An Imperative for Higher Education* (New York: McGraw-Hill, 1972), p. 113.

2. "On Full-Time Non-Tenure-Track Appointments," *AAUP Bulletin,* September 1978, pp. 267-73.

3. National Research Council, *Employment of Humanities Ph.D.'s: A Departure from Traditional Jobs* (Washington, D.C.: National Academy of Sciences, 1980), p. 44.

4. National Center for Education Statistics, *Digest of Education Statistics* (Washington, D.C.: Government Printing Office, 1979), p. 104.

5. David W. Leslie, Samuel E. Kellams, and G. Manny Gunne, *Part-Time Faculty in American Higher Education* (New York: Praeger, 1982), p. 19.

6. *Special Labor Force Report No. 244* (Washington, D.C.: Department of Labor, Bureau of Labor Statistics, 1981), p. 7.

7. Richard Edwards, *Contested Terrain: The Transformation of the Workplace in the Twentieth Century* (New York: Basic Books, 1979), pp. 163-99.

8. There is no uniformity among the salaries of part-time faculty. Adjuncts earn the most at universities, somewhat less at four-year colleges, and the least at community colleges; however, even within one type of institution, their wages vary significantly. (Howard P. Tuckman and Jaime Caldwell, "The Determinants of Variations in Earnings among Part-Time Faculty," in *Part-Time Faculty Series*, ed. Howard P. Tuckman, William D. Vogler, and Jaime Caldwell [Washington, D.C.: American Association of University Professors, 1978], p. 55.)

9. Howard P. Tuckman, Jaime Caldwell, and William D. Vogler, "Part-Timers and the Academic Labor Market of the Eighties," *The American Sociologist* 13 (November 1978):187.

10. Leslie, Kellams, and Gunne, *Part-Time Faculty*, p. 31; Tuckman, Caldwell, and Vogler, "Academic Labor Market," p. 192.

11. Tuckman, Caldwell, and Vogler, "Academic Labor Market," p. 187.

12. In fact, some institutions that provide fringe benefits to adjuncts teaching over 50 percent are careful to ensure that most part-timers work less than half-time.

13. Tuckman, Caldwell, and Vogler, "Academic Labor Market," p. 187.

14. Leslie, Kellams, and Gunne, *Part-Time Faculty*, p. 49.

15. Ibid., pp. 88-89.

16. Howard P. Tuckman and William D. Vogler, "The 'Part' in Part-Time Wages," *AAUP Bulletin*, May 1978, p. 74.

17. I use this term advisedly. Although the word generally is reserved for the termination of a midterm contract or the removal of a tenured faculty member, the nonreappointment of a part-timer who has served an institution for several years in succession should be considered the equivalent.

18. Leslie, Kellams, and Gunne, *Part-Time Faculty*, p. 143.

19. "City University of New York: Mass Dismissals under Financial Exigency," *AAUP Bulletin*, April 1977, p. 65.

20. Chancellor's Office, California Community Colleges, "Summary of Proposition 13 Impact on Community College Programs, Students, Faculty, and Finance," January 1979, p. 3.

21. For an account of this merger, see Robert L. Jacobson, "Massachusetts System Thrown into Turmoil by a Wrangle over Finances and Governance," *Chronicle of Higher Education*, 10 February 1982, pp. 1, 4, 5, 6. Nevertheless, the number of part-time faculty in higher education may not decline despite the deepening financial crisis. In fact, administrators clearly are torn between two competing pressures. For political reasons, they first have to fire faculty members without job security. But they also have strong incentives for maintaining a large corps of adjuncts. Studies of the impact of Proposition 13 on California community colleges demonstrate how administrators resolved this dilemma. Although they dismissed a large proportion of all part-timers, they also converted full-time positions into part-time slots at an accelerated rate. During the first six months after the passage of Proposition 13, the community colleges hired six times as many part-timers as full-time faculty. ("Summary of Proposition 13 Impact.")

22. Leslie, Kellams, and Gunne, *Part-Time Faculty*, pp. 81-82.

23. Ibid., p. 103.

24. Ibid., p. 84.

25. Ibid., p. 78; Tuckman and Caldwell, "Variations in Earnings," p. 66.

26. See Leslie, Kellams, and Gunne, *Part-Time Faculty*, p. 44.

27. Howard P. Tuckman, Jaime Caldwell, and William D. Vogler, "Part-Time Employment and Career Progression," in *Part-Time Faculty Series* (Washington, D.C.: American Association of University Professors, 1978), p. 82.

28. Seventy-five percent of adjuncts in community colleges teach introductory courses, 52 percent in four-year colleges, and 40 percent in universities. (Tuckman and Vogler, "Part-Time Wages," p. 71.) In the California State University and Colleges system in 1976, 45 percent of the classes taught by part-timers were lower division courses, compared to only 31 percent of those taught by full-time faculty. (Office of the Chancellor, California State University and Colleges, *Task Force on Temporary Faculty*, Appendix II, December 1977, p. b.)

29. Leslie, Kellams, and Gunne, *Part-Time Faculty*, p. 78.

30. Ibid., p. 83.

31. National Center for Education Statistics, *The Condition of Education* (Washington, D.C.: Government Printing Office, 1978), p. 120.

32. *Digest of Education Statistics*, p. 89.

33. *On Campus with Women*, no. 26, Spring 1980, p. 8.

34. See, for example, Samuel Bowles and Herbert Gintis, *Schooling in Capitalist America* (New York: Basic Books, 1976), pp. 191-95.

35. Higher education in California traditionally has been concentrated in the public sector. During the past decade, public institutions throughout the country have been enrolling an increasing proportion of all undergraduates. (*Digest of Education Statistics*, p. 81.)

36. California Postsecondary Education Commission, *Information Digest 1979: Postsecondary Education in California* (Sacramento, 1979), p. 38.

37. California Postsecondary Education Commission, *Equal Educational Opportunity in California: Postsecondary Education*, Part II (Sacramento, 1977), p. 36.

38. *Information Digest*, p. 38.

39. *Equal Educational Opportunity in California*, p. 36.

40. Ibid.

41. Jerome Karabel, "Community Colleges and Social Stratification," in *The Educational Establishment*, ed. Elizabeth L. Useem and Michael Useem (Englewood Cliffs, N.J.: Prentice-Hall, 1974), p. 110.

42. Connecticut Commission for Higher Education, *Preliminary Draft of Master Plan for Higher Education in Connecticut, 1974-79*, Document 17 (Hartford, 1973), IV, p. 1.

43. Legislative Analyst [William G. Hamn], *Analysis of the Budget Bill of the State of California for the Fiscal Year July 1, 1978 to June 30, 1979* (Sacramento, 1979), p. 992.

44. *Information Digest*, p. 38.

45. *Analysis of the Budget*, p. 1168.

46. See Burton R. Clark, *The Open Door College: A Case Study* (New York: McGraw-Hill, 1960); Karabel, "Community Colleges," pp. 117-45; L. Steven Zwerling, *Second Best: The Crisis of the Community College* (New York: McGraw-Hill, 1976), pp. 75-103.

47. *Information Digest*, p. 38; *Analysis of the Budget*, p. 1168. In addition, very few of the transfer students from community colleges succeeded in graduating. (Office of the Academic Vice President, University of California, Berkeley, *Report of the Task Group on Retention and Transfer* [June 1980].) In the Los Angeles Community College District, the state's largest community college district, only 3 percent of all students transferred to either UC or CSUC in 1979-80. (Jack McCurdy, "California Colleges Attacked: Too Much Growth in Wrong Direction," *Chronicle of Higher Education*, 4 November 1981, p. 11.)

48. Karabel, "Community Colleges," p. 126.

49. Ira Shor, *Critical Teaching and Everyday Life* (Boston: South

End Press, 1980), p. 24.

50. See Stanley Aronowitz, *False Promises* (New York: McGraw-Hill, 1973), p. 90.

51. Neil J. Smelser, "Growth, Structural Change, and Conflict in California Public Higher Education, 1950-70," in *Public Higher Education in California*, ed. Neil J. Smelser and Gabriel Almond (Berkeley: University of California Press, 1974), p. 66.

52. *Los Angeles Times*, 2 May 1980, p. 3. It is, of course, extremely difficult to compare per student expenditures at these different types of institutions. The University of California has expensive research and graduate programs. Nevertheless, the argument could be made that the greatest amount of money should be allocated for community college students, who often lack basic skills and require individual tutoring.

53. Leslie, Kellams, and Gunne, *Part-Time Faculty*, p. 19.

54. Tuckman, Caldwell, and Vogler, "Academic Labor Market," p. 185. A few community colleges now operate entirely with part-time faculty. (Clara Lee R. Moodie, "The Overuse of Part-Time Faculty Members," *Chronicle of Higher Education*, 10 March 1982, p. 72.)

55. In the fall of 1981, the University of California employed 1,500 lecturers, constituting 19 percent of the total faculty. Many are full-time teachers on short-term appointments, not part-timers. (Letter from Jeff Lustig, Field Representative, U.C. Council, A.F.T., to Gary Hart, Chairman of the State Assembly Education Committee, December 4, 1981; see also *Off the Track*, Bulletin of Non-Academic Senate Faculty, U.C., vol. 1 [Fall 1981].)

56. Figures obtained from the Office of the Chancellor, California State University and Colleges system.

57. "Summary of Proposition 13 Impact," p. 3.

58. See Smelser, "Growth," p. 96.

59. *Analysis of the Budget*, p. 1031. According to the American Association of University Professors, elite universities throughout the country would have to increase the number of their faculty members by 25 percent if they dispensed with the services of teaching assistants. (Ernest R. May and Dorothy G. Blaney, *Careers for Humanists* [New York: Academic Press, 1981], p. 89.)

60. Robert H. McCabe and Jeffrey I. Brenzer, "Part-Time Faculty in Institutional Economics," in *Employing Part-Time Faculty*, ed. David W. Leslie (San Francisco: Jossey-Bass, 1978), p. 66.

61. Emily K. Abel, "The Academic Proletariat: Part-Time Teachers in Community Colleges," *Radical Teacher*, no. 5, July 1977, pp. 1-2.

62. Leslie, Kellams, and Gunne, *Part-Time Faculty*, p. 81.

63. A major survey of part-time faculty was conducted by Howard

P. Tuckman, Jaime Caldwell, and William Vogler for the American Association of University Professors (the results of this study are reported in a series of articles, most of which are reprinted in *Part-Time Faculty Series*). Although I have used information they provided about institutional policies, their data about the demographic characteristics of part-timers are less reliable. Their study is marred by their division of part-time faculty into the following seven categories:

> *Semi-Retired*—those reporting their primary reason for becoming part-time is that they are semi-retired (2.8 percent of the sample).
> *Students*—persons employed in other departments than the one in which they are registered to receive a degree (21.2 percent).
> *Hopeful Full-Timers*—persons who report that their primary reason for becoming part-time is that they could not find a full-time position (16.6 percent).
> *Full-Mooners*—persons who in addition to their part-time job held a full-time job of 35 hours a week or more for 18 weeks or more (27.6 percent).
> *Homeworkers*—persons who report that their primary reason for becoming part-time is to take care of a relative or child (6.4 percent).
> *Part-Mooners*—persons holding two or more part-time jobs of less than 35 hours a week for more than one week (13.6 percent).
> *Part-Unknowners*—persons whose motives for becoming part-time do not fall into any of the other categories (11.8 percent). (Tuckman, Caldwell, and Vogler, "Academic Labor Market," p. 189.)

Although the authors claim these categories are "mutually exclusive," they are, in fact, overlapping: some are based on motivation, others on objective work situations. The distinction between "Hopeful Full-Timers" and all other groups is particularly unclear. The authors acknowledge that "Part-Mooners" include people who are "concerned about future employment at an institution" and who therefore are "hedging by developing work contacts in several places." (Tuckman, "Who Is Part-Time in Academe?" *AAUP Bulletin*, December 1978, p. 308.) Similarly, many students apply for full-time positions. Even people who hold full-time nonteaching jobs might prefer full-time academic appointments, should they be available. In fact, a sizable proportion of people in *every* category have applied for full-time academic positions. (Tuckman, "Who Is Part-Time," p. 313.) At the same time, only 62.5 percent of the "Hopeful Full-Timers" have sought full-time academic positions. (Tuckman, "Who Is Part-Time," p. 313.) One wonders why the other 37.5 percent were included in this category. An additional problem is that the category "Homemakers" includes both women whose incomes are simply supplementary and those who are the sole support of their households. (Tuckman, "Who Is Part-Time," p. 308.) There are critical differencesC between these two groups, and including them in the same category obscures more than it clarifies.

A final criticism of this study is that the questionnaires were distributed by the administration. As one observer commented, "It is a little like sending a questionnaire on working conditions to J. P. Stevens and asking that it be distributed to the workers, please." (Judith Bronfman, "Letter to the Editor," *Academe*, February 1979, p. 82.) Another major study of part-time faculty (Leslie, Kellams, and Gunne, *Part-Time Faculty*) relied heavily on interviews with part-timers specifically chosen by the administration. This might explain the large number of respondents holding full-time jobs (almost twice as many as in Tuckman's study) and the high proportion who expressed satisfaction with their conditions of employment. (Leslie, Kellams, and Gunne, *Part-Time Faculty*, pp. 40-46.)

64. Questionnaires were sent to 3,086 lecturers at seven of the campuses. These campuses were selected to ensure a representative distribution in terms of size, location, urban-rural nature, teaching area emphasized, and student composition. The lecturers who were surveyed at each campus were selected randomly. The number of surveys sent to the campuses was determined by a formula estimating the number of returns needed to secure representative results from each location and then increasing that number proportionate to an expected return rate of 50 percent. Follow-up postcards were sent out two weeks after the questionnaires were distributed.

Forty percent of the surveys, representing a total of 1,223, were returned. The return rate undoubtedly would have been higher had current lists been available. However, the chancellor's office provided lists only for the fall of 1980, a semester prior to the distribution of the questionnaire.

The representativeness of the returns can be determined in a number of ways. About 20 percent of the surveys were returned from the two rural campuses, while 20 percent of all temporary faculty in CSUC were located on rural campuses in the fall of 1980. More full-time lecturers than part-timers returned the questionnaires. Full-time lecturers constituted 15 percent of the 7,950 lecturers employed in the fall of 1980 and 26 percent of the respondents to the survey. The lower return rate from the part-time group was probably a consequence partly of the fact that semester-old lists were used; the turnover rate between semesters is higher for part-time than for full-time lecturers. In addition, the latter tend to be more involved in campus affairs.

The proportions of women and racial and ethnic minorities among the respondents were very close to those in the actual population. Women constituted 43 percent of the respondents and 39 percent of the lecturers as a whole. Minorities constituted 17 percent of the temporary faculty and 14 percent of the respondents to the survey. As the following table indicates, the returns were well distributed among the various disciplines:

Discipline	Number of Respondents	Percentage of Total Respondents
Humanities	212	17
Social Sciences	162	13
Natural Sciences and Math	173	14
Other Liberal Arts	78	6
Physical Education	37	3
Engineering	113	10
Education	97	8
Business/Management	160	13
Other Professional	155	13
Discipline not stated	36	3
Total	1,223	100

Although the category of part-timers officially includes tenure-track faculty members who temporarily teach on a part-time basis, I did not include them in the sample because they typically receive the status and rewards of other regular faculty.

65. Figures from the Chancellor's Office, CSUC.

66. See Joan Smith, *Social Issues and the Social Order: The Contradictions of Capitalism* (Cambridge, Mass.: Winthrop, 1981), p. 132.

67. *Analysis of the Budget*, p. 1113.

68. However, many part-time faculty object to their assignment of such classes, complaining that their jobs do not make full and proper use of their educational backgrounds and professional skills.

69. The latter figure also suggests that many of these teachers do not hold part-time appointments by choice. In the labor force in general, two-thirds of the part-time employees would not prefer full-time jobs.

However, a rapidly growing segment of the part-time work force wants full-time employment. Between 1970 and 1982, the number of "voluntary" part-time workers rose only 33 percent, from 9.3 million to 12.4 million; the number of "involuntary" part-time workers jumped 166 percent, from 2.19 million to 5.8 million. (*New York Times* [August 14, 1983], p. 1.)

It is also important to note that, although 60 percent of the part-time faculty would accept full-time tenure-track positions, a similar proportion would prefer to hold part-time jobs if they carried security of employment and pay proportional to that of full-timers. This indicates that part-timers are more dissatisfied with their lack of security and advancement than with their reduced teaching loads as such. Moreover, administrators occasionally speak of the desirability of eliminating part-time positions should adjuncts gain all the perquisites of tenure-track faculty. In fact, part-timers themselves often advocate the conversion of all part-time slots into full-time positions. Such a policy clearly runs counter to the wishes of significant numbers of part-time faculty.

70.   Although administrators justify the low salaries of part-timers by arguing that they have other sources of incomes, the great majority of tenure-track professors also add substantial sums to their teaching salaries. (Jack Magarrell, "Extra Work Found to Add 21 Pct. to Base Salaries of Most Professors," *Chronicle of Higher Education*, 15 November 1980, pp. 1, 7.) Moreover, the most highly paid professors—those who teach in business, law, and medical schools—earn the most from outside sources. (*Chronicle of Higher Education*, 1 December 1980, p. 7.)

71.   *Work in America*, Report of a Special Task Force to the Secretary of Health, Education and Welfare (Cambridge, Mass.: MIT Press, 1973), p. 15.

72.   According to a study conducted in 1976, about 60 percent of the entire faculty in CSUC favored collective bargaining. (Joseph W. Garbarino, "Proposition 13 and Faculty Organizing under HEERA," California Public Employee Relations, No. 39, December 1978, pp. 23-32.)

73.   Women also are concentrated in part-time work in the economy at large. Half of the million women who entered the labor force between 1967 and 1979 obtained part-time jobs. Among workers in the age group 25 to 54, women part-timers outnumber men seven to one. (Jerry Flint, "Growing Part-Time Work Force Has Major Impact on Economy," *New York Times*, 12 April 1977, pp. 1, 56.)

74.   It could be argued that this is the only statistic we should use to determine economic need; wages should be sufficient to enable every adult to be economically independent of other members of the house-

hold. Nevertheless, because men and women derive virtually the same proportion of their *household* incomes from their teaching jobs, it is clear that the women rely more heavily on the incomes of other family members.

75. The distribution of the minority faculty among the various ethnic and racial groups is as follows: Black/Afro-American—34; Asian/Asian-American/Pacific Islander—59; Hispanic/Latino/Mexican-American—31; American Indian/Native American—7.

76. Three doctorates noted in writing that they had "given up" the search for regular academic employment and one job hunter stated she was looking for a faculty position but "without much hope."

Chapter 4
THE ACADEMIC PROLETARIAT

When I was going to graduate school, I had an image of
myself as a professional. But the way I'm treated as a
part-timer is more like a hired hand, a person who
doesn't count.
> —*A man who has worked as a part-time teacher since
> receiving a Ph.D. in history in the early seventies.*

At every place I taught, there was some possibility of a real job
opening up. These are the words in the English language about
which I'm now most cynical.
> —*A woman with a Ph.D. in philosophy who taught on a
> temporary basis in both full-time and part-time academic jobs
> for five years.*

As professionals were subjected increasingly to capitalist
relations of production during the recent decade, their autonomy
was eroded. Within the academic framework, marginal employment represents the extreme of this process of proletarianization.
The response of displaced academics to temporary jobs in institutions of higher education thus illuminates the reactions of professionals to the transformation of their work, if in a more intense
form. This chapter first will discuss academics who teach part-

112

time in colleges and universities[1] and then will examine Ph.D.s with terminal, full-time appointments.

ADJUNCTS

Not all displaced academics regarded part-time teaching as a viable option. When their hopes of obtaining regular faculty positions were shattered, some preferred to leave higher education entirely. Like other workers, academics who had held full-time appointments strongly resisted demotion.[2] One man, interviewed shortly after his dismissal from a full-time job as a result of budget cutbacks, explained why he refused to drop into the ranks of part-timers:

> I toyed with the idea of taking a job part-time, but as a full-time faculty member I had been with full-time people when they discussed part-time people. Full-time tenured faculty have an attitude of despising part-time people. I wasn't going to put up with being insulted on top of everything else. I was not about to be treated as a second-class citizen.

For this academic, a reduction in status was an unacceptable humiliation.

More women than men obtained part-time employment. According to the National Research Council, only 10 percent of the men awarded Ph.D.s in the humanities between 1972 and 1976 and still seeking employment when they graduated were employed part-time in 1977, compared to 28 percent of the women.[3] In this study, men represented 37 percent of the displaced academics teaching part-time when interviewed, although they constituted almost half of the respondents as a whole. (Some of the reasons for this disparity are discussed in Chapter 6.)

Despite this sex differential, most displaced academics gravitated toward part-time employment. Thirteen were teaching part-time when I interviewed them, and seventeen others previously had held fractured appointments. Thus, thirty, or 70 percent, of the displaced academics had had some experience as part-time teachers. Traditionally, academics taught part-time only before completing their degrees. Indeed, five of the academics in this study had relied on part-time employment to support themselves while writing their dissertations, and four other part-timers were interviewed while still doctoral students. However, since the collapse of the academic job market, increasing numbers of academics have remained in the part-time circuit after graduation. Three of the interviewees who had begun teaching on a part-time basis as graduate students retained their jobs when they failed to convert their degrees into tenure-track appointments. The majority of displaced academics sought part-time positions only after they had been awarded Ph.D.s.

Like most other part-time faculty, the adjuncts in this study sharply resented their conditions of employment. The lack of job security was the strongest grievance for the interviewees, as it was for the respondents to the survey. One woman commented:

> I can't begin any research that will extend beyond a year or two because I don't know where I will be to finish it up. Everything gets foreshortened into these six month segments and you don't plan on anything more than six months ahead of time.

As members of the middle class, these academics had high expectations of security, and they found it intolerable not to be able to engage in long-term planning. The vicissitudes of part-time work affected even more profoundly those adjuncts who relied solely on their teaching salaries. A woman who had been teaching part-time for seven years described her life as follows:

> I have to live very much in the present. I don't think about things I am going to do in the future. I don't have anybody or anything to fall back on, so this means I can only count on something as far ahead as four months before my life can be totally disrupted and changed. There is a sense of tenuousness about my whole life.

Uncertainty about the future compelled one part-timer in Los Angeles to give up her apartment and store her furniture when she returned to the Midwest in June to defend her dissertation. She later recalled:

I finally got a part-time job late in August at eleven-thirty at night. Until then, I didn't know where to go. I was house-sitting in someone's apartment, my dissertation was finished, my stuff was in California, my car was in California. I had some medical problems so I thought I was going to need minor surgery and I didn't know how I could afford that. I didn't know how I could live any place on unemployment. So I really was desperate.

Despite their lofty aspirations, these academics experienced the instability that historically has been the fate of the working-class.

However, a steady job was not the only goal of these displaced academics. A primary reward of professional success is steady and predictable increments in prestige, salary, and rank,[4] and they wanted careers with prospects of continuous and orderly advancement. One woman imposed her own sense of progressive order on the random series of jobs she held. Because her pay increased slightly each year, she was convinced that "things were getting better all the time" and that the quality of her life would continue to improve. But the majority of part-timers spoke of "treading water," of feeling "frozen," or of "being on a treadmill." Like Alice in Wonderland, they saw themselves running very fast just to stay in place.

We have seen that adjuncts rarely are promoted to the ranks of the full-time faculty. In addition, many displaced academics were convinced that the longer they remained part-timers, the more elusive any regular position became. No matter how glowing their past records, they incurred some of the stigma of part-time employment. In addition, academic selection committees rank applicants according to the number and quality of their publications, not their experience and skills as teachers. But publishing was particularly difficult for part-timers. First, they generally were denied access to research support. Moreover, the large number who shuttled between campuses had little time for scholarship. One part-timer spoke directly to this point:

I did have a good publications record in the past but...now I don't have the money to fly to major conferences. Of course full-time tenure-track position people get that from their departments to go to one and sometimes even two major conferences. And of course there's also soft money and money that comes from the internal university structure, but I don't have access to any of these things and I can't afford to go on my own....Also, when I teach three courses in three places I don't have time to write. It's a vicious circle—with more publications I would have a better chance to get a job, but teaching this way, there's no chance to turn out publications....My future looks bleak and scary because I know publications are important.

Finally, as people remain in the part-time circuit for several years, their Ph.D.s depreciate in value. Although they may become better teachers, they are likely to be surpassed in the competition for a coveted job by a candidate who can display a late model degree.

The low pay and lack of fringe benefits also created serious hardships for many displaced academics. One part-timer at a large state institution described her financial situation in this way:

I bring home less than six hundred dollars a month. In order to go to graduate school, I had to borrow money and I have enormous debts. I owe two thousand dollars on one and four thousand dollars on another. Also, I keep just one step ahead of things that could really do me in. I'm terrified about getting sick. I don't have any insurance and I recently saw both my mother and father get catastrophically ill. I'm also concerned about being able to stay in my apartment which has a low rent. If I get kicked out, where will I go? Another thing that weighs heavily on me is my brother. He is nine years younger than me and I've been responsible for mothering him since he was nine. I think that if I could give him some kind of financial help it would make all the difference in the world for him. He might be able to go to college and really learn something that could help him get a better job. But I'm afraid that he is going to have to stay working-class.

Many were more fortunate. Of the thirteen academics who were teaching on a part-time basis at the time of the interviews, only five had no other source of income. One man lived with another part-time teacher, and together they managed "to make ends meet, though just barely." One woman supplemented her meager earnings with savings and another with both a postdoctoral fellowship and a part-time blue-collar job. Five part-timers relied on partners who had stable incomes and provided health insurance. Nevertheless, all of these academics depended on their own wages for substantial portions of their livelihoods. Even those who considered their own salaries secondary stressed that their earnings were crucial to sustain their life-styles. The social devaluation of their work also was critical. After emphasizing the "absolute necessity" of her salary for her family's welfare, one woman mused:

> I don't know that I would feel differently about my salary if I married a man who was able to support us easily. I put a lot of sweat and blood and tears into my work, into my degree and being able to do the work that I care about....Certainly it would make a difference in terms of security and comfort, but for my own goals I don't think so.

The comment of a man who had worked part-time for a year was more acerbic:

> The pay was just an outrageously low salary. You wouldn't believe it. It was just so embarrassing. You were paid like you were a janitor.

In a society that measures people's value by their wages, part-timers inevitably felt demeaned.

Other aspects of part-time academic employment were equally humiliating to adjuncts who had aspired to professional status. Although most of the part-timers in this study had hoped to enjoy a sense of community at the institutions where they taught, their full-time colleagues treated them with disdain. A typical comment was: "I kept getting all these signals early on that we really don't belong here, that we're very much less than second class." In addition, adjuncts were denied the visible signs of occupational success. Many lacked office space and access to secretarial services, mailboxes, and duplicating equipment. The last-minute hiring represented an even greater affront. Part-timers frequently had to wait throughout the summer to learn whether or not they would be reemployed and, if so, how many courses and which subjects they would teach. Nancy Henley has argued:

> Keeping someone waiting probably does more to reduce someone's stature than telling the person verbally how you feel. Time is far from a neutral philosophical/physical concept in our society: it is a political weapon.[5]

Furthermore, the expectation that part-timers could begin teaching at a moment's notice revealed the low value attached to the work of preparing syllabi and other course materials. As Magali Sarfatti Larson has explained, professionals in this society typically are granted control over the pace at which they work:

> The central characteristic of expert intellectual work is that it cannot be established from the outside *that a given result should be obtained in a given time.* This characteristic is tied to the experts' monopoly of knowledge, which makes it even more difficult for non-experts to "see" or to replicate the productive process in which experts actually engage.[6]

Thus, part-timers who had little warning about the nature of their teaching assignments tended to feel that they were being treated more like unskilled workers than professionals.

Eight of the academics who currently were teaching part-time held jobs at more than one institution. Just as the itinerant academics in the survey were especially dissatisfied with their working conditions, so these commuters were particularly vituperative about their employment situations. Even if they succeeded in putting together a schedule in which they taught a full-time load, they generally earned much less than the full-time teachers and received no fringe benefits. Their jobs also were more costly, in terms of both the out-of-pocket expense and the psychological strain of commuting between different campuses. Because they believed their rehiring was contingent on their willingness to accept every course they were offered, and they lacked control over teaching times, they found themselves locked into difficult, sometimes impossible, schedules. A "freeway flyer" in Los Angeles described the logistics of her week:

> During the fall term I was driving to three places. One is one and a half hours to the north, a little more than sixty miles from here. The second is just twenty miles from here and the third is seventy-five miles from here. Sometimes I could go from one to the other, but, in general, I was driving at least forty and frequently eighty miles a day.... I've hardly met any of my colleagues because I drive to a place, park, and run up to teach and then get back in the car and drive some place else and run up to teach. I can't publish because half of my time is spent driving from one place to the other.

The schedule of an itinerant academic in New York compelled him to rely on his fiancée to ferry him from one class to another:

> There were some amusing if sad vignettes last fall. Our one horrible extravagance is that we have a Toyota. My fiancée would take me down to one campus and read for the hour she was there, all the while making sure she was under a street light because it was November or December and it was getting dark early and I had a four o'clock class. Then she'd hustle me down to the other campus, so I could teach there. By the same token, if there were some days that I wasn't teaching and she was, I'd have the car waiting for her. It was almost like a get-away car. It was ridiculous, really absurd.

Finally, these academics had to familiarize themselves with a variety of regulations, memorize several campus maps, obtain different sets of keys, library cards, and parking stickers, and prepare materials appropriate to students from vastly different backgrounds. A man who taught simultaneously at U.C. Berkeley and a community college portrayed himself as "going through some very difficult contortions."

Although most part-time faculty felt themselves drifting farther and farther away from the world of established academics, many initially exhibited enormous concern for their jobs. Several spoke of giving their "heart and soul" to their courses. Studies of many different kinds of workers have emphasized their desire to produce high-quality work and their anger at company policies that restrict their ability to do good jobs.[7] Similarly, the part-timers I interviewed employed various devices to circumvent the obstacles placed in their paths by the administration. Although they received their assignments shortly before the beginning of the semester, they expended extra effort on class preparation. If they lacked access to a typing pool or a Xerox machine, they typed their own course materials and had them copied at their own expense. After enumerating both the problems she encountered and her efforts to overcome them, one part-timer reflected, "Sometimes I think I'm in a conspiracy to teach." Some adjuncts also assumed tasks outside the scope of their assignments, such as advising students, developing curricula, and serving on committees.

Part-timers gave several reasons for working so hard. Some were motivated by the hope that their diligence would be rewarded, as it had been in the past, and they would be able to move into full-time positions. Many also were convinced that, in a buyer's market, they would only be rehired if they displayed clear superiority as teachers. They also sought to prove their competence to themselves. One former part-timer had wanted to deny the reality of her employment situation and to assert her claim to the title of professional:

> By working hard at registration and going to graduation and advising students, I was able to really perceive myself as a full-time professional, even though I was a part-time employee.

Some displaced academics devoted themselves to their courses and campus activities precisely because they received insufficient material rewards; the intrinsic satisfactions they derived from their jobs served to counterbalance the low salary. For several, teaching clearly was a calling as well as a job. A woman who had been unemployed for over a year after losing a tenure-track position described her first opportunity to teach again in almost lyrical terms:

> Being in the classroom was terrific. It's marvelous to do something you're good at, and I'm very good at teaching, I know how to do it. It was just lovely. I'm sure it's the way athletes feel; the muscles work just right.

Others sought to infuse their work with meaning and purpose; they were transmitting crucial information to students, teaching them to think more deeply or creatively, imparting values, or raising consciousness. Finally, notions of appropriate professional conduct, internalized during graduate school, compelled displaced academics to spend many hours preparing classes. Although paid a pittance, they wanted to fulfill the high standards they always had set themselves.

Nevertheless, intense involvement in part-time teaching also had disadvantages. The more part-timers behaved like regular faculty members, the greater dividends they expected from their work. At a minimum, they wanted recognition for their efforts. However, just as assembly-line workers gain attention only when they make mistakes, so these part-timers were noticed when they failed to turn in their grades or book orders on time, not when they delivered brilliant lectures or led engrossing discussions. Another difficulty was that they developed progressively deeper attachments to their jobs and institutions. One woman described her dilemma:

> Because I view my work at the college as more than just a part-time job, I am kept hooked into an exploitative situation. It's really double-edged. The more I put in, the more I care, the more I want to be there, and also the greater the extent to which I subject myself to exploitation.

An even more serious problem was that the task these part-timers set for themselves was impossible. By redoubling their efforts, adjuncts could overcome some of the barriers to effective teaching, but they could not eliminate them altogether. Moreover, the intrinsic rewards of teaching were never as great as anticipated. The institutions at which part-timers were most likely to find jobs—community colleges and the less prestigious state universities—were those that tend to emphasize rote learning rather than analytical reasoning. Adjuncts often were assigned only lower-level introductory courses that had standardized syllabi and preordered texts and were populated largely by students motivated solely by the need to satisfy requirements. One European historian, who had taught at least three courses each semester for the past year and a half, feared he was becoming deskilled:

> As a scholar I feel that the adjunct racket has taken a lot out of me. I'm not nearly as sharp as I was as a graduate student and I feel that I've lost my grip on the material. Apart from the occasional foray into American history, I've taught the same European survey course over and over. The entire history of the world, from the lower Paleolithic era till Jimmy Carter has really become flattened out in my mind.... If you teach the same introductory course three or four times a semester, there's a tendency for the material to lose any real meaning and it's difficult to maintain an intellectual relationship with the material.

Like the detail workers Harry Braverman has described, this historian performed the same operation over and over.[8] His continuing sense of himself as an academic rested on his ability to use his expertise as a teacher, but even in the classroom he was expected to perform only routine and repetitive tasks. Thus, he was deprived of any feeling of accomplishment. David Moberg has argued:

> Most workers would like to have interesting work. Increasingly they feel, however, that they are denied the opportunity to use their talents, to pursue whatever would make their work more satisfying and to have work that is challenging and interesting. The notorious cases of worker disinterest in doing good quality work are in part an inarticulate rebellion.[9]

As adjuncts became increasingly aware of the distance between the reality of their employment, with its subordinate status and limited autonomy, and the image of professional work that had sustained them through graduate school, they tended to reduce their commitment to their institutions and withdraw some of their energy from the classroom. Some part-timers left at this point. Those who remained invested the minimum effort possible in their teaching, despite the idealism that originally had inspired them.

Nevertheless, part-timers typically eschewed more collective forms of opposition. Theorists of the "new class" have expected the proletarianized sectors of the professions to come to resemble the industrial working class and, if not make common cause with the latter, at least imitate their modes of resistance.[10] The survey demonstrated that the majority of part-time faculty believe that collective bargaining can ameliorate their conditions of work, and that part-timers with Ph.D.s in the humanities and social sciences are particularly supportive of unionization. Nevertheless, some displaced academics responded to their experiences as part-timers by grasping even more tightly the last vestiges of professional identity. To become a union member would be to relinquish any claim to superiority over other workers. Although the majority of part-timers interviewed for this study were willing to join unions, few were activists.[11] As the following two quotes demonstrate, some were inhibited from protesting because they feared their treatment accurately reflected their true worth:

One reason I didn't become active in a union was basic insecurity. I felt that since I wasn't a full-time person, then obviously I wasn't good enough.

All the ways we're treated add up to the message that what we have is irrelevant and they don't care about it. This makes it harder to fight back because it's much easier to say you're wonderful when everyone else is saying you are and that your skills are valued and what you know is important. Instead the message we get is that no one needs us and they can find someone else to replace us.

Some viewed themselves as exceptions. Although all other adjuncts had shortcomings as scholars and teachers, they themselves had been misclassified. One man who taught part-time at an institution where he previously had held a full-time position explained why he refused to attend union meetings for adjuncts: "I don't consider myself a part-timer." By viewing part-time status as a state of mind, he could salvage his pride and hold himself aloof from his colleagues. Several others believed their success in securing a few privileges reflected their greater value. For example, two part-time faculty members proudly noted they had received research funds generally reserved for tenure-track teachers. Another boasted that her placement at the top of the pay scale for adjuncts demonstrated she had more in common with tenure-track faculty than with other part-timers. Yet another contended that his superior worth had been affirmed when a department that had had to fire most of its part-time staff retained him. Because these academics remained sensitive to fine gradations of rank and privilege and saw themselves as having been singled out for small favors, their sense of common or shared grievances was weakened.

Displaced academics also were deterred from challenging the system by the lingering hope that they would become part of it one day. Most continued to enter the job market each year despite the low probability of obtaining regular academic positions. A few placed their faith in the promises of upward mobility held out by department chairs. Looking back at her stint as a part-timer, one woman recalled that she continually had been "beguiled" by the belief that she was about to be promoted to full-time status. A number of part-timers had abandoned hope of securing niches in academia but still sought professions befitting their backgrounds, education, and aspirations. They devoted their primary efforts to obtaining, or training for, alternative careers in which they expected to obtain the status and remuneration denied them in higher education. Although many academics remained in the part-time circuit much longer than they originally intended, they perceived their work as temporary, enabling them to view their grievances as ephemeral discontents.

Another barrier to organized protest was the lack of models of effective change. We will see that unionization has benefitted few part-time teachers. Many adjuncts assumed that competition inevitably resulted from the dearth of academic positions and that any form of collective activity thus was doomed to failure. One man articulated the sense of hopelessness shared by many:

> We're divided and conquered by this situation. People are fighting for those jobs desperately and there's not a lot of

cooperation. I've never found a lot of, "Let's get together and change things." There are ten people for every job. You want to break a union, just have these conditions. If it was the opposite, then we could get together and demand changes. But we can't, it just won't work.

Nevertheless, the few part-timers who did seek to express their anger and frustration in collective action reported that their efforts helped to mitigate feelings of powerlessness and to prevent the internalization of disparaging comments and humiliating treatment. One part-time faculty member explained how her participation in an association of adjuncts enhanced her self-esteem:

I have an increasing sense of being proud of being a part-timer. It's like now there's a cause to champion. We're saying there's injustice there and there is a group that has been mistreated and oppressed and it's time that something be changed. And being part of that group, I suddenly see that that group of people really is valuable and important and the conditions under which we live really ought to be changed. We really ought to be recognized and validated. Also, even though things are bad for us, there's a sense in which we're all in it together.

DISPOSABLE DONS

Seven of the academics in this study were employed on short-term, nonrenewable, full-time contracts when they were interviewed, and eight others previously had held such jobs. All had completed their degrees at the time of their appointment. Although two of these lecturers viewed teaching simply as a means of supporting themselves while investigating alternative careers, the great majority approached their jobs with high expectations. They assumed either that their selection as lecturers was a prelude to even greater success in the job market the following year or that their jobs would be converted automatically into tenure-track positions.

Department chairs often nourished the hopes of these faculty. Some academics were guaranteed promotions; others were assured of priority when tenure-track positions became available; still others interpreted vague promises from department chairs as firm commitments. The hiring process also heightened expectations of imminent career success. Nonladder positions typically are advertised through the same channels as tenure-track jobs, and recruitment follows the same forms. As a result, some candidates are not even aware until after the search process is complete that the junior faculty positions for which they apply are temporary slots.[12] One lecturer in this study took pride in having been selected from hundreds of competitors for the job, and another remarked that her department had interviewed over twenty candidates before choosing her. Thus, unlike part-time jobs, these positions tended to be viewed as marks of distinction, and academics who obtained them had renewed faith in their ability to emerge as winners.

Their working conditions also helped to foster the illusion that their careers had been launched. Many were paid at the same level as other junior faculty and were eligible for most of the same benefits. Moreover, the great majority taught at elite institutions, where all faculty enjoy substantial privileges. Of the fifteen lecturers I interviewed, eleven currently were employed or previously had taught at major research universities and three others at four-year liberal arts colleges; only one had worked at a community college. One woman described her year as a faculty member at a prestigious university in glowing terms:

> It was superb! That was a year that stands out in my memory as really one of the best years of my life....I was treated really decently. I had a secretary; people took messages for me and put them in my mailbox; people typed things for me....Also, the students were outstanding...and it's a wonderful thing to teach students who are interested in your subject....Also...there was a sense of being a colleague, a sense of being accepted as an equal....It was just a jewel of a year.

Nevertheless, most lecturers rapidly discovered that their temporary status set them apart from other junior faculty. Although some were expected to participate in department meetings and were invited to informal gatherings, others complained they were treated as though they were invisible. Their jobs often were readvertised shortly after they arrived on campus, and lecturers who sought reemployment felt under enormous pressure to demonstrate instant superiority. The few lecturers who did succeed in ignoring the distinctions between themselves and other junior faculty found the end of the year an acutely painful time. One woman, who had taught at a large university, commented:

> Nothing they did ever made me feel out of place. But there comes that point at the end of the spring quarter when they're planning for next year. You feel like the little match girl out on the porch, while they're all inside warm and toasty.

Five of the academics in this study had held a series of one-year appointments at different institutions and thus had moved annually to new parts of the country. The costs of such a peripatetic existence are described by a woman who had taught at three different schools during the past three years:

> The cumulative effect of moving is really devastating. The worst thing is being constantly new to some place. I had accumulated a lot of student kinds of furniture, but it wasn't worth it to move it, so when I got to my first job I had a TV set and I bought a mattress, and that was it. I finally decided to buy a couple of pieces of good furniture and, whether or not it was worth it, I've paid to have them moved because they symbolize some kind of continued existence....
> But, still, every fall for three years I had to find a bank, decide what kind of checking account I wanted, find a doctor, change my driver's license, license plates, and car insurance. I figure it takes at least a month, counting packing and unpacking and trying to settle in.

Others focused on the disruption of personal relationships. For example, a woman who had been employed by two different universities in two successive years could neither maintain an ongoing relationship nor establish roots in her new environment:

> I had been involved with somebody just before I went to the first place and we were tentatively planning to be married....I came back and lived with him over the summer, but by then it was all gone. We grew apart because we just didn't see each other every weekend....I didn't want to get together with him every weekend because I felt like I had to spend time making friends at the university. Because I had hoped the job would be permanent, I wanted to take time to get to know the faculty. I felt very much pulled in two directions, wanting to spend time with him and feeling a need to have some kind of social network at the university. Both failed.

Another woman, interviewed shortly after she had moved to her second job, asserted, "Just as I'm really settled in, I have to be moving again. It's a terrible way to live."

However, displaced academics did not remain on the lecturer route more than a few years. The likelihood of finding permanent positions decreased with each passing year. Thus, as the dislocation of moving intensified, both the immediate returns and the future prospects diminished. One part-timer decided to change careers because she "got tired of chasing rainbows."

The point at which lecturers realized their expectations of advancing rapidly to tenure-track positions were unfounded represented a critical juncture. They acknowledged that they were vulnerable, often for the first time, and that the grim statistics about academic jobs could apply to them as well as their classmates. Thus, if they ever were to try collective activity, this was a likely occasion. In fact, we will see that some academic women do file sex discrimination charges when they are denied promotion to tenure-track positions. Nevertheless, most of the academics in this study placed their faith in individual solutions; they quietly abandoned their dreams of academic success and searched for jobs in other fields.

NOTES

1. For accounts of Ph.D.s teaching part-time see Cara Chell, "Memoirs and Confessions of a Part-time Lecturer," *College English* 44

(January 1982):35-40; John E. Cooney, "The Gypsy Scholar," *Wall Street Journal,* 13 March 1979, pp. 1, 16; Joanne Spencer Kantrowitz, "Paying Your Dues, Part-Time," in *Rocking the Boat: Academic Women and Academic Processes,* ed. Gloria DeSole and Leonore Hoffman (New York: Modern Language Association, 1981), pp. 15-36; Susan O'Malley, "Nonworking or Speak Bitterness," *Radical Teacher* 1 (n.d.):19-26; Tim Spofford, "The Field Hands of Academe," *Change,* November-December 1979, pp. 14-16.

2. James R. Green, *The World of the Worker: Labor in Twentieth-Century America* (New York: Hill and Wang, 1980), p. 136; Teresa A. Sullivan, *Marginal Workers, Marginal Jobs: The Underutilization of American Workers* (Austin: University of Texas Press, 1978), p. 5.

3. National Research Council, *Employment of Humanities Ph.D.'s: A Departure from Traditional Jobs* (Washington, D.C.: National Academy of Sciences, 1980), p. 33.

4. See Magali Sarfatti Larson, *The Rise of Professionalism: A Sociological Analysis* (Berkeley: University of California Press, 1979), p. 229.

5. Nancy M. Henley, *Body Politics: Power, Sex and Nonverbal Communication* (Englewood Cliffs, N.J.: Prentice-Hall, 1977), p. 43.

6. Larson, *Professionalism,* p. 235.

7. Barbara Garson, *All the Livelong Day: The Meaning and De-meaning of Routine Work* (Harmondsworth, Eng.: Penguin, 1977); David Moberg, "No More Junk: Lordstown Workers and the Demand for Quality," *The Insurgent Sociologist* 3 (Fall 1978): 63-69. In addition, studies of part-time workers often demonstrate that they are more productive than full-time workers. For example, according to a study of social workers employed on a half-time basis for a state agency, these employees handled 85 percent as many cases as their full-time counterparts, not 50 percent. (Carol S. Greenwald, "Part-Time Work and Flexible Hours Employment," cited by Project on the Status and Education of Women, "Part-Time Faculty Employment," April 1976, p. 1.)

8. Harry Braverman, *Labor and Monopoly Capital: The Degradation of Work in the Twentieth Century* (New York: Monthly Review Press, 1974).

9. David Moberg, "Work and American Culture: The Ideal of Self-Determination and the Prospects for Socialism," *Socialist Review* 10 (March-June 1980):30.

10. See André Gorz, *Strategy for Labor* (Boston: Beacon Press, 1967); Serge Mallet, *Essays on the New Working Class,* ed. Richard Howard and Dean Savage (St. Louis, Mo.: Telos Press, 1975).

11. Chapter 7 will discuss the reluctance of part-time faculty in general to devote time or energy to union activity; here I am focusing on the part-timers interviewed for this study.

12. National Research Council, *Career Outcomes in a Matched Sample of Men and Women Ph.D.s* (Washington, D.C.: National Academy Press, 1981), p. 46.

Chapter 5
OFFICIAL SOLUTIONS

Anyone venturing into the annual meeting of an academic association would have reason to assume that the worst of the unemployment crisis is over. Because warnings of the paucity of job interviews have been circulated prior to the meeting, most of the unemployed have been dissuaded from coming. Hence, their plight is not the focus for anxious debate. Although a few unemployed Ph.D.s stalk the halls, scanning bulletin boards for notices of job openings, hoping to be summoned for an interview, and providing embarrassing reminders that all is not well in the profession, their anxiety and bitterness seem out of place in the genteel surroundings. As the large number of sessions on esoteric subjects attest, business is proceeding as usual.

The atmosphere of these meetings exemplifies the attitude of some established academics to the collapse of the job market. Just as individual graduate students have looked to their own advisers to lead them into the ranks of the profession, so displaced academics as a group hold the older generation of scholars responsible for solving the job crisis.[1] Nevertheless, many tenured faculty take no action in response to the job crunch. Some argue that the severity of the crisis has been grossly exaggerated. They note that, although the number of positions has declined drastically during the past decade, the present academic employment situation is not without precedent. Before the heyday of the 1960s, job offers for recent graduates were extremely scarce. In fact, these professors also point out, during the 1930s the job prospects for new Ph.D.s were even bleaker than they are today. New doctoral recipients tend to hold inflated expectations because they entered graduate school when jobs were unusually plentiful. The anger they turn on their mentors is misplaced because many forged careers for themselves under equally adverse conditions.[2]

In addition, these professors contend, the imbalance between jobs and applicants may not be nearly as great as the figures imply. The ranks of the job seekers are swollen by the large group of people who cannot reasonably hope to obtain academic appointments. Although they may display the requisite diplomas, they lack the qualities of mind that would entitle them to enter the ranks of most university faculties.[3] Opportunities remain for graduates who really excel: in all fields some jobs are advertised each year.[4] This argument has a familiar ring. Since the beginning of capitalism, jobless workers have been viewed as inferior. A basic tenet of any society with a deep commitment to free enterprise and individualism is that people rise according to their merits. As we have seen, many displaced academics themselves refuse to view the causes of academic unemployment as structural.

But even those professors who acknowledge that the shortage of jobs is rooted in social and economic forces claim that academics are powerless to correct them. They have little access to government officials, and their own fields of expertise generally bear little relationship to the issue of unemployment.[5] Unlike the American Medical Association or the American Bar Association, the professional societies of academics exert little clout. Although they can pass resolutions, they lack the ability to enforce them.[6]

Nevertheless, many established professors do view the job crisis as their legitimate concern and propose two major remedies —restricting the number of new graduate students and encouraging the unemployed and underemployed to seek nonteaching positions. The first is consistent with other trends in higher education. Just as undergraduates increasingly are channeled into vocational majors, so students seeking graduate education can be directed into more practical professional programs. One method of restricting enrollments is to publicize information about the deteriorating job market. Indeed, since the early seventies, the professional societies in the humanities have encouraged departments to send prospective students warning letters about the job crisis.[7]

But more direct methods of limiting enrollments also are advocated. For example, some professors have recommended that no new graduate programs be founded, that some of the existing programs be dismantled, and that others restrict their intakes.[8] We might expect this solution to be endorsed widely. The primary way in which all professions establish their monopolies is by regulating entry.[9] Moreover, some academics argue that this remedy may offer an auxiliary benefit: because standards for admission and retention in graduate school would be tightened, the quality of the profession would rise.[10]

Nevertheless, two drawbacks have been cited. First, there is no consensus about which programs should be disbanded. Some insist that elite institutions should maintain their enrollments at current levels, while "second-rate schools" either drastically reduce the number of students admitted or cease producing Ph.D.s altogether.[11] Others, however, point out that diversity is important at the graduate as well as at the undergraduate level: different institutions attract different clienteles and serve very different purposes. Should the cuts fall disproportionately on less prestigious schools, higher education would return to the elitist model that it repudiated, albeit ambivalently, during the sixties.[12]

A more serious problem is that professors have a self-interest in maintaining the size of their graduate enrollments. A steady stream of graduate students enables them to teach their own fields of study. Instead of lecturing undergraduates, they can hold seminars in areas related to their own research and direct dissertations in topics of special interest to them. As teaching assistants, graduate students release senior professors from the burden of staffing introductory courses and grading exams and papers. The time saved can be spent on activities that enhance their professorial reputations and thus, indirectly, earning power. Professors who do succeed in placing protégés improve their own standing in the profession. Moreover, university faculty, like members of other professions, acquire prestige partly on the basis of the status of the clients they serve. Professors in Ph.D.-granting departments attain higher esteem than faculty members who teach only undergraduates, notwithstanding the current emphasis on basic skills. Finally, because the budgets of departments in many schools are tied closely to enrollment, professors want to attract as many students as possible. Thus, graduate faculty are in a bind. Their own privileges rest on contributing to the "overproduction" that has led to the erosion of the status of their profession as a whole.[13]

Because many academics are unwilling to control supply, the more popular remedy is to encourage surplus doctorates to seek alternative employment, primarily in business and government. Proponents of alternative careers frequently portray business as the new frontier; although the number of jobs in higher education is contracting rapidly, opportunities in business are said to be virtually unlimited. An anthropologist writing in the newsletter of the American Anthropological Association encouraged "enterprising" doctorates to "carve out new domains of employment."[14] A book on careers published by the American Sociological Association urged displaced academics to explore "the unexploited...labor market."[15] Similarly, the director of an association of historians spoke of corporations as the "untapped area" for members of her profession.[16]

Publications of the various professional associations also present case studies of Ph.D.s employed outside academia, who can serve as role models for disappointed job seekers. For example, the *Anthropology Newsletter* frequently includes a column entitled "Profile of an Anthropologist," which features members of the profession holding nonteaching jobs. The upbeat tone of the column of October 1979 is representative. Although a young anthropologist had "considered nothing other than academic employment" while working on her Ph.D., she realized she would be forced to alter her goals when her first foray into the academic job market proved unsuccessful. Initial contacts with anthropologists employed by government agencies convinced her that a job in the civil service could be challenging and satisfying, and she "pursued federal employment aggressively." Within a few months, she found a position that suited her. Soon afterwards, she was able to move to Washington, D.C., and to a better job by following "the same aggressive methods." Happily employed as a government anthropologist, she has few regrets about her move away from academia.[17]

The same revivalist optimism—listen and heed and you too can be saved—is contained in articles written by Ph.D.s themselves in the publications of the Modern Language Association. In one, a veritable Horatio Alger story, a man described his experiences after leaving his family behind in order to look for work in a new city. At first his search yielded nothing more promising than a temporary job loading newspapers on a truck, and his lodgings consisted of a furnished room in which he slept with two other men. He became so discouraged that he began to fear for his sanity. Nevertheless, he persevered and eventually found an editorial job on a business journal. He counseled academics who follow his example to remember that, although "they face a struggle,...talent and resourcefulness are not long denied an opportunity."[18] The recurrent message to unemployed academics is that the search for nonacademic work may be long, frustrating, and discouraging, but there are plenty of jobs for people who are determined, aggressive, and eager for a challenge.

Proponents of nonacademic employment also seek to upgrade the image of nonteaching jobs in order to enhance their appeal. Jobs that academics traditionally have viewed with disdain now are hailed as honorable pursuits for new Ph.D.s.[19] Recent doctorates are urged to stop romanticizing academia. Universities are no purer than any other social institution; they serve similar ends and operate in similar ways. Moreover, university and college professors increasingly have been compelled to emulate the techniques of profit-making enterprises; at many institutions, faculty members advertise their courses before the beginning of term and adapt their lectures, syllabi, and grades to student preferences. In a book entitled *Careers for Humanists*, Ernest R. May, professor of history at Harvard, and Dorothy G. Blaney, of the New York State Education Department, quote, apparently with approval, the response of a graduate student at the University of Pennsylvania to a classmate's criticism of a job as a salesperson:

I come from a business family. I play the same damn games my father does. We are trying to sell education now. We are selling ourselves all the time. Do you think people need literature any more than a paper towel?[20]

But, it is stressed repeatedly, Ph.D.s who seek jobs in government and business are not just pursuing self-interest. Like many of the actions taken by members of professions on their own behalf, the movement into nonacademic employment is couched in the language of altruism. Doctorates bring with them the qualities of mind and character that enabled them to succeed in academia. They are determined, hard-working, resourceful people who have a high level of verbal and analytical skills and an extensive body of knowledge upon which to draw.[21]

In fact, it is asserted, the benefits that derive from employing Ph.D.s extend beyond the specific companies that hire them. Because doctorates can exert an "uplifting" effect on the organizations they enter, their employment will be good for society at large. Although some advocates of nonteaching jobs exhort displaced academics to cease exaggerating the distinction between higher education and the surrounding society, others wax eloquent about the possibility of infusing business and government with the values of academia. The claims held out for doctorates in the humanities are particularly exalted. According to Dorothy G. Harrison, commissioner for postsecondary policy analysis in the New York State Education Department, the "dispersion of their scholarly talent throughout society" will result in the "enrichment of commercial or public activities."[22] Similarly, Ernest R. May envisages an "increase in the sensitivity" of government and business "to the values and needs of the people whom they affect."[23] Paula Backscheider, a professor of English, urges her colleagues to "learn to rejoice" as their students "infiltrate" the world around them: "I think we will feel better about Gulf Oil and Westinghouse and the Center for Government Research when we know that the people who work there share some of our values, our education, and our delights."[24]

Many activities have been designed to facilitate the entry of Ph.D.s into nonacademic careers. For example, several universities have established special summer sessions to retrain doctorates in the humanities and social sciences for management positions in business and industry. The first of these programs was "Careers in Business," organized by the Graduate School of Business Administration at New York University in 1977. Within a few years, the University of Virginia, UCLA, the University of Texas, the University of Pennsylvania, and Harvard University had emulated that model. Lasting between four and twelve weeks, the programs at these various universities provide classes in marketing, accounting, finance, and business organization; help students develop business resumés; introduce them to representatives of the business community; and arrange internships and job interviews.[25]

All the academic associations endorse these "retooling" programs, but their own activities have been directed toward manufacturing demand for academic expertise and redesigning graduate curricula in order to prepare students for employment outside universities. Thus, the American Sociological Association has placed renewed emphasis on applied sociology. In 1979, it established an ad hoc committee on Professional Opportunities in Applied Sociology, which has sought to enhance the prestige of applied research, strengthen the links between academics and practitioners, and examine the training required for positions in industry, research organizations, and consulting firms.[26] Similarly, the American Anthropological Association has taken steps to improve its relationship with the Society for Applied Anthropology, reserved two seats on its executive board for practicing anthropologists, and established a Committee on Anthropology as a Profession which, among other goals, seeks to explore and expand employment opportunities in the field of applied anthropology.[27]

Although the humanities lack the same tradition of applied work, members of these disciplines have adopted similar techniques in order to enlarge job options for new scholars. English departments have instituted courses in technical writing and actively encouraged Ph.D. recipients to establish writing programs for corporate executives.[28] Philosophers have campaigned for the inclusion of philosophy courses in the high school curriculum.[29] A subcommittee of the American Philosophical Association's Committee on Placement deals specifically with nonteaching jobs; it recommends that unemployed Ph.Ds find positions in academic administration.[30] Historians have developed the new field of applied or public history, which they view as, perhaps, a partial solution to the career difficulties of young historians. The first public-history programs were established at the University of California, Santa Barbara, and at Carnegie-Mellon University in 1976. Four years later, over fifty colleges and universities were teaching courses in such aspects of public history as archival management, historical preservation, museum curatorship, and scholarly editing.[31] During the same period, a new national journal, *The Public Historian*, was launched, and public historians began holding annual conventions.[32] In 1979, the National Council on Public History was founded to coordinate the work of public historians and publicize their activities.[33] Public historians also enjoy a close relationship with the National Coordinating Committee for the Promotion of History, an association sponsored by the major professional associations for historians, which disseminates information about positions for historians outside universities and seeks to generate demand for their services in both public and private enterprise.[34] The ultimate goal of public historians is "the establishment of an historical office in every organization of significant size."[35]

Many public historians seek to democratize both the creation and study of history. Freed from the need to write works of history that satisfy the narrow definitions of scholarship imposed by many tenure committees, they have produced documentary films, photographic exhibits, and popular articles. Some of these newer history projects have been undertaken in conjunction with both community and trade union groups. All reach a wider audience than traditional scholarly articles.

Nevertheless, the public-history movement also illustrates the difficulties confronting those who seek to send unemployed Ph.D.s into nonteaching jobs.[36] First, the optimistic assertions that myriad opportunities await historians who venture outside higher education to seek employment may be greatly exaggerated. Museums, libraries, local history societies, and historic preservation projects all are plagued by severe shortages of funds. Furthermore, even were they able to hire additional staff, they might not grant priority to applicants with advanced degrees in history. The recent attempts to carve out new domains for academic historians have generated considerable resentment among the people already employed in these fields.[37]

Partly by default, many proponents of public history now look to business as the source of new jobs.[38] However, although the National Council on Public History and the National Coordinating Committee are waging a campaign to demonstrate that the expertise of historians can be of value to business, most corporations remain unconvinced. One of the most widely publicized exceptions is Wells Fargo Bank, which established an historical office with a staff of thirteen to administer the corporate archives, arrange exhibits in the bank's mini-museum, collect and evaluate

Wells Fargo memorabilia, and conduct research for both legal cases and public relations. Their long-range plan is to write a book-length history of the bank. Although these historians perform a wide range of services, the impetus behind the establishment of an historical office was a desire to enhance the image of Wells Fargo as an institution with a long and distinguished pedigree.[39] Other private enterprises have far less incentive to hire a staff of historians.[40]

Part of the problem in persuading either the public or private sector to hire historians may lie in the vagueness of the services historians purport to provide. It is not clear whether they are well-educated generalists or command special skills. If the latter, how can their expertise be distinguished from that of doctorates in other fields? This difficulty is exacerbated by the fact that some leaders of the public-history movement argue that historians have a unique competence and that their work therefore cannot be performed adequately by sociologists and other social scientists.[41] Others, however, encourage historians to encroach on the turf of other disciplines. For example, an article in *The Public Historian* contends that historians should move into cultural resource management, a field formerly monopolized by archaeologists.[42] Another article exhorts historians to seek jobs advising multinational corporations about the political situation in various parts of the world, a type of work to which both geographers and political scientists have laid claim.[43] Prospective employers thus may have difficulty understanding why they must hire historians.

Second, the rapid expansion of courses in public history could result in the development of a two-tiered system of graduate education, replicating the hierarchical arrangement at the undergraduate level. We have seen that practical, job-oriented courses constitute the lower track of many nonelite colleges. Students deemed unworthy of learning to engage in critical inquiry are directed into more vocational courses. This model may be adopted by graduate schools. Although large numbers of college graduates would be encouraged to enroll, professors would transmit the traditions of scholarship only to the top stream. The rest would acquire a variety of technical skills. Moreover, many public-history programs award an M.A., rather than a Ph.D., thus reinforcing any incipient stratification.

Two other issues pertain specifically to the campaign to send surplus historians into corporations. For one thing, the direction of historical studies could well be distorted. During the past decade, large numbers of historians radically have altered our notions about what is significant in history. Whereas earlier generations of historians focused on the lives of a few celebrated individuals, social historians turned their attention to groups such as women, ethnic minorities, and workers. Should the historical profession succeed in its aim of placing an historian in every major corporation, history writing might revert to the elitism that previously characterized it.

Furthermore, although bold claims are being advanced for the value of historical analysis to corporations, institutional constraints may well intervene. In fact, most articles exhorting historians to find employment in the private sector contain a basic contradiction. They contend that business requires the broad perspective and deep understanding of historians, but they also insist that the behavior and attitudes of university-trained historians must be reshaped. In order to fit into corporate settings, academics need to learn to work as members of teams,[44] to meet deadlines,[45] to answer questions posed by others,[46] and to create products that are suited to the demands of their employers.[47] These requirements would involve a total reorientation of historians, transforming them from intellectuals into technicians.[48]

Of course, it would be wrong to draw a dichotomy between the "pure" research conducted in universities and the "tainted" research carried out under corporate auspices. A number of notable academics serve on the boards of directors of major corporations;[49] others have established research ties with private enterprise. As the economic problems of institutions of higher education intensify, many are relying even more heavily than before on business and industry for support. Although the consequences of this shift in funding generally have been ignored, it is doubtful that schools that depend on corporate revenues will be scrupulous defenders of academic freedom.[50] Nevertheless, historians employed by corporations would lack even the minimal independence university-based researchers possess.

For example, historians working as team members in corporate settings would be collaborating not with academics from other disciplines whose analyses could enrich their own, but rather with

business people, whose emphasis on practical results is antitheti-
cal to the basic aims of historical inquiry. The premium placed on
efficiency and speed in corporate settings would further undermine the autonomy of historians. Historians customarily work
without time constraints, not simply because they are concerned
unduly with "looking up every source," as one advocate of public
history snidely put it,[51] but also because they seek to understand
the ramifications of their findings and to relate them to a broader
context. Working under strict deadlines, few historians would be
able to ponder the theoretical implications of their research.

The requirements that practicing historians answer questions
framed by others and hold themselves accountable to their employers rather than to the broad academic community are even
greater threats to their independence. Many who would channel
historians into business believe that the promulgation of a code of
ethics would guarantee the integrity of such historians,[52] but such
confidence is unwarranted: numerous studies have documented
the irrelevance of written codes to the behavior of the professionals they are supposed to regulate.[53]

Nevertheless, some proponents of public history go so far as to
claim that works of history produced directly under corporate
auspices could be more objective than those of university-based
academics. Ignoring everything that has been written about the
crucial role of outsiders in research, they contend that staff
historians would gain "the perspectives and understanding" that
comes only from "operating inside a corporation."[54] In addition,
they assert, corporate historians would be able to document their
studies more thoroughly than any other scholars. Here the argument approaches sophistry. They contend that corporate executives are understandably outraged by the "sensationalism" of most
academic histories of business and therefore are justified in
closing their archives to scholars. Because historians hired by
corporations would endorse the activities and goals of private
enterprise, they would be permitted to examine any records they
chose and thus would be in a position to write the first truly
impartial business histories.[55] The defects of this argument are
readily apparent. First, demanding a prior commitment to particular conclusions totally invalidates the scientific claims of any
research. Second, were corporations sincerely interested in ob-

taining accurate accounts of their pasts, they would open their archives to scholars of diverse political persuasions.

It clearly is vital that displaced academics reassess the "marketable skills" they possess and transfer them directly to other, more remunerative fields. But we should acknowledge the social costs of channeling large numbers of teachers and scholars into careers in business and industry and seek alternative employment that responds to genuine social needs. We also should recognize that it is not inevitable that the effects of retrenchment in academia fall disproportionately on younger scholars and reassess the distribution of privilege in the profession. Simultaneously, we should call for the continued expansion of higher education. Because the job crisis stems from political decisions as well as demographic trends, it is necessary to challenge government policies that place defense before social services. Finally, we should make explicit the connections between the collapse of the academic job market and larger problems of work and unemployment in this society and seek to address these broader issues.

NOTES

1. *Outside Academe: New Ways of Working in the Humanities* (New York: Haworth and Institute for Research in History, 1981), p. 18.

2. See Stuart Tave, "The Guilt of the Professor," in *Profession 79,* ed. Modern Language Association (New York: Modern Language Association, 1979), p. 23.

3. See Lawrence H. Martin, Jr., "Suicide by Letter Bomb," *ADE Bulletin,* no. 67, Spring 1981, p. 25.

4. Interview with Mack Thompson, Executive Director, American Historical Association, Washington, D.C., December 1980.

5. See Albert E. Gollin, "Comment," *American Sociologist* 13 (November 1978):225; see also George T. Karnezis, "A View from the Other Side," *Employment and the Profession,* Special Joint Issue, Bulletins of the Association of Departments of English and the Association of Departments of Foreign Languages, September 1976, p. 7.

6. Ernest R. May and Dorothy G. Blaney, *Careers for Humanists* (New York: Academic Press, 1981), p. 89.

7. American Historical Association, *Newsletter* 12 (April 1975):3; Modern Language Association, "A Statement on the Academic Job Market in Language and Literature" (n.d.); Lewis C. Solmon, Laura

Kent, Nancy L. Ochsner, and Margo-Lea Hurwicz, *Underemployed Ph.D.'s* (Lexington, Mass.: Lexington, 1981), p. 38; interview with Ann G. Kirschner, Assistant to the Coordinator, Department of English, Modern Language Association, New York City, March 1980. Many proponents of restricting enrollments claim that the primary problem is the "overproduction" of Ph.D.s, not the shortage of jobs. Similarly, the Victorians spoke of "overpopulation," not of unemployment. (John F. C. Harrison, *The Birth and Growth of Industrial England, 1714-1867* [New York: Harcourt Brace Jovanovich, 1973], p. 98.)

8. See John Algeo, "After the Fall: Some Observations on Graduate Curricula," in *Profession 78*, ed. Modern Language Association (New York: Modern Language Association, 1978), pp. 16-18; H. M. Blalock, "Comment," *American Sociologist* 13 (November 1978):219-20; Ward Hellstrom, "Academic Responsibility and the Job Market," in *Profession 80*, ed. Modern Language Association (New York: Modern Language Association, 1980), p. 24; Quentin M. Hope, "Notes on the Profession," *Employment and the Profession*, p. 19; Paul Kay, "The Myth of Nonacademic Employment: Observations on the Growth of an Ideology," *American Sociologist* 13 (November 1978):216-19; Marilyn Williamson, "Give Them More than They Seek," *Employment and the Profession*, p. 27; Neal Woodruff, "Only Connect," *Employment and the Profession*, pp. 73-76.

9. Magali Sarfatti Larson, *The Rise of Professionalism: A Sociological Analysis* (Berkeley: University of California Press, 1979).

10. Blalock, "Comment," pp. 210-20; J. Paul Hunter, "Facing the Eighties," *Profession 80*, pp. 1-9; Williamson, "Give Them," p. 27. The legal and medical professions adopted similar strategies earlier in the twentieth century. (Harry First, "Competition in the Legal Education Industry (1)," *N.Y.U. Law Review*, no. 53, [May-June 1978], pp. 354-55.)

11. See Tave, "Guilt," pp. 23-28; see also William G. Bowen, *Graduate Education in the Arts and Sciences: Prospects for the Future*, Report of the President (Princeton University, 1981).

12. See Solmon, Kent, Ochsner, and Hurwicz, *Underemployed Ph.D.'s*, p. 36.

13. Algeo, "After the Fall," pp. 18-19; Hellstrom, "Academic Responsibility," pp. 24-25; Hope, "Notes," p. 20; Tave, "Guilt," p. 25; see David G. Brown, *The Mobile Professors* (Washington, D.C.: American Council on Education, 1967), p. 120. According to a recent survey conducted by the Modern Language Association, six more English departments offered doctoral training in 1977-78 than in the previous year. (Jasper P. Neel and Jeanne C. Nelson, "Doctoral Programs Awarded in English, 1977-78: The MLA Placement Survey," *Profession 79* [New York: Modern Language Association, 1979], p. 51.)

14. Steve Barnett, quoted in "Profile of an Anthropologist," *Anthropology Newsletter* 21 (April 1980):6.

15. Sharon K. Panian and Melvin L. DeFleur, *Sociologists in Non-Academic Employment* (Washington, D.C.: American Sociological Association, n.d.), p. 35.

16. Comments of Arnita Jones in "First National Symposium on Public History: A Report," *The Public Historian* 2 (Fall 1979):13.

17. "Profile of an Anthropologist," *Anthropology Newsletter* 20 (October 1979):20.

18. Richard H. Gamble, "Hitch Your Wagon to a Star: Confessions of a Postacademic Job Seeker," *Profession 80* (New York: Modern Language Association, 1980), pp. 20-23.

19. See Neal Woodruff, "Only Connect," p. 77.

20. May and Blaney, *Careers*, p. 61.

21. See Paula Backscheider, "Into All the World," *ADE Bulletin*, no. 68, Summer 1981, p. 17; Kenneth W. Haas, "The Value of a Professional English Education," *Employment and the Profession*, p. 62; see also Rita D. Jacobs, *The Useful Humanists: Alternative Careers for Ph.D.s in the Humanities* (New York: Rockefeller Foundation, 1977), p. 21. Many displaced academics also assert that their abilities and accomplishments entitle them to special consideration in hiring. For example, the Association for the Full Employment of Doctorates, founded in Los Angeles in 1972 by unemployed and underemployed Ph.D.s, urged the administration of a local community college to establish an affirmative action program, requiring department chairs to hire Ph.D.s in all faculty openings, and requested the personnel officers of city and local governments to grant special preference to applicants with doctorates. The group also asked the United States Department of Labor to adopt policies to aid the highly educated who lacked jobs. When the Department of Labor replied that it focused only on individuals with limited educational backgrounds, the leaders undertook legal action to have Ph.D.s recognized as a "protected" group; if successful, they intended to press for the establishment of relief programs specifically for unemployed doctorates. (Interview with Delina Halushka, Founder, Association for the Full Employment of Doctorates, Santa Monica, November 1980.)

22. Dorothy G. Harrison, "The Nonacademic Job Market," *Employment and the Profession*, p. 68.

23. Ernest R. May, "Nonacademic Career Possibilities," *Employment and the Profession*, p. 72.

24. Backscheider, "All the World," p. 19. For a discussion of similar arguments employed to convince community college students to enroll in vocational programs, see Fred L. Pincus, "The False Promises of

Community Colleges: Class Conflict and Vocational Education," *Harvard Educational Review* 50 (August 1980):332-61.

25. Interview with Patricia Katsky, Program Coordinator, Careers in Business for Ph.D.s, U.C.L.A., Los Angeles, August 1980; interview with Ernest Kurnow, Director, Careers in Business, N.Y.U., New York, December 1980; Jill Felzan, "Retooling the Historian: Careers in Business Programs," *The Public Historian* 3 (Summer 1981):133-43.

26. Interview with Howard Freeman, Chairman, Ad Hoc Committee on Professional Opportunities in Applied Sociology, American Sociological Association, Los Angeles, May 1981; interview with Russell Dynes, Executive Director, American Sociological Association, Washington, D.C., December 1980; American Sociological Association, *Footnotes*, February 1980, p. 7; August 1980, p. 20; December 1980, pp. 1-4; see also Beverly Watkins, "'Applied' Sociologists Find Gaps in Training for Non-Academic Jobs," *Chronicle of Higher Education*, 10 September 1979, p. 12.

27. Interview with Robert Cimino, Director, Departmental Services Program, American Anthropological Association, Washington, D.C., December 1980; Rayna Rapp, "Focusing on Non-Traditional, Non-Academic Anthropology: History, Science, Politics, Ethics," (paper delivered at the annual convention, American Anthropological Association, Los Angeles, November 1981.)

28. Interview with Kirschner; see Andrew D. Turnbull, "Wanted: Humanists to Write Computer Manuals," *Chronicle of Higher Education*, 20 October 1982, p. 23.

29. Janet Hook, "Students of Popular Culture Try to Recruit Philosophers," *Chronicle of Higher Education*, 6 January 1982, p. 9.

30. American Philosophical Association, *Proceedings* 51 (August 1978):761.

31. Nina Kressner Cobb, "Necessity Was the Mother: The Institute for Research in History," *The Public Historian* 2 (Spring 1980): 78. However, some of these programs are at the undergraduate, not the graduate, level.

32. See G. Wesley Johnson, Peter N. Stearns, and Joel A. Tarr, "Public History: A New Area of Training, Research and Employment," American Historical Association, *Newsletter* 18 (March 1980): 7.

33. See "Formation of the National Council on Public History," *The Public Historian* 2 (Fall 1979):83.

34. Arnita Jones, "The National Coordinating Committee: Programs and Possibilities," *The Public Historian* 1 (Fall 1978):49-60; interview with Page Miller, Director, National Coordinating Committee for the Promotion of History, Washington, D.C., December 1981. For an analysis of demand creation in the field of law, see Richard L. Abel,

"Toward a Political Economy of Lawyers Services," *Wisconsin Law Review* (1981), pp. 117-87.

35. Robert Kelley, "Public History: Its Origins, Nature, and Prospects," *The Public Historian* 1 (Fall 1978):22.

36. Two articles that criticize some aspects of the public-history movement are Howard Green, "A Critique of the Professional Public History Movement," *Radical History Review*, no. 25 (Fall 1981):164-71; Ronald J. Grele, "Whose Public? Whose History? What Is the Goal of a Public Historian?" *The Public Historian* 3 (Winter 1981):40-48.

37. See Jerry George, "Take a 'Public Historian' to Lunch," *History News*, no. 34, May 1979, p. 1; Green, "Critique," pp. 165-66.

38. See, for example, Kelley, "Public History," p. 22.

39. Harold P. Anderson, Comments in "First National Symposium on Public History: A Report," *The Public Historian* 2 (Fall 1979):50-52; Anderson, "The Corporate History Department: The Wells Fargo Model," *The Public Historian* 3 (Summer 1981):25-29; Janis MacKenzie, "Wells Fargo and Company: Banking on the Past," National Coordinating Council Supplement Number 25.

40. See Richard Forman, "History Inside Business," *The Public Historian* 3 (Summer 1981):49; Albro Martin, "The Office of the Corporate Historian: Organization and Functions," *The Public Historian* 3 (Summer 1981):11; Robert W. Pomeroy, "Historians' Skills and Business Needs," *The Public Historian* 1 (Winter 1979):8; Ernest Swiger, Jr., "Historians and Corporate Consulting," *The Public Historian* 3 (Summer 1981):101.

41. See "First National Symposium on Public History," p. 47.

42. See Theodore J. Karamanski, "History as an Empowering Force in Cultural Resource Management," *The Public Historian* 2 (Spring 1980):71-72; see also David A. Clary, "Historic Preservation and Environmental Protection: The Role of the Historian," *The Public Historian* 1 (Fall 1978):61-75; see also W. Ray Luce, "Jobs for Historians in Historic Preservation," National Coordinating Council Supplement Number 27.

43. See Stephen J. Kobrin, "Political Assessment in International Firms: The Role of Nontraditional Specialists in Business Organization," *The Public Historian* 3 (Summer 1981):87-94.

44. Comments by Anderson, "First National Symposium," p. 52; "Editor's Preface," G. Wesley Johnson, *The Public Historian* 1 (Fall 1978):7.

45. See "First National Symposium," p. 41; Lawrence DeGraaf, "Summary: An Academic Perspective," *The Public Historian*, 2 (Spring 1980):69; *Outside Academe*, p. 30.

46.   See Johnson, "Editor's Preface," p. 8; Kelley, "Public History," p. 18; see also Edward D. Berkowitz, "The Historian as Policy Analyst: The Challenge of HEW," *The Public Historian* 1 (Spring 1979):17.

47.   See "First National Symposium," p. 41; DeGraaf, "Summary," p. 69.

48.   For the distinction between intellectuals and technicians see Alvin W. Gouldner, *The Future of Intellectuals and the Rise of The New Class: A Frame of Reference, Theses, Conjectures, Arguments, and an Historical Perspective on the Role of Intellectuals and Intelligentsia in the International Class Contest of the Modern Era* (New York: Seabury, 1979).

49.   See Ellen K. Coughlin, "Scholars See Possible Conflict in Academics' Business Ties," *Chronicle of Higher Education*, 21 October 1981, p. 23.

50.   See Craig Kaplan and Ellen Schrecker, eds., *Regulating the Intellectuals: Perspectives on Academic Freedom* (New York: Praeger, 1983).

51.   DeGraaf, "Summary," p. 69.

52.   See Johnson, "Editor's Preface," p. 9.

53.   See Abel, "Political Economy," pp. 117-87.

54.   Forman, "Business," pp. 44-45.

55.   See comments by Anderson, "First National Symposium," p. 52; Forman, "Business," p. 44; Barbara Benson Kohn, "Corporate History and the Corporate History Department: Manufacturers Hanover Trust Company," *The Public Historian* 3 (Summer 1981):36; W. David Lewis and Wesley Phillips Newton, "The Writing of Corporate History," *The Public Historian* 3 (Summer 1981):65-67.

Chapter 6
CHANGING CAREERS

LETTING GO

The number of Ph.D.s entering nonacademic employment has risen sharply. In 1981, almost one-quarter of the humanities doctorates who received their degrees between 1973 and 1976 were working outside higher education, compared to 6 percent of the 1960-64 cohort![1]

Nevertheless, about half of the academics interviewed for this study resisted the pressures to find alternative employment. Some believed the campaign to send doctorates into work in business and industry was fueled not by concern for their well-being, but rather by the desire of senior professors to avoid responsibility for placing former students. One man, who had searched unsuccessfully for a tenure-track position for more than five years, explained why he responded angrily to the suggestion that he change careers:

My adviser thinks that the most dignified solution would be for me to suddenly transform myself into a businessman and blow away into Arkansas or someplace like that where he wouldn't have to think about me. His attitude is · very difficult because I had a relationship with him. I was a bright young graduate student who looked like he had a promising future. But at this point I'm just excess ballast.

Others were reluctant to sever links to disciplines with which they identified closely and in which they had made enormous investments of both time and money. One woman, who continued to conduct independent research after receiving her degree, staunchly refused to "dismantle everything I have done for the past fifteen years." A part-time teacher, asked whether she had any plans to leave academia, responded:

> I keep saying, one more year, and then I'll think about it, but I feel a real resistance. I can't think concretely about the future at all because it makes me too angry. I've invested so much in my career—I shouldn't have to change.

Despite the disadvantages of their present lives, such people hesitated to abandon academic work for any of the alternatives.

Several also reacted angrily to the specific career options the academic associations have endorsed. Some had been involved in the political movements of the sixties and, although no longer active, felt that business careers would betray fundamental values. A few saw themselves as temperamentally unsuited for management positions. Still others refused to accept jobs at the entry level or those that required additional training: "I've already paid my dues," a recent graduate declared.

However, many displaced academics did look for jobs outside higher education. At the time they were interviewed, twenty-one had either found alternative employment, entered some type of retraining program, or made firm decisions to leave higher education. Almost all of these academics restricted their job searches to other professional work. Although they had relinquished their dreams of finding faculty positions, their expectations continued to be shaped by their images of professional status. In fact, they spoke with assurance of obtaining new careers that would provide the security, social recognition, and opportunity for advancement they had sought in academia. Some hoped, above all, to be protected from the "helplessness" and "vulnerability" they recently had experienced. One man, for example, acknowledged his decision to apply to medical school was "a real reaction" to his dismissal from a tenure-track job:

> I felt victimized by the system, abandoned by the people I trusted. There is a real emotional need on my part to never, never again put myself at the mercy of such a victimizing system. Medicine, like very few other fields, will give me the independence I want.

Despite his recent setback, he remained confident that he could parlay educational credentials into an autonomous work life. Others assumed they could find professions governed solely by the meritocratic principles they missed in higher education. One man explained why he applied to business school immediately after learning that a candidate with inferior credentials had been awarded a job he sought: "I was determined to find a field where dedication and work and performance would be rewarded." Although disenchanted with academia, he continued to place his faith in a professional career.

Statistics compiled by the National Research Council demonstrate that business and industry are the largest employers of humanities doctorates working outside of their fields.[2] Similarly, seven, or one-third, of the displaced academics who had decided to change careers had either entered or were seeking work in business or industry; three had selected law; two had chosen each of public-school teaching, government, and academic administration. Other choices included publishing, medicine, and work in social service agencies.

Although most displaced academics mentioned the possibility of finding nonprofessional jobs, they did so only to indicate just how low they could fall. Work as a "shoe salesman," "secretary," "filing clerk," "cab driver," or "gas station attendant" was totally unacceptable. One woman, recently denied tenure at a large university, described her "worst fear" in the following way:

> Because I had failed in my one good opportunity in life to succeed, my punishment would be that I would have to take a series of humiliating jobs which would basically substantiate the view of my department that I was a failure or incompetent.

A man who worked briefly as a waiter in order to supplement his meager earnings from part-time teaching recalled his sense of shame:

> I was always scared that one of my old students would come in. It seemed like such a demeaning thing, after all these years and all these degrees, to be doing what any eighteen-year-old could do. In fact, one of my former students did come in, and I'll never forget her surprise.

During the 1950s and 1960s, numerous social commentators contended that rising levels of affluence had blurred class lines, and that industrial workers increasingly were resembling middle-class professionals and managers.[3] But, just as blue-collar workers continue to believe that they live in a world totally different from that of professionals,[4] so the academics in this study resolved not to cross the barrier separating them from the mass of workers. Anecdotes circulating about Ph.D.s driving cabs or serving hamburgers at McDonalds indicate the horror such job placements arouse, not the statistical likelihood that doctoral recipients will end up in this type of work.

But even the transition to another professional job is not easy. For one thing, people who have spent several years looking for academic jobs must recommence the long, humiliating, and discouraging process of contacting and submitting resumés to potential employers. Moreover, although an increasing number of university placement centers and "how-to-do-it" books help to ease the path of faculty into nonteaching careers,[5] many people leave academia with little information about other options or about appropriate behavior when applying for them. In addition, the range of possibilities is much narrower than it was when most made their first career choices. The economic and political forces that have decimated the academic job market have also restricted the possibilities for other types of employment. Even in business and industry, often portrayed as a world of golden opportunities for Ph.D.s, qualified applicants exceed the number of openings.[6] Employers are not anxious to hire doctorates in the humanities and social sciences. Not only do they lack appropriate credentials, but it is widely assumed that they are looking for temporary work and are not committed to new careers. Finally, displaced academics do not fit easily into any job category. They are too old and too well-educated for most entry-level positions but too inexperienced for those in the upper ranks. Thus, many academics who seek work outside higher education conclude that, once again, they are in the wrong place at the wrong time.

In addition, doctorates who change careers must discard old habits and adopt new ones. All professions develop distinctive cultures that serve as barriers to outsiders,[7] and many displaced academics complained that accustomed patterns of behavior no longer made sense. Some focused on nuances of social behavior, such as styles of dress and patterns of speech. A woman who had gone to New York in search of work after her dismissal from a tenure-track job recalled:

> I didn't know how to dress, I didn't know how to talk to people the way people in New York talk to each other, I didn't know how to banter. People would ask me questions and I would begin to answer them in these very elaborate and serious ways, and that's not how people talk, so I felt constantly that I didn't belong in that world.

A second woman, only partly in jest, described the new vocabulary she had to acquire before she was ready to apply for jobs in business:

> One of the problems for academics is the problem of language because business communities use a lot of language that those of us in the humanities find repulsive, like "interface"—everything is "interfacing" now with everything else—and "energize" and "utilize." They will not use simple verbs and nouns but instead go off into this jargon that one has spent a good part of one's life teaching students not to use and excising from one's own language and papers and that offends the ear of anyone with a decent respect for language.

Even after a year in business this woman was forced to recognize she was not yet fully acculturized:

> Appearances are very important to business people, including the appearance of one's desk. My desk for a while was considered to be too messy. Actually it resembled, I suppose, more of an academic's desk, with stuff

piled in various piles....The people I worked with were afraid that other people coming into the division would think I was disorganized. And I looked around me and, it's true, all the other desks are clean in the evening and people have just little piles on them. I had tried setting my piles at ninety degree angles; it wasn't a clutter on my desk, they were defined, clear piles, so I thought it was clean. When I got the promotion, it was said to me more than once—so finally I had to take it seriously—that I had to unclutter my desk, that it was unbefitting my new position. Now I would have thought that having clutter meant at least I was doing work....When occasions like that happen I am aware that I am still in a whole new culture and I don't know how long it will take me fully to assimilate.

Still another woman, who had worked for a year in a government agency after teaching at various colleges on short-term contracts, commented:

One of the hardest things is that I spent many years thinking it was worth it to work very hard and then to go out and take a walk or play tennis. But in a nine to five job you can't work at a really high pace all day; otherwise you'd be just exhausted. So what you do is to work at an even pace all day and there's no incentive to hurry up and get things done because you still have to stay there. My whole work habits were just completely inappropriate for survival in that kind of world.

Like earlier generations entering the factories, she had to learn to work at a totally new pace.[8]

Moreover, although it frequently is asserted that academic skills are applied readily to a wide variety of occupations, several former academics discovered their new positions called for radically different modes of reasoning. For example, a historian, interviewed shortly before completing law school, reported:

Going to law school was like going to another planet. I found that none of the kinds of intellectual talents I had were of much use there. A different set of cognitive skills were required. Moving from the specific to the general is what I always did in history, coming up with a theory that explains a lot of different data. That doesn't operate in the law. Instead, you're given a law and told to apply it to a set of facts. Also, in the social sciences, I was always concerned about finding *the* answer, the truth, what is the best explanation, what is the best theory. In law, you're taught that there is no best answer, everything is to be questioned and you're taught to argue both sides of every issue and that both sides are of equal value. I wasn't used to doing that kind of thinking.

Academics who change careers must also relinquish the roles that furnished the bases of their social identities. Most professionals feel strongly bound to their occupations as a result of the long process of socialization and training. A historian who recently had completed a year of premed courses spoke to this point:

I *am* a historian. Everything I have done for ten years has been connected to the field. There has been no such thing as free time since I went to graduate school; summers were an extension of research. To go into my house, for example, is to see who I am. The walls are full of books, and they happen to be books on history, and it's very obvious who this person is. It's going to take some wrenching to make the change.

Suspended between careers, many displaced academics were uncertain how they should define themselves and their lives.

Nevertheless, most disenfranchised academics do succeed in finding nonteaching jobs and in adjusting to their new work lives. Furthermore, almost all the academics who had left higher education were certain they had made the right decision. Several spoke with contempt about former classmates who continued to hope for futures in higher education. One man, who recently had applied to law school, described doctorates who remained in the part-time circuit as "stray dogs hanging on to a dump truck that's going down hill. It's craziness, they're ruining their lives."

Certain benefits of leaving academia were emphasized repeatedly. Some were pleased to have an opportunity to make new life choices. One woman discussed her sense of liberation when she realized that her life need not be forced within an academic mold:

> I had never been anything other than an academic, never perceived myself as anything other than as an academic and certainly if I had been five years older and entered the job market at a different time, I would never have been anything other than an academic. But suddenly I was like someone who had been in prison on a diet of bread and water and was suddenly let loose in Zabar's; just the variety of possibilities of things I could do. I kept running over to the lox counter and then running over and looking at the cakes.

It was exhilarating to many former academics to regain a sense of personal power and competence. By going back to school or taking jobs in new fields, they discovered capabilities they never knew about and acquired skills to replace those discarded by society. In addition, they obtained the validation and approval that had been withheld in academia. One woman, working in business, felt vindicated when she received her first promotion just nine months after assuming her post and exactly two years after an unfavorable tenure review. A few weeks later, another company invited her for an interview and offered her a job: "For someone who was told two years ago she was irrelevant and unworthy, it's really nice to go out on an interview and be hounded for a full month afterwards to take the job." Others noted with pride that their salaries far exceeded those of assistant professors. Finally, there were satisfactions intrinsic to the jobs: stimulation, challenge, and a sense of purpose could be found outside the halls of academia, the exacademics were happy to discover.

But there were also disadvantages to changing fields. None considered returning to academia on the only terms available— part-time teaching or a succession of lectureship positions—but a few continued to regret they had not fulfilled their original aspirations. Even some who spoke most enthusiastically about their new jobs missed many aspects of academic life. First, they were now tied to nine-to-five days and had little control over the quantity and timing of their work. In addition, they were supervised more closely. A woman who had begun working in private industry after teaching at a university for seven years commented:

> At my university there were deadlines for turning in grades, but no one took them seriously. But here they use the word "accountability" a lot and it offends me. I may come out of a meeting with a bunch of consultants and a line manager will take me aside and the tone of authority is there and the implication is that I will do what it is suggested that I do: "Your role will be so and so and so." People in the academic world don't talk to each other that way, with that kind of authoritative direction.

A more serious complaint was that skills arduously acquired in graduate school were wasted. Lewis C. Solmon found that almost half of the humanities Ph.D.s employed in business are convinced that workers with inferior academic credentials can perform their jobs equally well.[9] A woman I interviewed who became a bank officer observed:

> A lot of what I do is interesting, but only because it's varied....It doesn't really command all of my skills. Someone else could do it, it just depends on ordinary competence. I'm aware that a whole reservoir of what I have encouraged myself to do is not tapped.

Reading the book review section of a newspaper sharpened her realization that she was "intellectually hungry." As she commented:

> I found myself being filled with the joy of the written word. It was like discovering something that I had previously had but had temporarily lost. Because I don't get that at work. I don't get this realization of, this is a book that is well worth reading, or this is a thought that's a wonderful thought.

Like many other doctorates who had left academic employment, she also felt keenly the loss of a field of study to which she had devoted many years. Despite the satisfactions and sense of fulfillment she had found in her new job, she believed she had had to abandon an important part of herself.

One response to feelings of loss was to seek to maintain links with the past. Some academics hoped to find careers that utilized their academic skills and interests. Two men who had specialized in foreign area studies were looking for employment with multinational corporations. An anthropologist who had conducted research in Latin America was retraining to become a bilingual teacher, a job that would permit him to employ his foreign language skills. A former English professor, interviewed shortly before completing business school, had plans to develop computer systems for use in university writing programs.

Other displaced academics sought to convert academic work into avocations. Pointing to the long tradition of independent scholars, a few men claimed that their primary reason for entering business was to obtain the time and resources to conduct research. Teaching evening classes in the extension programs of nearby colleges and universities was another option. One woman hoped that such a job would serve as a means of easing her entry into another occupation; she sought a "gentle transition" from her life as a philosophy professor, a "waning" of her scholarly interests. But most former academics viewed part-time teaching as a means of preserving skills and establishing continuity with their fields of expertise. In fact, although all the displaced academics were drawn to jobs that would allow them to exercise creativity and critical judgment, several continued to believe their true vocations lay in scholarship. Thus, they adopted the solution of the vast majority of Americans, who work primarily for material rewards and seek authenticity and meaning in the realm of leisure.[10] Significantly, one ex-musicologist discovered he enjoyed playing piano far more after he had left academia and begun to train for another field. When music lost its instrumental character, he could derive far more pleasure from it.

Nevertheless, it is not easy for most academics to ply their crafts part-time. Unlike jogging, pottery, or collecting stamps, writing articles on medieval history and teaching courses on analytic philosophy demand full-time commitments. These are not activities that easily can be interspersed with the real business of life. The attempt to transform academic work into an avocation may appear to deny one's training as a professional.

Moreover, many displaced academics felt ambivalent about establishing continuity with higher education. If they still were adjusting to the loss of their careers, they tended to have conflicting desires. They wanted both to sustain a connection to the interests and pursuits that previously had been basic to their lives and to avoid everything associated with academia. Peter Marris has argued:

> Grief…is the expression of a profound conflict between contradictory impulses—to consolidate all that is still valuable and important in the past, and preserve it from loss; and at the same time, to re-establish a meaningful pattern of relationships, in which the loss is accepted….
>
> A sense of continuity can…only be restored by detaching the familiar meanings of life from the relationship in which they were embodied, and re-establishing them independently of it….
>
> Thus grief is mastered…by abstracting what was fundamentally important in the relationship and rehabilitating it.[11]

This passage helps to explain the behaviors and attitudes of two women dismissed from tenure-track positions in history. Although they embarked on different career paths after leaving academia, they clearly were responding to similar pressures.

Marilyn Sorrel was 35 when she received an adverse tenure decision from a large research university. She immediately applied for other teaching positions:

> I didn't even dare hope that I would find another academic job where I would be able to pursue my research and my teaching—it would have been beyond my wildest dreams—but sure, I would have loved it. You don't train as many years as I have or do the type of research I did unless you are very deeply committed to the field.

But she also decided that she could not "afford to engage in those fantasies. I had to gear all my psychological resources toward the end of carving out a career for myself in another area." Thus, she moved to another city, joined a career planning seminar at a nearby university, and searched systematically for work in business. A year after her teaching job ended, she did find a management position. Interviewed several months after the beginning of this job, she spoke enthusiastically about her opportunity to acquire expertise in a new field and the security derived from a clearly defined career ladder. Convinced she had found the right job, she planned to provide practical tips to others seeking to change careers: "I almost have a zeal about it. It's so nice on the other side—I want people to share in that."

Although she had expected originally to gain just enough business experience to enable her to find a position in academic administration, she realized she might prefer not to return to a university setting. The woman who "wrote and taught history" seemed like "another person entirely." She did want to finish the book she originally had hoped would win her tenure, but she stressed that her primary motivation was to separate from, not to preserve, a connection to academia: "Off and on that book consumed six or seven years of my life, and I think that when one has done that, one wants to get closure." The preface would include a statement that she was "publishing the book not only as a testimonial to the people who acted in the story, but also to the author at a certain period in her life."

However, she was unwilling to repudiate completely the values of the past. Despite her talk of "closure," she acknowledged that old interests still were compelling. After mentioning her central role in plans to establish a local institute for independent scholars, she commented, "Maybe I'm just not willing to cut the cord yet." Moreover, she realized her determination to sever her links to higher education was partly self-protective. Because she was "in a state of transition," she was wary of threatening her fragile readjustment. Thus, she refrained from widely discussing her experience as a university professor in order not to "stir up a lot of painful feelings." The possibility of teaching an evening course in her field provoked an intense conflict. She was ecstatic about a guest lecture she delivered in a course taught by a friend:

It was just an exhilarating experience. I put together the lecture in just a few minutes and talked for three hours. It was just fantastic. I was very flattered: at the end, people came up and said I should go into teaching because I do it so well and I was just so excited, I might do that.

But she also feared succumbing to the temptation of part-time teaching:

I think the trick for me is to work out a compromise, so if I go back and teach a class in my field I won't feel regretful that I can't do the real thing. Because even if I teach a Western civilization class in an extension program, that's not really the level I am accustomed to teach at. I was doing upper division and graduate stuff, I was leading Ph.D. students, and I will never be able to do that again. Never. So that's hard and there's part of me that's still very self-protective. I want to ease into my new life an association with my former academic life to the extent that I am comfortable with that. If at any time it feels like it's releasing the floodgates, if going back into this other world is going to make me dredge up the old feelings, then no way.

In sum, Marilyn wanted both to escape from everything associated with her loss and to sustain her connection to activities and interests that had infused her life with meaning for many years.

But she also realized that part-time teaching and scholarship were not the only means of retaining continuity in her life. Another option might be to use the skills she brought from the past in her present job. Her experience interpreting autobiographies had given her an "ability to get behind what people think they are saying to what they really mean." Because she had been a teacher, she knew how to help others learn. She had spent many years "not only physically living in foreign countries but intellectually living in a very different culture"; as a result, she had a heightened sensitivity to cultural diversity. She described "the ideal resolution" to her career progression in terms very similar to those used by Marris to refer to the mastery of grief:

> What I hope to do is to integrate the past and present not by staying within the old mold, teaching a course or publishing a book, but breaking the mold and then seeing what was the essence of what I did and then putting it together in a new way.

But she also acknowledged that she could not attain this goal until she had accepted her loss. As she commented, "Right now there is a block between the old and the new me which is necessary for my survival."

Elizabeth Geller also illustrates the ambivalence of many who change jobs. After receiving a negative pretenure review at an elite Eastern women's college where she had taught for four years, she resolved to leave higher education: "I felt very strongly that I didn't want an academic career, that if this was what happened, if this was your reward for doing things right and working so hard, then forget it." Thus, she adamantly refused to look for other teaching positions. When another college asked if she were willing to be considered for a tenure-track position, she agreed to apply and be interviewed, but she turned down the job when it was offered. Nevertheless, she had no other clear sense of direction:

> Wouldn't you think that under the circumstances I would be out beating the bush and looking for jobs in other fields? I wasn't. I was just paralyzed, I couldn't do anything. I would look for jobs sporadically, but never pursued anything.

It was much harder for Elizabeth than for Marilyn to extract from her academic experience the sense that she was masterful and talented and apply it to another area. As she noted, "I constantly felt that the world in which I had been solid and competent had just totally faded away."

Perhaps as a consequence, she did not break abruptly with academia. She worked first for a scholarly journal in a field related to her own. When this journal moved to another city, she found an editorial position in a small publishing house that also specialized in a subject similar to her previous area of expertise. The most gratifying aspect of her second job was its connection to the world she had left: "A lot of the work has to do with putting ideas together in a way that's close to academia." The long-term goal she eventually embraced was to write works of nonfiction.

Nevertheless, she too initially sought to distance herself from academia. Although her first job involved reading scholarly articles, she eschewed new books in her field: "I felt a great deal of bitterness and a great deal of uncertainty about what those books still meant in my life." She sought to reestablish her ties with academia only after she grew more confident about her ability to create a new life for herself. Four years after the termination of her teaching position, she was surprised to find that she still identified herself as an historian in a job interview. As she subsequently remarked:

> The longer I hang out in other circles, the more it strikes me that I am an academic by training and that that's not a world whose values I entirely accept but I am very much shaped by that world and I ought to own [up to] it.

Thus, she began tentatively to read new scholarly books that appeared in her discipline. She also began a relationship with a professor whose course load included the class she had most enjoyed teaching:

> He taught "the course" this spring. It's fascinating to hear what he's assigning and how it's working and what the conversation is and seeing the papers he's getting and comparing them to the papers I got. We spend a lot of time talking about the books I'm reading and the books he's reading, the personalities of people in the field, and that feels just fine.

Although she still did not consider herself settled in a new career, she had a much clearer sense of her own goals and a renewed faith in her own capabilities. Perhaps because she had been away from teaching two years longer than Marilyn, she no longer yearned to be back in academia. As a result, she was able to incorporate what she had found most meaningful in the academic world into her new life and to accept the remnants of her identity as an academic.

Changing careers was not so disruptive for all displaced academics. As we have seen, some were excited by the prospect of making a fresh beginning; others already had found work that suited them better than teaching and research. Nevertheless, for many, the process of readjustment to an alternative career was extremely difficult, and it lasted long after they had found satisfactory work outside higher education. It could be considered complete only when they could both attach new meaning to their new careers and maintain connections with whatever aspects of academia still were important to them.

GENDER DIFFERENCES

Men alone have been responsible for the recent increase in nonacademic employment among doctorates. If, in 1977, we look at all male Ph.D.s in the humanities who held nonteaching jobs as a fraction of all men who received humanities doctorates, the percentage is three times as high for the class of 1975-76 as for the classes between 1934-68. However, the same proportion of women in both the 1975-76 and the 1934-68 cohorts held jobs outside higher education in 1977.[12] Thus, although women who obtained doctorates in humanities fields during the earlier period were more likely to enter nonacademic work than their male counterparts, a higher percentage of the recent male Ph.D.s have found alternative work.[13]

A larger fraction of the men than of the women I interviewed also entered nonteaching careers. Most of the displaced academics had begun to explore tentatively other options. However, whereas thirteen, or about two-thirds, of the men had made firm commitments to leaving academia, only five, or just over a fifth of the women had done so. Moreover, six, or almost a third, of the men were either enrolled in law, business, or medical school or had applied to one of these institutions.[14] Although several women had considered seeking additional training, none actually had applied to a professional school.[15] As we have seen, a higher proportion of the women remained in marginal academic positions. This section examines several possible reasons for these gender differences.[16]

One explanation could be that men placed greater significance on careers than did women. Although both male and female displaced academics had invested the same number of years preparing for professional positions, they may have brought different motivations and expectations to the graduate school experience. As numerous studies have demonstrated, men are encouraged to direct their energies toward career goals, but women are socialized to place personal relationships at the center of their lives. One writer contended, "Occupation is a man's major role, unemployment or failure in his occupation the worst disaster that can befall him."[17] Life crises for women, this author noted, are connected to the loss of the roles of wife and mother. According to one argument, then, men enter alternative employment sooner than women because they tend to be affected more profoundly by career loss.

However, during the past decade, the women's movement has challenged traditional definitions of women's identity. Feminist writings have encouraged women to seek a sense of mastery and competence and to cease living for and through others. Work, especially in the privileged form of a professional career, has been presented as the primary means of self-determination and independence.

In assessing the influence of this brand of feminism on the women, it is important to consider both the ages of the women and the types of family responsibilities they have assumed. Of the women I interviewed, the two in their late twenties were committed firmly to pursuing professional careers; their goals were indistinguishable from those of men in the same age category. But most of the women over thirty already had made major life choices by the time they were affected by feminism. Their decisions to go to graduate school, to complete dissertations, or to enter the job market frequently represented attempts to reorder priorities in line with expanded notions about women's roles. Although all but four of the men, or about a fifth, had followed unbroken career paths, eighteen of the women, or just over three-quarters, had interrupted their schooling at some point after receiving B.A.s. Several of these women had found employment in traditional female occupations. Two had worked as secretaries, and seven others had taught in elementary or secondary schools. As many of the latter explained, they loved to teach and believed they were gifted in transmitting knowledge and exciting the curiosity of students, but the women's movement had encouraged them to raise their aspirations. By obtaining Ph.D.s, they hoped to continue to practice their crafts while receiving the rewards of professional status.

In addition, many of the older women initially shaped their lives around family responsibilities. Eleven women were married, and two were divorced; ten had children. One spoke for many others when she observed, "My personal life has been intertwined with my professional life and I cannot take the threads apart." Several had interrupted their graduate training for a period in order to follow their husbands to jobs in other locations. While graduate students, seven had been married to academics who were one or two years ahead and whose careers automatically took precedence. The criteria employed by some of these women to choose fields of study also demonstrated their willingness to accommodate themselves to the lives of others. For example, one woman "scrambled up a thesis topic I could do in the Philippines," where she had accompanied her husband on his field work. Another selected a dissertation topic that she hoped would enhance her marketability in the small southern town where her husband taught.

Children also had determined the timing and pace of the careers of several of the older women. Two women in their mid-forties had postponed graduate school entirely when their children were young; other women had taken extra time to complete dissertations or delayed applying for full-time jobs while they cared for small children.

However, heterosexual women were not the only ones whose careers had been broken by family obligations. A lesbian in the study had dropped out of graduate school for a year in order to care for her dying mother. As she noted, class as well as gender explained her action: her mother had lacked the money to pay for adequate nursing care. Nevertheless, it is noteworthy that the caretaking function fell to this woman rather than to any male member of her family.

Two case studies demonstrate that women who returned to school after interruptions tended to place enormous significance on their careers. Maureen Ross initially entered graduate school immediately after college, but she left before receiving an M.A.

because her husband obtained a faculty position in another part of the country. For several years she worked at jobs considered appropriate for college-educated women—teaching junior high and writing a series of children's books. Shortly after the birth of her first child, she decided to return to graduate school. However, she encountered numerous barriers. First, she could not transfer credits she previously had earned. More seriously, the university did not provide child care, and she thus worked with a group of parents to establish a day-care center before enrolling in school. Although she won a fellowship, university regulations prevented her from accepting it because her husband taught at the same institution: "The dean told me that if they gave me this award, every faculty wife who was taking a summer class could apply for this grant, and they couldn't have that." Nevertheless, she spoke almost lyrically about her experience as a doctoral student:

> I loved graduate school, it was a very wonderful thing for me. It was a completion of a segment of my life which I had begun earlier. My dissertation year was a very exciting year for me. It was just a wonderful, wonderful year. I felt very triumphant finishing that dissertation.

Diligence and outstanding performance convinced her that she would receive just rewards:

> I didn't doubt that I would have a job at the end of all that. It's like I used to believe in equity in the world. I worked so hard. I did very, very well. I was in the upper echelon of graduate students, I'd come back after all those years. It was inconceivable to me that I wouldn't have a job at the end.

Julia Benson left graduate school after completing an M.A. to follow her husband, who had joined the Foreign Service. She lived abroad for five years, when she taught high school and adopted two children. She was divorced soon after returning to the United States and entered a Ph.D. program almost immediately. Like Maureen, she viewed her return to graduate school as a means of fulfilling a goal she earlier had set herself: "This was what I wanted to do in the first place and gave up in deference to my husband's career." Nevertheless, her graduate career also was impeded by major problems. She had sole responsibility for two children, one of whom was emotionally disturbed. In addition, she had to teach part-time at nearby colleges throughout graduate school in order to support her children. She, too, did not doubt that hard work would pay off, and she was shattered to discover that she could secure only a series of part-time jobs:

> I was furious, just miserable, crying and screaming and hollering. I had not worked so hard for so long and tried so hard and waited so long—I had not done all that for these jobs and I was very angry.... It was just so large in my mind that I had had such hopes and aspirations and goals.

Because she already had made a career change, she refrained from considering beginning in yet another field:

> Every year I go through wondering whether I should do something else and that's very upsetting to me. I went back to graduate school in my thirties with two little children and very little money and I busted my ass to get my Ph.D. to do the thing I wanted to do.

Both women, then, overcame enormous obstacles to complete their graduate studies, and they approached the job market with inflated expectations. Failure to secure a tenure-track position provoked a crisis for each.

Although change was a pervasive theme in the interviews of a majority of women, many aspects of their lives remained the same. In order to explain why a smaller proportion of the women sought alternative employment, we also must understand the ways in which legacies from the past continued to affect them. For example, despite their histories of academic success, some had residual doubts about their capabilities as scholars and their entitlement to professional careers. As Jane Flax has pointed out, even successful women often carry within themselves the fear that they are in fact frauds, that momentarily they will be "found out"; any setback threatens an already shaky sense of self-esteem.[18]

One woman believed that her inability to achieve her career goals was proof that she had been "too uppity." The comment of a second woman, interviewed a few weeks before filing her dissertation, was particularly telling: "In some ways it is more comforting not to have an academic job because I can go back to being a high-school teacher, which is basically how I see myself." Although she had spent seven years preparing to enter the ranks of university faculty, she was not yet accustomed to viewing herself as a professional and reluctant even to put herself to the test.

Significantly, two women invoked diametrically opposed reasons to explain why they may have been assessed fairly in the job market. One stated:

> I should never have been an academic. I see myself as a good technical researcher if someone else has the brilliant ideas. I'm not a hotshot scholar.

The second defined herself as inadequate because she lacked the skills of the first:

> Intellectually I always felt like an imposter and I always thought that the kind of history I did, which was intellectual history, was second-rate, that it was what the people who didn't have the patience and the professionalism to sit in libraries did....I could get by on a lot of razzle-dazzle.

Many of the women also were aware that other family members were ambivalent about their past accomplishments. One woman noted that her mother had been "uneasy" about her earning a Ph.D.: "So, in succeeding and yet failing I think I've been making her feel a bit better." Thus, many women still were struggling to convince themselves that, despite traditional notions about women's roles and the attitudes of the people closest to them, they belonged in the professions; failure served to confirm their worst fears.

Men's responses to career loss were more difficult to interpret. Although all displaced academics acknowledged that their lack of career success had eroded their self-respect, men were more likely to exude a strong sense of confidence. But they also steered conversations away from topics in which divulging feelings of worthlessness might have been appropriate. When asked how they reacted to their inability to fulfill their aspirations, a few answered other questions entirely. Far more men than women spoke in the second or third person, "You begin to think...," "One tends to feel...." Is it possible that the men expressed less self-doubt because they were unwilling to acknowledge such feelings? Did they need to flee academia immediately in order to avoid confronting a sense of inadequacy? Such questions are difficult to answer on the basis of interviews lasting only a few hours, but they make us exercise caution before concluding that women necessarily had lower self-esteem. In other words, the responses of men and women to failure may not differ although the socially acceptable reactions clearly do.

Nevertheless, the men did tend to have more distinct visions of themselves on career tracks and they did not doubt their right to professional status. The ones who had hesitated before applying to graduate school generally had been considering other professional options, not questioning their entitlement to professional careers. Almost none of the women had viewed law, medical, or business school as an alternative to graduate school but, as one man put it, professional school represented "the route not originally taken."[19] Because these fields meshed with the men's self-definitions, the men could move more easily into them.

Still another reason some women may have hesitated to change careers is that they assumed they could not act decisively on their own behalf. As we have seen, all disappointed job seekers strive to regain control over at least some parts of their lives, but many of the women who had accommodated themselves to others had little faith in their power to become masters of their fate. Looking back over their past experiences, these women tended to emphasize their reliance on others to shape the course of their lives. Although such women as Maureen and Julia clearly chose to focus on academic advancement, several others described themselves as having "stumbled" into academia. Numerous studies have shown that even high-achieving women often attribute their success to luck.[20] Similarly, one woman interviewed for this book portrayed her life in strikingly passive terms. Although she had demonstrated unusual initiative in carving out a niche for herself in a new field, she claimed she "just sort of fell into a doctoral program"; her choice of a thesis topic was "fortuitous," and the acceptance of her first seminar paper by the most prestigious journal in her field simply "a lucky break." Summing up her experience, she noted that there had been "many chancey things." A second woman also viewed herself as incapable of assuming responsibility for her life because "things have turned up in the past." After moving to a small college town, when her husband received a faculty appointment, she was "invited to teach" at a nearby university. Although she had intended to spend the year completing her dissertation, she felt powerless to refuse this offer: "I would never turn down a job that walks up to me." The following year she was "called" to teach at her husband's institution. Perceiving herself as the passive recipient of job offers, she had difficulty deciding what to do next.

> Subconsciously I may just be waiting for something to turn up again. That's not really very wise, but it's threatening to make some decisions about a career. They're awfully big decisions. It's much easier to slip into something, to have it open up for you.

A third woman conveyed an even deeper sense of discomfort about seizing control of her own destiny. Her decision to enter graduate school had been made "foolishly or at least haphazardly." Because she had always "fit into" her husband's life, she did not even consider applying to the university with the strongest reputation in her field: "This would have been the time to make long-range plans, but I just ended up going to X [the school closest to her home]." When she graduated, she realized that she had grown accustomed to letting others plan her life: "It would be wonderful to say, 'I'm going to do this,' but after years of adjusting my life to someone else's, I don't even know how to act like an independent person; I've become incapable of making decisions."

But situational as well as attitudinal factors explain the different rates at which men and women entered alternative employment. For one thing, previous decisions to grant precedence to husbands' careers were not reversed easily. Many of the women had husbands already ensconced in career positions. Thus, as a group, the women felt less free than the men to apply to professional schools or move to jobs in other parts of the country.

Although a slightly higher proportion of the men were married, relatively few had wives with professional or managerial jobs, and most of the married men considered themselves geographically mobile.

Children also imposed more serious constraints on the lives of the women than of the men. Eight, or almost three-quarters, of the married women had children; in addition, two of the single women were mothers. By contrast, only five, or less than half, of the married men and none of the single men had children. Moreover, three of the fathers had only one child, but almost all of the mothers had at least two. These figures can be explained partially by the slightly lower ages of the men. The median age of the men was 35 and of the women 38; additionally, many of the men were married to women considerably younger than themselves. More significantly, several men reported that they intentionally postponed children until their careers were launched; they wanted to feel both financially and emotionally secure before embarking on the critical task of child rearing.[21]

Such considerations may be particularly compelling to members of what Barbara Ehrenreich and John Ehrenreich have dubbed "the professional managerial class." As these authors have argued:

> The interior life of [this class] is shaped by the problem of class reproduction. Unlike ruling-class occupations,...occupations [of the professional managerial] class are never directly hereditary: The son of a research scientist knows he can only hope to achieve a similar position through continuous effort....
>
> As a result of the anxiety about class reproduction, all of the ordinary experiences of life—growing up, giving birth, childraising—are freighted with an external significance unknown in other classes.[22]

Thus, capitalists transmit class privilege by passing on capital, professionals by conferring education and culture. Not surprisingly, many of the men bitterly resented the fact that the academic job market had dictated the timing of their children. One of the promises of professional status is autonomy over basic life decisions; the necessity to defer children demonstrated clearly their inability to insulate themselves from economic forces.

But it also is important to note that the few fathers in the study did not view themselves primarily within the context of child-rearing obligations. True, two men described the heavy parenting responsibilities they had assumed because their wives were the primary wage earners. Nevertheless, these men expected to curtail the amount of time spent on child care as soon as they obtained full-time careers. Diane Ehrensaft has found that, even among the small fraction of couples who attempt to share parenting, men and women do not become equally involved in the process:

> Contrasted to mothers, the sharing father more likely enters the parenting experience with a notion that parenting is something you *do* rather than something you are....If parenting is something you *do*, then it is something you can stop doing. But it is much harder to stop being someone you are.[23]

Although all the women I interviewed directed some of their energies toward career success, many continued to view parenting as basic to their identities, and some still planned their lives around what they perceived to be their children's needs. Several mothers volunteered information about the ages of their children but not of themselves. When her youngest child was in school, a woman would be able to do X; by the time all the children were grown, she would feel free to pursue Y. Such women clearly viewed themselves as tied to the rhythm of the lives of others.[24]

But the emphasis placed on child rearing also may have stemmed from the women's career disappointments. Ehrensaft claims that she has seen "many a sharing mother—undervalued, sexually harassed, or discriminated against at the workplace—waffle on her outside identity and refocus on the pleasure, reward, and fulfillment that one can find in identity as a mother."[25] However, she notes, the "flight into parenthood is not a likely one" for most men.[26] Two women did acknowledge that they viewed child rearing as compensation for their lack of satisfying careers. When one was particularly discouraged about her employment prospects, she considered adopting children "so I wouldn't have all my eggs in the one basket of a career." The second acknowledged that her adoption of two children had been "a bit of a surrender, a form of defeatism." On the other hand, one woman desperately sought a job because she had allowed herself to be engulfed by the demands of others:

> I often feel pressed from two directions. My parents are getting old, my father is showing signs of senility, my daughter is in emotional distress. I feel so selfish, so guilty about wanting to do my own work and about resenting being bothered by these family problems of my father's health and my daughter's mental health. There are times when I have wanted to scream and just go away from my family altogether.... It's much easier if you have a job because then you can either physically separate yourself or throw yourself into preparing your lectures and tell yourself, "this is what I'm involved in now."

The most obvious explanation for the greater determination of the men to seek alternative employment is that they have more responsibility for supporting families. The fact that so many men postponed child rearing until after they were settled in careers lends weight to this argument. In addition, one man who recently had applied to law school declared:

> One of my major reasons for going into law is that I intend to have a wife and family. If I didn't have to worry about supporting a family, I could probably stay in the field and enjoy it. I notice a lot of women doing that. But it's not part of their world view to see themselves supporting a family. They're freer. They're competent enough to know they can get something each year and survive, but it's not enough for me.

This man's envy of the broader options of his female counterparts shaded quickly into contempt: he would not settle for the lives he envisions for them. Moreover, his derogatory attitude is shared by the society around him; his female colleagues who remain in the crevices of academia will command far less social recognition than he expects to receive.

More significantly, this quotation serves to remind us that a decade of feminist activity has not erased the notion that every woman will marry and that her husband's income will be sufficient to support her. Half of the female interviewees were neither married nor in long-term heterosexual relationships. Single women were less than half as likely as single men to leave academia. Four, or just a third, of the single women had decided to change careers, as opposed to five, or almost three-quarters, of the single men. Furthermore, the single women who had found alternative employment tended to hold "noncareer" positions; as already noted, none had applied to law, business, or medical school.

In addition, most of the married women claimed that their earnings were essential to their families' support. One woman stated that her family went into debt during the months she was unemployed. Two others needed full-time jobs in order to make mortgage payments. Still another woman was determined to remain financially independent although her husband earned enough to support her comfortably. At the same time, marriage to women with high incomes did not deter men from attempting to find their own professions.

Nevertheless, it is true that four of the women were able to rely entirely on their husbands' earnings and to view not working as an option. Furthermore, some of the married women regarded themselves as secondary wage earners, not the primary ones. In addition, single women were far more likely to seek alternative employment than were married women; four of the single women but only one of the married women had left academia. The different economic constraints on men and women thus may be one factor in the greater alacrity with which men changed careers.

But the above quotation points to still another distinction between men and women. This man's quest for a high status career is predicated on the assumption that a wife and children will materialize once he has attained his goal. When asked about the woman with whom he intended to produce a family, he replied he had no particular one in mind. In this respect he was typical of many of the single male displaced academics. They were convinced they easily would find appropriate mates once their careers were launched. In other words, one of the rewards of occupational success would be personal fulfillment.[27] This man enumerated the traits that would establish his value in the marriage market:

> By the time I'm 34, I will have a Ph.D., a law degree, three years of teaching experience, a broad background; I will have more to offer my family than most 34 year olds. I work out every day so I will be in good health. I'll still be running three to four miles a day.

He described himself as a prize he would offer a woman who in turn would provide him with a satisfactory personal life.

Single women viewed professional achievement in a different light. They did not equate personal fulfillment and career success, and they frequently resented their past emphasis on professional goals. One woman who had taught at a large research university resolved to place personal relationships at the center of her life:

> I am never again going to take a job that consumes so much of my personal life because I don't think it's worth it any more. I think maybe that's what one does once in one's life and from here on out it's my personal growth and my friendships and other aspects of my life that I'm primarily concerned with.

Another woman explained her determination to restrict her job search to large metropolitan areas: "My decision about graduate school was made on a narrowly professional basis. I don't want other decisions to be made that way." Unlike many male academics, these women did not compartmentalize their lives or expect personal happiness to result automatically from career advancement.

Finally, it is important to remember that the fields unemployed academics are encouraged to enter remain male dominated, despite affirmative action regulations and the striking gains women have secured during the past decade. Feminist writings have amply documented both the formal and informal barriers encountered by women in most professions.[28] Furthermore, statistics compiled by the National Research Council demonstrate that a Ph.D. does not furnish adequate protection against discrimination. In 1977, men with doctorates in the humanities and social sciences who were employed in business and industry earned an average of $21,000 a year; the average annual salary of women was $13,100.[29] According to a study conducted by the Higher Education Research Institute, women Ph.D.s in the humanities who find employment in government are less satisfied with their jobs than are men.[30] In other words, the payoff for changing careers may be less for women than for men.

The reluctance of many women to enter alternative employment clearly stems from a variety of factors. Some women were uncertain about their entitlement to professional status or their ability to engage in long-term planning. Many expected more limited rewards from professional success than did the men. The inequitable division of caretaking functions in this society was especially critical in determining the actions of the men and women.[31] Embedded in family obligations, married women felt less free than married men to devote themselves to career advancement. Unlike several single men, no single woman assumed she would find someone else to undertake the tasks of nurturance for her. Indeed, as long as the essential roles of caring for the young and the old remain gender-linked, we can expect men and women to view occupational success from different perspectives and thus to respond differently to the loss of careers.

NOTES

1. National Research Council, *Departing the Ivy Halls: Changing Employment Situations for Recent Ph.D.s* (Washington, D.C.: National Academy Press, 1983), p. 61.

2. National Research Council, *Employment of Humanities Ph.D.'s: A Departure from Traditional Jobs* (Washington, D.C.: National Academy of Sciences, 1980), p. 23.

3. See Robert A. Nisbet, "The Decline and Fall of Social Class," *Pacific Sociological Review* 2 (Spring 1959):11-17; Kurt B. Mayer, "The Changing Shape of the American Class Structure," *Social Research* 30 (Winter 1963):460-68.

4. Andrew Levison, *The Working-Class Majority* (Harmondsworth, Eng.: Penguin Books, 1975); Lillian Breslow Rubin, *Worlds of Pain: Life in the Working-Class Family* (New York: Basic Books, 1976).

5. The most widely recommended book is Richard Nelson Bolles, *What Color Is Your Parachute? A Practical Manual for Job Hunters and Career Changers* (Berkeley: Ten Speed Press, 1975).

6. See René D. Zentner, "Business and the Humanities: A New Look at Two Cultures," *ADE Bulletin*, no. 68, Summer 1981, pp. 14-15.

7. See Randall Collins, *The Credential Society: An Historical Sociology of Education and Stratification* (New York: Academic Press, 1979), p. 17; Magali Sarfatti Larson, *The Rise of Professionalism: A Sociological Analysis* (Berkeley: University of California Press, 1979), p. 228.

8. See E. P. Thompson, *The Making of the English Working Class* (London: Victor Gollancz, 1963), pp. 305-6.

9. Lewis C. Solmon, Laura Kent, Nancy L. Ochsner, and Margo-Lea Hurwicz, *Underemployed Ph.D.'s* (Lexington, Mass.: Lexington, 1981), p. 112.

10. See Stanley Aronowitz, *False Promises: The Shaping of the American Working-Class Consciousness* (New York: McGraw-Hill, 1973), pp. 51-133.

11. Peter Marris, *Loss and Change* (Garden City, N.Y.: Doubleday, 1975), pp. 35-38.

12. National Research Council, *Employment of Humanities Ph.D.'s*, p. 51.

13. Only 7 percent of the men awarded doctorates in the humanities between 1934 and 1968 held nonteaching jobs in 1977, compared to 23 percent of those receiving Ph.D.s during the academic year 1975-76. However, 14 percent of both the 1934-68 female Ph.D. recipients and the 1975-76 cohort held nonacademic jobs in 1977. (National Research Council, *Employment of Humanities Ph.D.'s*, p. 51.)

14. In addition, one man was enrolled in a school of education, preparing to become a special-education teacher.

15. Many women Ph.D.s do, of course, enter professional schools after unsuccessful attempts to secure faculty positions.

16. Although I am differentiating between male and female attitudes, a few men conformed to the pattern I have defined as female and a few women fit the male model. For a different explanation of the rates at which men and women sought alternative employment, see Arnita A. Jones, "The Humanities Labor Force: Women Historians as a Special Case," paper presented at the Annual Convention, American Historical Association, New York, December 1980.

17. Inge Powell Bell, "The Double Standard: Age," in *Women: A Feminist Perspective*, 2nd ed., ed. Jo Freeman (Palo Alto: Mayfield, 1979), p. 237.

18.   Jane Flax, "The Conflict Between Nurturance and Autonomy in Mother-Daughter Relationships and Within Feminism," *Feminist Studies* 4 (June 1978):181.

19.   Lewis C. Solmon, Nancy L. Ochsner, and Margo-Lea Hurwicz also found that men were more likely than women to consider professional school an option when they applied to graduate school. (*Alternative Careers for Humanities Ph.D.s* [New York: Praeger, 1979], p. 50.)

20.   See Irene Hanson Frieze, "Women's Expectations for and Causal Attributions of Success and Failure," in *Women and Achievement: Social and Motivational Analyses*, ed. Martha T. Shuch Mednick, Sandra Schwartz Tangri, and Lois Wladis Hoffman (New York: Hemisphere, 1977), pp. 164-65.

21.   Higher proportions of other groups of male doctorates have children. For example, the National Research Council reported that 79 percent of the men who earned Ph.D.s between 1970-74 and who were married had children in 1979. (*Career Outcomes in a Matched Sample of Men and Women Ph.D.s* [Washington, D.C.: National Academy Press, 1981], p. 31.) According to a recent study of junior faculty at two northeastern universities, less than a third of the married men, but two-thirds of the married women, had children. (Cathy Spitz Widom and Barbara W. Burke, "Performance, Attitudes and Professional Socialization of Women in Academia," *Sex Roles* 4 [August 1978]: 549-62.) These figures lend weight to the contention that the men I interviewed postponed children because of their unsatisfactory employment situations.

22.   Barbara Ehrenreich and John Ehrenreich, "The Professional-Managerial Class," in *Between Labor and Capital*, ed. Pat Walker (Boston: South End, 1979), p. 2.

23.   Diane Ehrensaft, "When Women and Men Mother," *Socialist Review* 10 (January-February 1980):55.

24.   For a discussion of the way in which the identity of women is enmeshed in their personal relationships, see Carol Gilligan, "Restoring the Missing Text of Women's Development to Life Cycle Theories," in *Women's Lives: New Theory, Research and Policy*, ed. Dorothy G. McGuigan (Ann Arbor: University of Michigan, 1980), pp. 17-33.

25.   Ehrensaft, "Women and Men Mother," p. 52.

26.   Ibid.

27.   He may, in fact, have assessed his prospects accurately. As Jean Baker Miller has written, "There is reason to believe that self-development will win [men] relationships. Others—usually women—will rally to them and support them in their efforts, and other men will respect and admire them." *Toward a New Psychology of Women* (Boston: Beacon, 1976), p. 95.

28. See, for example, Cynthia Fuchs Epstein, *Women in Law* (New York: Basic Books, 1981); Rosabeth Moss Kanter, *Men and Women of the Corporation* (New York: Basic Books, 1977); Michelle Patterson and Laurie Engelberg, "Women in Male-Dominated Professions," in *Women Working*, ed. Ann H. Stromberg and Shirley Harkess (Palo Alto: Mayfield, 1978), pp. 266-92.

29. National Research Council, *Science, Engineering and Humanities Doctorates: 1977 Profile* (Washington, D.C.: National Academy of Sciences, 1978), p. 53; see also Solmon, Ochsner, and Hurwicz, *Alternative Careers*, p. 115.

30. Solmon, Ochsner, and Hurwicz, *Alternative Careers*, pp. 138-40.

31. See Gerda Lerner, *The Majority Finds Its Past: Placing Women in History* (New York: Oxford University Press, 1979), p. 140.

Chapter 7
FIGHTING BACK

We have seen that displaced academics generally eschewed collective activity. Avoiding contact with other unemployed or underemployed academics, they viewed their own problems as personal and unique. Although they did not deny the existence of structural barriers, most blamed themselves for failure to fulfill their goals. Some continued to pursue academic aspirations; others placed their faith in alternative professional careers through which they expected to obtain satisfying work and economic security. Both groups were unwilling to jeopardize their prospects by engaging in any form of protest. In addition, displaced academics typically believed collective action was a waste of time. Intensified competition, not cooperation, they frequently declared, was the inevitable result of diminishing resources.

This chapter will examine the validity of that contention. The two primary methods of protest in academia are unionization and lawsuits. Because sex discrimination suits by women faculty are the most common form of legal action in higher education, the first section will assess their effectiveness. The second will evaluate the extent to which faculty unionization has benefitted part-time teachers.

FACULTY WOMEN AND
SEX DISCRIMINATION LAWSUITS

The pursuit of sex discrimination grievances by faculty women in institutions of higher education involves a conflict between two competing images of society: the individualism that underlies both the legal and the educational systems, and the collectivism inherent in any political protest. In order to assert that they have suffered discrimination on the basis of gender, women must recognize the commonality of their interests with those of other women. Moreover, their chances of success are greater, and the significance of their action is enhanced if their protest is waged collectively. Such a strategy, however, is inconsistent with the meritocratic ideal of the educational selection system, according to which rewards are distributed solely on the basis of individual talent and effort. Women who have derived real benefits from this system are often reluctant to question its basic tenets. Collective aims are also undermined by the grievance process itself. Complainants are often forced to couch their cases in individualistic terms, focusing more on their own personal and professional qualities than on systemic patterns of discrimination.

These themes will be explored in the following section, which is based on interviews with sixteen faculty women who filed charges of sex discrimination against colleges and universities.[1] These women relied on laws and regulations passed during the late sixties and early seventies that promised a significant improvement in the status of women in academia. The first federal measure to prohibit sex discrimination in higher education was Executive Order 11246, which requires all colleges and universities receiving at least $10,000 in federal contracts to implement an affirmative action plan in hiring.[2] The Equal Pay Act of 1963, which mandates equal pay for equal work, was extended to cover executive, administrative, and professional employees in 1972.[3] Title IX of the Education Amendments Act of 1972 prohibits sex discrimination in educational activities in all federally assisted programs.[4] The most significant law for faculty women, however, is Title VII of the Civil Rights Act of 1964, prohibiting discrimination in hiring and establishing the Equal Employment Opportunities Commission (EEOC) to enforce its provisions.[5] This act often is heralded as one of the first tangible victories of the women's movement. True, the insertion of the word "sex" in the original bill was not just a result of pressure by feminist legislators and lobbyists, but also a consequence of the misguided machinations of conservative southerners, intent on dealing a deathblow to the entire bill. Nevertheless, women's groups could claim responsibility for the fact that sex as well as race discrimination subsequently came to be considered by the EEOC as a legitimate area of concern. Moreover, it was largely as a result of pressure from feminists, joining with civil rights advocates, that amendments were passed in 1972 strengthening the enforcement powers of the EEOC and including educational institutions as well as governmental bodies within its jurisdiction.[6] Although a few of the women interviewed for this study also asserted rights under several other laws, all relied primarily on Title VII.

Many academic women viewed Title VII as a powerful weapon with which to attack institutional sexism, and they began to take advantage of this measure almost immediately. Within the first year after passage of the 1972 amendments, 250 cases were filed against educational institutions.[7] But other women were more skeptical. Looking at the experience of the civil rights movement, they questioned the ability of laws to alter ingrained attitudes and patterns of behavior. Moreover, they pointed to aspects of Title VII that made it an ineffective agent for the redress of past injustice. First, the initiative for investigating discrimination has to come from an individual, who is then vulnerable to harassment and retaliation. Second, the law upholds the traditional liberal goal of fair competition but leaves unchallenged the structural sources of unequal opportunity.[8]

Title VII has not proven to be an effective mechanism for eliminating sexism in academic employment. Although there have been a number of major victories, faculty women have won only a small proportion of cases decided since Title VII was extended to educational institutions.[9] Furthermore, the condition of women in colleges and universities has not improved since 1972;[10] women continue to be concentrated in low-status and low-paying positions.

This section seeks to assess the effectiveness of Title VII as a vehicle for redressing injustice by examining how women who perceive themselves as having suffered discrimination experience the complaint process from the point at which they first decide they are victims of discrimination until their cases are concluded.[11] I will first discuss the position of faculty women in colleges and universities, the responses of the interviewees to the incidents they alleged were discriminatory, and the factors involved in their decisions to protest. I will then trace the complaint process, including campus grievance mechanisms, government enforcement agencies, and litigation. Next I will discuss the role of lawyers and the extent to which the grievants were successful in gaining the support of other women. Finally, the costs and benefits of filing a sex discrimination charge will be assessed.

Discrimination in the Ivory Tower

Although most of the interviewees filed charges as individuals, they all were challenging patterns of discrimination that have become the concern of a growing number of academic women. The position of women academics in four-year colleges and universities has not changed significantly since the passage of the 1972 amendments to Title VII: women continue to constitute only 24 percent of the full-time faculty, and they remain clustered in the lower levels of the academic hierarchy.[12] As we have seen, a disproportionate number of women begin their careers in part-time positions, not in full-time ones.[13] Furthermore, even full-time faculty women are concentrated in nonladder appointments. Women represent 37 percent of the lecturers and 49 percent of the instructors, as opposed to 18 percent of professors in the tenure track.[14] The proportion of women at each level within the tenure track also is inversely related to the status of that position: women constitute 28 percent of the assistant professors, 16 percent of the associate professors, and 8 percent of the full professors.[15]

The most serious problem, then, is not entry but advancement, and this is the issue raised by the women interviewed for this section. Two women challenged the termination of their contracts at the stage of pretenure reviews. Seven others claimed that unfair practices adversely had affected their tenure decisions. An additional seven alleged that discriminatory treatment had prevented their promotions from nonladder positions to regular academic appointments.

Response to Discrimination

The first step in filing a sex discrimination charge was recognition that an injustice had occurred. The women had to believe that they had been judged not as individuals, but rather as members of a group that generally is accorded a lesser value. Although a number of grievants claimed that they had long been conscious of sexism at their colleges or universities, others described the painful process of discovering the existence of institutionalized discrimination. In a few instances, the women's awareness of discrimination crystallized only after their appointments were terminated. One woman's testimony provides an exceptional example of how an understanding of the operation of discrimination can transform feelings of unworthiness into anger and a determination to seek redress:

> When I was fired, I went into a complete and total depression. Much of my trouble was that I needed a definition of my case. All I knew was that there was unfairness but I didn't know what had happened or why. I wasn't involved in women's groups, but if I had been, that might have helped me perceive at an earlier time what was going on.
>
> But then someone told me to go to EEOC and when I got there, they asked me questions about my salary, my working conditions, and how many other women were on the faculty. Then they said, "You've got a sex discrimination suit; you're just one of the others."
>
> Then NOW contacted me, and people began calling me who also had problems at the university and I began to realize it wasn't just me. Now I have strength both physically and emotionally. I know what took place and so I can defend myself.

This woman's discovery that her personal problems originated in the structure of the university made her determined to challenge her treatment and gave her the courage to do so.

Nevertheless, as we have seen, it often is difficult for academics to question the fairness of the educational system. Because they are accustomed to succeeding in school, they have a stake in believing that academic rewards are distributed equitably. Moreover, an important part of their own jobs is evaluating the work of others, and they want to believe that they can do so without being influenced by subjective factors.

Some women academics may be particularly resistant to perceiving themselves as victims of social and economic forces.[16] Although many faculty women have formed active support networks, others cling to the illusion that they, as individuals, can transcend collective social constraints. Even when they owe their positions to pressure from the women's movement, such women persist in believing that they have "made it" on merit alone. They take pride in being "special" and "exceptionally deserving" and focus on elements that separate them from other women on campus, whether students, secretaries, research assistants, librarians, or teachers. The discovery that they share problems with other women threatens this sense of uniqueness.[17]

Thus, self-respect may depend on recognizing the systemic causes of their present plight, but challenging the meritocracy calls into question a system that rewarded them in the past. In fact, many of the women never completely resolved the issue of whether their problems originated in personal failure or social forces. They were forced to reconsider this question at many stages during the grievance process. In turn, this ambiguity affected both their goals and their strategies.

Deciding to Protest

The women reported a variety of motives for filing grievances. Several had been involved in the civil rights and antiwar movements, and they viewed the present protest as a natural extension of their earlier social activism. Many women described themselves as having a "combative personality" or being unable "to pass up a good fight." A black interviewee stated: "All blacks learn that they have to keep fighting for what's rightfully theirs." Almost one-half of the plaintiffs turned to the example of a female relative—an aunt, a mother, or a grandmother—whom they characterized as a fighter. In addition, a number of women stated that they had been aware of the psychic costs of taking no corrective action; had they done nothing, they would have internalized the judgments against them. Finally, at least four women mentioned that they were strongly impelled by revenge, "a much underrated emotion," according to one.

But above all, when asked why they had decided to protest, the women stressed the goals they hoped to accomplish. In fact, the interviewees can be divided into two groups on the basis of their aims. A few women claimed that personal considerations were primary. One woman, for example, insisted: "Initially I was concerned with my own particular oppression, my particular instance. My grievance was filed because of my own situation, not because of any principle. I didn't think about other women." A second woman similarly denied the link between the details of her case and larger patterns of discrimination: "I saw my case as a personal thing. If it had had some social benefits that would have been all right, but essentially it was a personal fight. There were a lot of unique factors." Women such as these will be characterized as "apolitical." They emphasized the idiosyncratic or accidental aspects of their own cases, and they confined their vision to their own specific concerns. Furthermore, they generally wanted to attain greater power or higher status within the university without necessarily questioning traditional methods of operation or calling into doubt any of the assumptions underlying the educational system.

The majority of women interviewed dwelled on the larger purposes of their individual protests. Although only one-quarter of the women defined themselves as committed activists, many claimed that they were motivated largely by idealistic concerns. They sought professional advancement but stressed the political significance of their action. They were "working for other women," "fighting for the principle," or "showing the university that it couldn't do whatever it wanted to women." In some instances, their cases had become moot by the time they were resolved. Three women who were contesting the termination of their contracts insisted that they did not want their jobs back. But most were motivated by an amalgam of personal and political aims and viewed these goals as inseparable. Thus one woman, who spoke of her need to convince herself that, as she put it, "my case, my battle was worth fighting for," assumed that her search for personal vindication was related to the shared experience of women as a group. Moreover, many of the women who I define as "political" sought to alter fundamental patterns in the university. For example, one woman explained: "My aim was not just back pay or promotion. My aim was to transform the entire system, to redistribute power, to change the status quo so that women could participate equally."

In sum, the grievants divided along the same lines as adherents of the women's movement in general. Some feminists emphasize the attainment of individual self-fulfillment and authenticity; others stress social change to improve the position of women as a group. Decisions these grievants made throughout the course of the complaint process reflected these different outlooks.[18]

What did most of the women believe would happen if they charged a university or college with discrimination? Both groups of women approached the grievance process with high expectations about the outcome.[19] One woman "truly believed that the law would work," and she noted how difficult it was to abandon the illusion of an early or easy victory: "At each stage what kept me going was the naïve belief that at the next stage it would all be settled." Some of these women had filed their cases soon after the passage of the 1972 amendments to Title VII, and they shared the general excitement surrounding that event. But the high expectations of the grievants also can be viewed as a consequence of their class position. Just as many academics have a stake in upholding the educational system that has rewarded them in the past, so most members of the middle class assume that the legal system will be responsive to any rights they assert; in the past, when they put forward a claim, they generally were rewarded.[20] Part of the outrage many grievants felt as their cases progressed stemmed from the disjunction between the privileges they previously had received and the poor treatment they experienced when protesting sex discrimination. But their class position also gave them confidence. Their heightened, even unrealistic, expectations were vital in sustaining them during the long, tedious, frustrating, and degrading grievance process.

The Complaint Process

Few women had definite notions about how to proceed when they decided to seek redress. Despite the prevalence of discrimination against women in academia, some faculty women are not connected to any networks that might furnish them with information about possible remedial action. Moreover, the grievants were naturally unable to obtain advice from university officials about how to file sex discrimination charges. University rules of confidentiality also impeded initial attempts to fight back. Many women reported that they were unable to obtain information about either the procedures that had been followed in their cases or the criteria on which unfavorable decisions had been based. One woman stated: "One of the most difficult things about these decisions is that no one will tell you what the vote was and who had been involved. It took me a year and a half just to find out what had happened."

Many women first appealed to various administrators, including the campus president and system-wide chancellor. Although these officials routinely expressed interest and concern, in no instance did they intervene on a grievant's behalf. Some administrators counseled the woman "not to make waves," warning that her career would be ruined irreparably if she proceeded to lodge any complaint. Affirmative action officers were similarly unhelpful. Despite the promise inherent in that title, these officers often report to personnel committees or deans; they have been criticized for contributing to a false appearance of equal opportunity that obscures the facts.[21] The verdict of many of the interviewees was that these administrators were "ineffective" or "useless."

Most women also requested internal grievance hearings. They reported, however, that the campus grievance committees were dominated by male senior professors; thus, their appeals were decided by those who either were responsible for the initial discrimination or who had a strong interest in refusing to acknowledge the existence of sexism on campus. Moreover, these committees typically had jurisdiction only over procedural irregularities and were unable to consider issues of racism or sexism. A few of the women who held nonladder appointments were shocked to discover that they lacked grievance rights entirely. Only two women reported that grievance committees had found in their favor, and in both cases these decisions were reversed by the administration.[22]

The next stage was equally frustrating. Most of the complainants filed grievances with EEOC, the regulatory agency established by Title VII.[23] Whenever there is a state agency, the case is automatically deferred to that agency for sixty days; however, over 85 pecent of the cases revert back to EEOC after this period has elapsed because the state agency has not resolved them.[24] EEOC investigates the charges and decides whether there is "reasonable cause" to believe that discrimination has occurred. If so, the commission seeks a settlement between the aggrieved party and the employer.

Since the passage of Title VII, women have criticized both state and federal enforcement agencies for unnecessary delays, ineptitude, and lack of diligence in pursuing sex discrimination cases.[25] The experiences of most of the women interviewed substantiate these charges. One woman concluded that EEOC "did nothing but push papers." Another characterized the commission as "very stuffy, very bureaucratic, very against rocking the boat." The main criticism was the length of time the investigation took. Since its inception, EEOC has been plagued by enormous backlogs and inadequate staffing. By 1974, the commission had 90,000 unresolved cases;[26] three years later, the backlog had grown to 126,000.[27] Thus, although the commission is supposed to settle cases within 120 days, most women reported that their complaints took at least two or three years. The inadequate qualifications of the investigators were another cause of complaint. Two women did report that their cases were handled expeditiously by dedicated and diligent investigators, but most grievants were convinced that their complaints were processed by investigators who knew little about academic employment practices and did not consider allegations of sex discrimination very significant.

Whether or not EEOC has taken action on a particular case, it routinely will issue a "right to sue" letter after 180 days if requested.[28] Five of the women chose to go into court without waiting for determinations by EEOC. The others were advised by their attorneys to exhaust administrative remedies before proceeding with litigation.

In all but one of the seven cases in which EEOC rendered a decision, the finding was favorable to the complainant. In other words, the agency discovered that there was "reasonable cause" to believe discrimination had occurred. Nevertheless, the outcome was disappointing to the grievants. Although conciliation proceedings are supposed to follow a ruling by EEOC, the agency has no power to compel a university to participate. One woman remarked: "I received my certified letter from EEOC stating that they found in my favor. It all seemed so promising. But then the university refused to conciliate and that was the end." Then, too, the conciliation process tended to focus exclusively on the issues in the specific case under consideration.[29] Thus, despite the desire of a significant number of grievants to alter campus policies and practices, institutional reforms were never part of the final agreement. One woman did design a new tenure-review procedure which was then written into the agreement, but the university was required to follow it only in her case. Moreover, the most common form of relief was a cash settlement. Women who were seeking goals other than pecuniary compensation were outraged: "They tried to buy me off," was one woman's reaction. Even the less political women had sought moral satisfaction or personal vindication, but this often was explicitly denied. In one instance, a grievant was asked to sign a statement that the university had never discriminated against her. In another, the university refused to sign the final agreement if it contained a statement asserting that the claimant was competent. Finally, none of the women thought that the award was adequate compensation for the pay she had lost or the damage to her career.[30]

When conciliation attempts fail, the Civil Rights Division of the Justice Department can take cases to court. However, the department chooses to handle only a few such cases every year and, as of late 1981, it had not yet intervened in an academic suit. Two interviewees reported that the division had "flirted" with their cases but then decided against intervention. Since 1972, EEOC also has had the power to file suit in federal court against intransigent private institutions. But EEOC, like the Department of Justice, will litigate only landmark cases. Hence the burden of filing a suit generally falls on the individual complainant.

The decision to litigate represented a critical point in the complaint process. Two women decided not to persevere after considering the time and energy that would be required and the slim likelihood of success.

Often the first step in litigation was to seek to obtain class certification. In order to do this, a plaintiff must demonstrate that her case is typical and that it adequately represents the class. Once a class is certified, the case has a greater potential to confer benefits on other women and to effect structural change. In other words, an individual claim is transformed into collective action.[31]

One type of evidence used in litigation also underlines the collective aspect of Title VII cases: statistical proof of a pattern of discrimination. The use of statistics illustrates the tensions inherent in this law between equal opportunity for individuals and the enhancement of the position of disadvantaged groups as a whole. In fact, even women who have not sought class certification generally rely at least partially on statistics. In such cases, evidence of group discrimination is used to prove an individual claim.

Nevertheless, faculty women, like professional women generally, have been notoriously unsuccessful in resting their cases on statistics. Instead, they are forced to rely on evidence of procedural irregularities or of their personal characteristics. The latter type of evidence is most commonly used, but, from the plaintiff's point of view, it has severe disadvantages. For one thing, the trial is diverted from the real issue at stake. Although the grievant went to court to protest a university's practices and policies, the trial focuses on her own qualifications.[32] Moreover, she is even less likely to receive a fair hearing than she was at her original review for promotion. She carefully produces evidence of her academic accomplishments, but the university summons all its power to prove that she is inadequate as a teacher, scholar, and human being. As many interviewees remarked, the process of taking depositions and answering interrogatories in the pretrial stage revived questions about individual worth that arose at the inception of the case. One woman noted:

> The interrogatories were even worse than the initial denial of a promotion....I began to question my own worth and wonder, well, maybe the college is right, look what they're saying. It's very hard to have people that you think highly of saying these things. I could hardly bear to read the answers to the interrogatories in the beginning because I took it so personally.

A woman whose case did go to trial recalled:

> It was very unpleasant when my own academic reputation was being scrutinized. I wasn't just a statistic. They

couldn't say, "she's terrible," because then it would have been clear that interviewing me at all was a sham. But there was always a sense that I wasn't quite good enough and that was very hard and it took me a long time to overcome that. And I of course had to say that I was wonderful. That was hard too, because you're taught to be terribly modest.

Of the ten women who undertook litigation, only one obtained a resolution that she considered satisfactory. In an out-of-court settlement, she was granted tenure; furthermore, the university agreed to institute a far-reaching plan of affirmative action. Two women lost their cases after trials. One other negotiated an out-of-court settlement that fell short of her original goals. The other women, still awaiting court hearings, tended to be less than sanguine about achieving their original expectations.

Lawyers

Most of the claimants first sought legal counsel when they appealed to enforcement agencies, although two women hired attorneys as soon as they filed charges with university grievance committees, and two others waited until they undertook litigation. As professionals, they often had better access than most women to information about legal services. Many had friends or relatives who were lawyers or could furnish the names of attorneys. In addition, the women's movement has served as an important source for disseminating such information. Four of the women either were referred to lawyers by an organization such as the National Organization for Women (NOW) or followed the recommendation of other women who had filed similar cases. Of the remaining interviewees who consulted lawyers, one received a referral from the campus chapter of a faculty union, and two others were advised by the EEOC investigators who handled their cases.

The major problem was not locating a lawyer, but convincing that lawyer to handle the case. For many women, the difficulty of obtaining legal counsel presented the first indication that suing a university would be a far more difficult and frustrating process than they originally had assumed. From the point of view of lawyers, Title VII cases have a number of disadvantages. Because most individuals lack large amounts of capital with which to pay a retainer, lawyers recover fees only if they are successful and the defendant pays them. Moreover, Title VII cases typically last a long time, and lawyers cannot expect to obtain any return on their investment for several years. Should the cases lose, the lawyers are paid nothing. All Title VII cases are difficult to win, but academic sex discrimination suits face unusually unfavorable odds. Thus, even lawyers who specialize in Title VII litigation refrain from taking such cases. Persuading a lawyer to accept a retainer requires a showing that success is not just likely, but is highly probable. Such success turns not on a showing of discrimination, but on whether or not the individual is unusual. One of the few attorneys who continues to represent a sizable number of academic plaintiffs explained the criterion of selection she uses: potential clients must demonstrate an academic record "of clearly outstanding excellence."

What did the women look for in their lawyers? The "apolitical" women were largely indifferent to the political orientations of their attorneys. They wanted specialists whose legal competence inspired confidence. Moreover, they tended to be pleased if their attorneys could relate to university officials and opposing counsel on terms of easy familiarity. Thus, one woman expressed satisfaction with her lawyer because he was "brash, aggressive, flirtatious and loud, just like the men at the college and the other lawyers, and so he could deal with them." She explained why it was essential for grievants to obtain legal counsel: "Government agencies must protect a whole class action, while a lawyer will work just for you as an individual."

The other group of women sought lawyers who shared their concern with the principled as well as the tactical aspects of litigation and who were willing to raise political issues in the trial. Moreover, they were suspicious of the relationship between their lawyers and the legal community:

> My lawyers are feminists and one is known as a civil rights attorney but they do first name [sic] the lawyers of the university system and they work with them and against them on different kinds of issues and cases and it sometimes makes me wonder.

These lawyers kept saying, "We can't antagonize the judge too much, because, he'll screw us in another case." I would say, "Well, you have to ask this." "We can't, it would upset him, we can't upset him," and on and on and on. So how I fit into their relationship to that judge — that was the most important thing for them.

As these quotations suggest, conflicts between lawyers and clients were built into their relationships.[33] Regardless of how strongly lawyers believed in the principles raised by particular cases, their primary allegiance was apt to remain with the legal community, and they were likely to avoid action that could undermine their standing with the judge or opposing counsel. Feminist lawyers, moreover, face the same dilemmas as the complainants; their own desire for professional success compels them to seek acceptance from other attorneys, even at the expense of the political purpose of the legal suit. Lawyers and clients were divided by other factors as well. For example, although many of the women worked closely with their lawyers, providing the latter with evidence and even discussing legal issues, at some point they had to relinquish control of their cases to experts whose judgment they could not question. One woman spoke of her difficulty in relying on someone else to "choreograph" her case in court. Financial arrangements also opposed the interests of lawyers and clients. As in most Title VII litigation, the lawyers in these cases usually worked without contemporaneous fees, hoping to be awarded statutory attorney's fees when they won. This arrangement had clear advantages for the plaintiffs, most of whom lacked the resources to pay legal fees in advance of or during the proceedings. But lawyers who were not reimbursed for each hour of work were strongly motivated to conclude the cases as quickly as possible.[34] Thus, the grievants' relationships with their lawyers tended to replicate their experiences with the enforcement agencies to which they had appealed. They found themselves under pressure to accept whatever the university officials offered, without regard to the principles that originally stimulated them to protest:

The university pressed me very hard to accept their offer and my lawyers said, "take the money settlement, take the money settlement," and I said, "My job, the principle," but they didn't listen. The whole fight I had been fighting on principle seemed to be restructured entirely and I was helpless. It was done with me standing outside and flailing and shrieking, "You can't do that to me, I've fought this fight for three or four years." The principle was lost entirely and this is what really caused my breakdown. After all that fighting the fight was being taken away from me and made into a sort of commodity for the lawyers and for that legal system of ours. That was too much.

Eliciting Support

Feminist consciousness begins with self-consciousness, an awareness of our separate needs as women; then comes the awareness of female collectivity—the reaching out toward other women, first for mutual support and then to improve our condition.[35]

We might assume that an academic woman engaged in a sex discrimination case would be strongly motivated to enlist the support of other women. Before a teacher could protest her situation, it was first necessary that she recognize she was oppressed as a woman, not simply mistreated as an individual. Moreover, the grievants faced overwhelming odds. Their opponents were institutions accustomed to litigation, which could not be hurt by delays and harassment and which had enormous financial resources at their disposal.[36] Most significantly, the women were fighting not simply against the actions of individual professors and administrators, but also against university policies and practices they believed systematically discriminated against women. When the grievants took their cases beyond the confines of the university, to government agencies and courts, they discovered that these institutions also were controlled by men and that they enforced male dominance. As the women's movement has constantly asserted, women cannot fight as individuals if they want to overcome the forces that oppress them as a group.

Nevertheless, asking for support runs counter to the individualism inherent in the educational system. Schools hold out the promise of upward mobility based on individual merit. Just as the "apolitical" woman viewed her prior academic success as a personal achievement, so now she was determined to continue to "make it" on her own. Moreover, she considered it inappropriate to ask others for help because she was fighting to rectify a personal injustice, not to further a cause. One woman explained how perceiving her case in highly individualistic terms inhibited her from seeking support from other women:

> My case was primarily personal and I suppose that might account for why it wasn't easy or necessary for me to feel that I should go out and find other people to give me money or to support it. Wives of friends [who taught at a nearby university] said, "let us know if there's anything we can do," and I found that sort of embarrassing. To ask somebody for help is a rather personally involving thing. I would have been in the position of saying to people, "take me on as your case."

She could not ask for assistance, then, because she did not believe her case had implications for others.

In addition, the primary loyalty of the apolitical woman was to the university, not the women's movement. Thus, she sought to placate the colleagues whom the protest might have offended and carefully avoided any connection with organizations that might be considered radical. One woman considered approaching the American Civil Liberties Union or NOW but then decided it would be unwise to consult "any of those propaganda groups." A second woman stated:

> I didn't connect myself with groups like NOW or something simply because this college doesn't like publicity, they do not like being hounded by groups. I wanted to protest, but I wanted to do it in the most civilized, quiet way that I could, meaning maintaining everyone's dignity if possible.

As this quotation illustrates, it was extremely important to many women to retain images of themselves as professionals; they regarded any form of collective activity as unbecoming to a faculty member. One woman explained why she did not discuss her case with students or colleagues: "I wanted very much to be completely professional these last weeks of school." Thus, these women sought to present themselves as embodying an ideal toward which others could aspire; they did not wish to work as one among a group of equals. When asked about her association with the women's movement, a woman responded:

> I considered myself one of the people who was helping the women's movement in the best way I knew how which was doing my work, teaching, publishing, simply by being the first woman at this university, but I wasn't doing it by being a banner waver.

Occasionally, the less political women rejected the few offers of help that were forthcoming, but several expressed bitterness about the isolation they had experienced once they filed complaints. When they had been most in need of friendship and affirmation, no women had come forward. Although they did not actively seek to organize support, they were hurt when others did not rally around them.

The more political women generally were determined that their protests not remain isolated events. Viewing their grievances as social in origin, not individual, they looked to group action for a remedy. Moreover, many of these women were accustomed to operating within collective contexts and had a strong sense of solidarity with others. One woman described herself as someone who "goes from group to group, taking care never to be isolated." She used her own experience to make the point that all support must be solicited actively: "I worked for my support, I earned it....I put myself on the line for a lot of people. I defended people when I did not have tenure and I took strong stands. So I didn't just come forward saying, support me because I've been treated badly....I did a lot for other people and in return I got support."

Like the less political grievants, they spoke of the anxiety they experienced when they had to ask others for help or when their cases formed the focuses for fund-raising activities. However, they coped with such anxiety by recognizing that it had a social base, just like the adverse decisions by their departments. Thus, one woman recalled the rallies organized on her behalf as initially painful: "As women, we are not socialized to be the center of our own rallies. I had to learn to say what was true about myself, even if it sounded like boasting."

These women were strongly motivated by the goal of politicizing other women on campus. One said she was "gratified" when some of her colleagues "started a Title VII fund" and used it "as a focal point for general organizing of other women." A second noted with pleasure that the women who helped her collect data "turned into conscious feminists." In a third instance, women faculty organized discussion groups in which they examined "the familiar but largely unexplored words like 'merit' and 'excellence.'" Thus, a primary function of these cases was to furnish a catalyst for the formation of new groups on campus.

Nevertheless, even the more political grievants were not very successful in securing support from other women. Many did speak gratefully of the activities of their former students and of secretaries. In a few instances, the interviewees were helped and sustained by the efforts of other women faculty. The following comment is representative: "Many of the people—some at the college and some who have left the college—have turned out to be just amazingly supportive, at the risk of their own careers, and that has made all the difference to me." However, such testimonials were relatively rare. Although women often mildly protested the injustice that had occurred, they generally stopped short of offering such help as providing financial assistance, speaking to administrators and other faculty members on the grievants' behalf, soliciting off-campus support, or furnishing necessary information.

Of course, in no case were there many women in a position to supply assistance. One interviewee was the first female professor at her university. Others were part of the small numbers of women in predominantly male faculties. It is easy to understand why nontenured women might be reluctant to support a colleague who alleges sex discrimination; as the job crisis intensifies, many junior faculty refrain from taking action that could jeopardize their careers. From the security of their tenured jobs, senior faculty women have less to fear from championing the cause of aggrieved sisters. Nevertheless, these women have the greatest stake in maintaining the belief in the meritocracy. Even if they owe their positions to pressure from the women's movement, they often perceive themselves as uniquely deserving. Thus, they view women who file sex discrimination charges as failures in the academic race, rather than as victims of a biased selection system.[37] In sum, the very factors that inhibited many interviewees from acknowledging sexism at their own universities or subsequently organizing support networks operated to deter other women from rallying around them.

The failure of most of the grievants to elicit support from their female colleagues can be explained in other ways as well. Grievants who had held only short-term temporary appointments had had no opportunity to develop collegial relations with other faculty members. Those few interviewees who did succeed in mobilizing others when they first filed grievances found this support slowly waning as their cases dragged on. Many of their supporters left the university when their own appointments ended, or they found employment elsewhere. Others lost interest in the cases as they slowly meandered through the labyrinth of government agencies and courts without producing any perceptible results.

When the grievants turned to off-campus groups and individuals, they were even less successful in generating support:

> I wrote to a large number of women off campus and only heard from one. This one woman was very nice, she sent about $10. But that was it. I wrote to about thirty women's groups, including women's caucuses and women's professional groups, and to the unions—AFT, NEA, and AAUP —and I didn't hear from any of them.

Two women did report that the Women's Equity Action League had provided some assistance in raising funds, and another stated that this association would write an amicus brief when her case went to trial.[38] In general, however, whatever support comes from outside sources tends to be sporadic and unorganized.

A few women did manage to wage a collective fight by filing their complaints together. One woman asserted that "we all became stronger working with each other." In addition, they were able to aggregate their financial resources, collaborate in the work of accumulating data, and share a lawyer. They were also less vulnerable to harassment and reprisals: "Nobody has been a martyr. There are just too many of us to try to pick off, and if someone did try, the pattern would be very clear." Moreover, group action permitted women to broaden the scope of their protest:

> Our suit is massive....It differs from the kind of case where only one person comes forward with a grievance. We are attacking many different causes—election of chairpeople, who's eligible to vote for the chairperson, initial appointment, rank, pensions, maternity benefits. We can cover so many areas, we're really moving to change the system.

These women, then, represented an important exception to the portrait of the isolated Title VII litigant. But few fought as a group.[39] For most, protesting sex discrimination in academia remained a lonely pursuit.

Costs

Women typically found themselves subjected to ridicule and disparagement as soon as their cases became public knowledge.[40] Many were surprised by the rapidity with which rumors began to circulate, discrediting them as scholars, teachers, and colleagues. One woman was known as "the crazy lady on campus," a second as "a liar and hysterical," and a third as "a bitch, a terrible woman, all-powerful, evil, and wicked." Others simply described themselves as "tainted." One woman described the way such charges affected her:

> I have begun to wonder: if six or seven or ten male people in my department say that I am this kind of person, is it possible that I really am? When they say that I said or did something which I do not believe I said or did but they all agree, is it possible I did? The self-doubt is enormous and you begin to think you're probably crazy.

But retaliation also took more serious forms.[41] A number of women cited instances of blacklisting. One woman heard reports that she "was being smeared." Another stated:

I applied for jobs for many years without getting any and I had indications that I was blacklisted. For example, people told me that they couldn't get me through their administrations because I was a troublemaker.

The clearest indication of this was when I went to a university for an interview and I gave a seminar talk and it all went very well, and the chairman walked me back to my hotel and he said to me, "Well, I'm certainly glad to meet you, I really pictured you with claws."

Why do women elicit such extreme hostility and retaliation when they complain about sex discrimination? One reason is undoubtedly that women traditionally have been punished for stepping out of line, and these women were deviating from prescribed conduct in two ways: they were demonstrating serious professional commitment, and they were confronting men in positions of power. As one woman recalled, "It was as if I had done the unthinkable. I had clearly transgressed." Moreover, it is definitely in the interest of the men on campus to deflect the charge from the institution by blaming the individual, proving that she is clearly unworthy of the job or promotion she is claiming; they insist that discrimination never occurs in the university. Some male administrators may also have feelings of guilt which they allay by exaggerating or even manufacturing faults of the plaintiffs. Specific instances of retaliation must also be viewed within the broader context of the backlash in academia, which takes such forms as resistance to mandatory affirmative action and charges of reverse discrimination.[42] But the frequency and extent of the reprisals also serve to remind us just how threatening these cases are to the members of university communities. Any complaint of bias challenges fundamental assumptions about the objectivity of the educational selection system. Indeed, as we have seen, some of the grievants themselves stopped short of recognizing that sexist behavior pervades academia.

There are a number of other costs entailed in filing a sex discrimination charge against an institution of higher education. Almost all the women spoke of the enormous amounts of time and money required and of the strains on both themselves and their personal relationships. Each step took much longer than the complainant originally anticipated, and years often elapsed between the initial filing of a grievance and the final resolution of a case.[43] Much of this slowness can be explained by factors previously discussed: the inefficiency and inertia of government bureaucracies and the accumulated backlog of EEOC in particular. But a persistent complaint was that the university purposely had tried to delay the proceedings in the hope that the plaintiff would grow discouraged and give up.[44] The deliberations of campus grievance committees occasionally dragged on for months without any resolution. Once cases went beyond the confines of the university, employers resorted to such delaying tactics as refusing to relinquish critical documents or requesting endless postponements of hearings.

Women also complained about the amount of time they had to spend preparing for trial. One litigant who was coordinating a large class action reported:

I have lost almost entirely any personal life. If I were married or if I had children or if I had any personal obligations, I couldn't do what I do. It's only possible because I'm single and my only obligation is to a cat. There are times when I work literally day and night, six and seven days a week.

More frequently, women spoke about the incursions on their work time. They often measured the amount of time spent on the case in terms of scholarship they might have produced. To two women, legal action represented lost articles; two others equated their cases with books. Nevertheless, it would be wrong to overstate the costs to these women of investing so many hours preparing their cases for trial. As a few of the interviewees noted, the ability to arrange their work schedules and to allocate time to court cases was one of the substantial privileges they enjoyed as members of the middle class.

The financial costs for women who undertook litigation were "unending and staggering." Although lawyers typically were paid on contingent fee bases, other costs mounted rapidly. One group involved in a massive class action against a major university spent $20,000 a year exclusive of attorneys' fees. A woman fighting an individual lawsuit estimated that she spent $7,000 for duplicating, depositions, computer time, and statistical analysis during the pretrial period. Some women noted that their ability to pay legal costs was a "luxury" made possible by a spouse's earnings or by savings. But it is important to note that the greater resources the employers could muster totally dwarfed the advantages of these litigants as middle-class women. The individual grievants were pitted against institutions that easily could spend huge sums of money fighting the allegation of sex discrimination.[45]

Finally, there are subjective costs of fighting a university.[46] A number of women spoke of "becoming the case," as they invested so much time and energy in it: "Your sense of who and what you are becomes eroded." A few also described physical ailments that they attributed to the tension of litigation. One discovered that she had become so anxious that her handwriting had altered.[47] Protest also takes its toll on personal relationships. The great majority of women spoke of the critical support they had received from their partners: "If there is one hero in the case it is my husband," said one. But they also acknowledged that they found themselves venting their rage and frustration on the people closest to them.

Gains

Despite the many costs of protest, most of the interviewees claimed they were glad they had decided to assert their rights. They pointed to the substantial gains their protest had achieved for other women. Although it is clearly impossible to measure precisely the impact of a particular case on the position of women faculty on that campus, the grievants frequently were convinced that their struggles had been responsible for major improvements in the position of other women.[48] In some instances, they pointed to an increase in the number of women who were appointed or promoted. One woman contended:

Because I went to court, things changed on that campus, even though I lost. They've become more careful. Women were promoted and their salaries were raised. I know that where I am now my department was famous for being abominable to women and many people suffered but I felt absolutely none of that because I came after someone else had sued the college. So I think things are changing and that we're changing them for each other.

New policies and practices also were adopted:

> Because of my questioning of things, there have already been many changes in the tenure process. There have been new procedures established for promotion and tenure.

> I'm sure that Title VII changes an institution even if women lose the case.... At the very least, this university knows that it can't just do anything it wants, that it is accountable. The university knows that it has to watch itself, that its power is limited, that there are definite constraints.

Ironically, then, despite the individualistic nature of the cases, institutional changes often resulted, and the individual complainants were led to assess their cases in collectivist terms.

There were also benefits for the claimants themselves. For one thing, during the course of their protests, most of the women acquired information that previously had been withheld, and thus they understood exactly why they had been denied promotions. In many instances, they were permitted to see their personnel files for the first time. Two women discovered that negative evaluations of their work had been solicited, another that positive letters of recommendation had been removed from her file, and still another that the letters on file had all been written by friends of the male colleague who was her competitor for the one tenured position in her department. Others were heartened to learn that the letters from outside referees were better than they had been led to believe:

> I had been told that the letters were marginal and that was one reason why I couldn't get tenure. But they had lied. I had to fight to see the letters, and when I finally did, I found that they were very good; in fact, they were embarrassingly good.

Some women also gained access to correspondence between department members. As a result, one woman learned that her family responsibilities had been used to justify her department's continual refusal to promote her. The revelations of another were far more dramatic:

> My lawyer asked if there was any private correspondence dealing with the case....The judge finally ruled on this and people had to divulge this. Of course there was a lot of faculty resistance and the chairman grumbled about the time it took. But through that I got hold of a set of letters from the chairman and the person who is not chairman with very good comments, nasty, sexist comments about me. It was terrific evidence. There had been a conspiracy between these two men to get me denied tenure on the basis of incredibly personalistic and sexist criteria. There was a lot of machinations back and forth.

Thus, the information acquired often removed any lingering suspicions that lack of advancement resulted from personal inadequacies.

In addition, university procedures were demystified:

> We forced the university to open up their confidential files,...and now we know what a dreadful shape these files are in. We know now that academic judgment is all too often a cover....There is no way you could make an academic judgment in large numbers of files we saw. It's done with whispers and in deals.

Another woman deepened her understanding of the meaning of sexism:

> I just didn't realize the dimensions of discrimination, and the connection between discrimination and power....The lawsuit has given me a chance to step back and look at my culture as though from the outside. It's been difficult to do because it's like looking at the air. I've had these moments when suddenly the air has color and I can see it. I have found out that sex discrimination permeates just

everything and that it has so many more dimensions than
I thought it did.

When the grievants had to decide how to make use of this
information, they divided along familiar lines. The more political
women were committed to sharing the information as broadly as
possible. As we have seen, they regarded the education of others as
a crucial aspect of their protest. In many instances, their lawyers
advised them to refrain from writing or speaking publicly about
the development of their cases. Nevertheless, they publicized their
cases as much as they could and encouraged other women to
attend any hearings that were conducted. To the "apolitical"
women, however, publicity had a more limited value. Less concerned about politicizing others, they spoke about publicity as a
"weapon" they could employ only strategically. Thus, one woman
agreed with a university request that the grievance committee
hearing be closed. She then informed university officials that she
intended to issue a press release if she did not obtain satisfaction at
this level: "I think that the university settled because of their fear
of publicity. This was my trump card." When a second grievant
gave her letter of determination from EEOC to university officials,
she agreed to avoid publicity if the university acted quickly in
accordance with the agency's findings. Her decided preference
was to refrain from "making a fuss out of my case. I didn't want a
turmoil in the newspapers. I did not want the university to be
publicly charged with discrimination."

When interviewees testified that the gains of protest out-
weighed the costs, they referred above all to their heightened
self-respect. Despite the charges that had been leveled against
them at various times, they gained a sense of their own power as a
result of fighting on their own behalf. A number of women who
had never before challenged injustice expressed pride in their
newfound ability to assert their rights. One stated: "This case has
made a fighter out of me. Now I make trouble when I find myself
abused." Others described their growth in self-confidence, for
example:

I know I'm a lot stronger now. People out there can no
longer define me. I think women have been defined so
long by roles, by husbands, by parents, by society, by other

women often. I think this case has freed me from a lot of that. It's almost intangible, but I have a sense of who I am. There's just some core that I recognize and know and no one can touch me at that core. They can't knock it down. They can't crumble it.

ORGANIZING A TRANSIENT LABOR FORCE

Service professionals find themselves in an ambiguous position. Although they act as agents of social control, they simultaneously are subordinated to bureaucratic authority.[49] University and college faculty issue instructions to students and evaluate their performance, but, even inside the classroom, their autonomy is circumscribed severely by rules imposed by administrators. As many of the privileges separating professionals from other workers were eroded during the 1970s, increasing numbers were willing to abandon their traditional self-image and engage in organized action.[50] Although the percentage of the entire work force that belonged to unions plunged during the late sixties and early seventies, the proportion of professionals represented by unions climbed. The number of colleges and universities with collective bargaining contracts tripled between 1970 and 1978.[51] By 1979, one-quarter of all faculty in institutions of higher education were union members.[52]

Because this process of proletarianization has proceeded at a different pace in different types of institutions, instructors have not joined unions at uniform rates. With respect to both status and social relations, community college teachers resemble secondary school teachers more closely than professors at elite institutions. Moreover, retrenchment in higher education has disproportionately affected faculty in the lower tiers. The size of their classes has swollen most drastically and their security of employment been jeopardized most severely. In addition, because administrators have responded to budget crises by seeking to "rationalize" their institutions, they have encroached on much of the remaining autonomy of instructors. Teachers in these schools have lost control over the subjects they teach, the shape of the curriculum, and the appointment process.[53] Not surprisingly, these faculty members have tended to join unions in greater numbers than their counterparts at elite institutions.[54]

But if the contradiction is propelling academics into unions, it also is forcing them to cling to the remnants of professional status. At many institutions, the majority of instructors continue to view unionization as inappropriate and unbecoming; they hope to advance by demonstrating individual merit, not through collective action. Moreover, workers in the United States historically have unionized in order to stratify the labor force, not to unify it. Even many faculty members who join unions fail to recognize the congruence of their interests with those of clerical and blue-collar workers within their schools. They see unionization as a means of retaining accustomed privileges, rather than of enhancing the well-being of the work force as a whole. Thus, they serve the interests of management by aggravating the fragmentation of staff and discouraging collective consciousness and action.

Few academics seek to erase the divisions within the faculty ranks. Only a minority of union members have challenged the hierarchical arrangement of higher education by organizing faculty members across the range of institutions. Nor have tenure-track faculty used unionization to overcome the fissure separating them from teachers in the nonladder positions. Thus, although part-timers are concentrated in institutions in which faculty unions predominate and are especially aggrieved about their conditions of employment, they have failed to reap significant rewards from the growth of academic unions.

Obstacles

Many full-time faculty attribute the failure of part-timers to benefit from unionization to the difficulties of organizing them. Part-time teachers are a fragmented work force, with a high rate of turnover. Some are fearful of speaking out because they lack job security. Others are reluctant to devote any efforts to improving jobs they perceive as temporary. At the end of each semester, a high percentage of union supporters simply disappear from campus. Moreover, the great majority of adjuncts hold other full-time or part-time jobs, and they cannot become deeply involved in union activity at each place they work. Dues also may be prohibitive for those who commute between several institutions. Indeed, the whole concept of separate "locals" is inappropriate for itinerant academics.

Part-timers also lack any sense of group identity. Whereas full-time faculty teach at similar hours, serve on the same committees, and work in neighboring offices, adjuncts rarely interact. Some do not have any space in which to meet each other. Even those assigned to the same offices tend to teach on different days or at different hours. Thus, they do not share experiences and resentments, an exchange that might promote the development of a collective consciousness. Opposing needs and expectations also divide part-time teachers. As the survey of lecturers in the California State University and Colleges system demonstrated, relatively few part-timers in vocational fields aspire to full-time positions. A majority of their counterparts in the humanities, however, yearn for regular academic careers. Framing policies that speak to the concerns of both groups may be virtually impossible.

Finally, a number of practical problems impede the process of organizing. Because administrators rarely release adequate information about their part-time staffs, organizing campaigns must begin with the onerous task of compiling accurate lists of names, home addresses, and phone numbers. On campuses where part-time faculty lack both offices and mailboxes, union organizers cannot easily communicate with those they hope to enlist. They also must make separate trips to contact one or two individuals because adjuncts generally stay at school just long enough to teach, and they often are scattered among several off-campus sites.

Response of Faculty Unions

These obstacles are compounded by the ambivalence of the major academic unions toward part-time faculty. Even if adjuncts enjoyed the full support of faculty unions, they still might be sparsely represented in them. However, because unions have offered few enticements to part-timers, it is premature to conclude that this sector of the teaching force is unorganizable.[55]

The rapid growth of part-time faculty placed conflicting demands on academic unions. They have been under pressure simultaneously to seek to restrict the use of adjuncts, improve their conditions of employment, and protect the advantages of tenure-track professors. The first goal is partly a response to the fear of unions that the proliferation of a cheap, transient work force can erode the gains from collective bargaining.[56] In 1976, the National Education Association (NEA) branded part-timers a "corps of unregulated personnel."[57] The American Federation of Teachers (AFT) concurred in this assessment, characterizing part-time faculty as a "reserve army of unorganized, noncontract teachers [who] can destroy the rights and prerogatives which faculty have fought for and have gained through collective bargaining."[58]

In addition, the widespread use of part-time faculty undermines the position of full-time faculty. Because many part-timers rarely advise students or perform departmental duties, additional burdens fall on tenure-track faculty. More seriously, their autonomy is reduced. Delegated responsibility for hiring and firing part-time staffs, some department chairs are elevated to the ranks of management.[59] But most full-timers lose control over the educational process because they cannot enforce decisions about academic standards or curriculum over teachers with whom they interact rarely, if ever.[60] In any dual labor market, employers are under pressure to replace their more expensive employees with cheap labor.[61] From the security of their tenured jobs, senior professors have little to fear, but some junior faculty worry they will be denied tenure by administrators who seek to cut labor costs by converting ladder positions into several part-time slots.

The policy of many unions also is guided by a desire to improve the status of part-timers. One means of stemming the rise in the number of these teachers is to reduce the benefits they provide administrators. If adjuncts gained pro-rata pay and job security, administrators would have little incentive to continue employing them. Strategic considerations also are important. Part-timers who have joined a union pose less of a threat than those who remain outside. On some campuses, the votes of part-time teachers have been critical in collective bargaining elections, and competing unions have courted their support by addressing their concerns. Finally, principles of trade unionism demand that unions espouse the cause of the most exploited workers.

But, though some forces spur unions to articulate the grievances of part-time instructors, still stronger pressures compel them to promote the interests of full-timers alone. Most full-time faculty set themselves apart from adjuncts and accentuate the gap between the two sectors of the teaching force. They draw a clear distinction between the "real professionals" and the substratum of part-time teachers whom they, like the administration, character-ize as unqualified, uncommitted, and unconcerned about the well-being of the school.[62] At a time when regular academics are acutely aware of their own declining status, they may take comfort in creating greater distance between themselves and part-time faculty. Thus, just as early craft workers violated the principle of labor solidarity by seeking to defend their privileges vis-à-vis unskilled workers, so full-time teachers resist efforts to equalize the conditions of the two groups of faculty and refuse to promote adjuncts to tenure-track positions.

Self-interest reinforces protectionist attitudes. During a per-iod of contraction, full-timers and part-timers assume they are competing for dwindling resources. Although some full-time faculty believe the low pay of adjuncts depresses their wages as well, others are convinced that their own relatively high salaries depend on the use of a large corps of cheap labor. Even those tenure-track professors who endorse the principle of pro-rata compensation are determined that part-timers not receive the major share of scarce salary increases.

Full-timers also are unwilling to relinquish the benefits they derive from the growing force of part-time help. Although some full-time teachers stress the disadvantages of employing part-timers, all profit to some degree from the use of this underclass. Adjuncts teach the classes their tenure-track colleagues do not want; they are assigned the least popular hours, the least attractive classrooms, and the most elementary subject matters. Thus, whereas many part-timers seek greater control over the selection of courses, full-timers are determined to reserve preferred assign-ments for themselves. Job security is a more serious source of contention. We have seen that the paramount concern of part-time faculty is their lack of security. But tenure-track faculty regard part-timers as their buffer against unemployment; as long as adjuncts are considered temporary workers, they will be dis-missed first during retrenchment.[63]

Academic unions have responded to these conflicting pres-sures in various ways. Although both NEA and AFT now support the principle of proportional compensation for part-timers,[64] individual locals are autonomous, and many disregard the official policy of the national organization with which they are affiliated. Some local unions continue to believe that the best defense against the threat posed by part-timers is to exclude them from membership and fail to address their needs. The policy even of unions that do encourage their participation can be described as tokenism. Many of their part-time members see themselves as engaged in two fights—one against the administration and the other against the union leadership.

California: A Case Study

The history of United Professors of California (UPC), an affiliate of AFT, demonstrates that a union controlled by full-time faculty can secure significant, but limited, benefits for part-timers.[65] Established in 1970, this union sought to become the exclusive faculty representative in the California State University and College system during the academic year 1981-82. As soon as it was founded, it demonstrated its distinctive commitment to part-time faculty. It welcomed them to membership and formed a committee on part-timers, consisting of representatives from each of the nineteen campuses.[66] In 1977, members of this committee wrote a handbook for part-time faculty, analyzing their role in higher education and demystifying many aspects of their employment situation.[67] The committee also facilitated the formation of grass-roots associations on several campuses. A particularly active group of part-time lecturers taught at San Francisco State, where they acquired leadership positions in the union local. When the paychecks of part-timers were delayed in the fall of 1980, this local filed an application for a writ of mandate in order to compel the university to pay salaries promptly.

Activists within this committee also pressed the union to address the concerns of adjunct faculty. Partly as a result, UPC publicized the conditions of part-time academic employment, campaigned for legislation to ameliorate the status of adjuncts, and helped them both file grievances and collect unemployment compensation. Shortly after college professors in California won the right to bargain collectively, UPC advocated that all faculty, regardless of class load or eligibility for tenure, be included in a single bargaining unit.[68] During the election campaign, the union endorsed the principle of parity pay and job security for part-timers and devoted special efforts to recruiting them.

Nevertheless, the solicitude of UPC for part-timers should not be exaggerated. Its insistence that adjuncts be included in the unit may have resulted from tactical as well as principled considerations. Because this union had taken the lead in organizing temporary faculty, it stood to benefit from a comprehensive unit.[69] Moreover, despite the official position of the union, many tenure-track members remained disdainful of part-time faculty and referred to them in condescending terms. Activists within the part-time committee frequently complained of the union's paternalistic attitude toward them. They were informed of the actions taken on their behalf, not invited to help define union priorities. Furthermore, the union focused on issues that were irrelevant to part-timers. Finally, part-time lecturers lacked representation in the union leadership. Although the president of the committee on part-timers had a seat on the executive board, no part-timer ever was elected to the state council, which was charged with establishing official policy. Tenure-track faculty monopolized leadership positions at the local level everywhere but San Francisco. Thus, part-timers were marginalized even within one of the few unions that tried to act as their champion.

Many tenure-track members of UPC ascribed the exclusion of part-timers from leadership positions to their low level of membership.[70] But part-timers responded that some union leaders appeared ambivalent about enlisting them. The argument could be made that a union with a firm commitment to representing part-time faculty would devote the bulk of its resources to recruiting these teachers because they are the most difficult to organize. But, even during the election campaign, UPC concentrated on tenure-track faculty. Furthermore, adjuncts understandably were reluctant to join an association they saw as insensitive to their needs.

Because UPC lost the election, it is impossible to know how forcefully this union would have supported the demands of part-time lecturers during contract negotiations. Nevertheless, by the end of the campaign, even some of the most devoted part-time union members had become skeptical that a UPC victory significantly would improve their status.

Defining the Unit

Another reason part-time faculty have reaped few benefits from collective bargaining is that they are excluded from the bargaining units of many campuses. The National Labor Relations Board (NLRB) first ruled on the issue of unit determination shortly after it assumed jurisdiction over private colleges and universities in 1970. Applying industrial precedents, the board held that workers should be included in a single bargaining unit if they shared a community of interest.[71] In a case involving C. W. Post of Long Island University, the board decided that part-time and full-time faculty belonged in the same unit because they had similar qualifications and performed similar duties. Although part-timers lacked tenure, sabbatical leaves, fringe benefits, and votes in academic governance, the chief function of both groups was teaching, and in this area their tasks were virtually identical.[72] In the case of the University of New Haven, the board again found a community of interest justifying the inclusion of both sectors of the faculty in a single unit; part-timers who were teaching at least one-fourth of a full-time load or had done so at least one semester each year for two of the previous three years should be included.[73]

However, in 1973, the board reversed itself in a landmark case involving New York University. Placing diminished weight on teaching, the board found that part-time and full-time faculty did not share a community of interest because of differences in compensation, university governance, eligibility for tenure, and working conditions. In addition, the board asserted, part-timers did not rely on their salaries from teaching.[74] The NLRB has continued to rule in favor of excluding part-timers in most subsequent cases.[75]

State labor boards have jurisdiction over collective bargaining in public institutions. Although they often cite decisions by the NLRB, they are not bound by them, and there is wide variation among the states on the issue of unit determination.[76] In general, however, state boards have tended to be more disposed to form comprehensive units.[77] In some instances, part-timers have been included if they have taught for a specified number of years. For example, in a case involving the Los Rios Community College

District, the Public Employment Relations Board in California ruled that part-timers should be members of the unit if they had taught at least three of the previous six semesters.[78] In 1976, the Massachusetts Labor Relations Commission decided that part-time faculty who had taught at least one course for three consecutive semesters should be included in the bargaining unit of the University of Massachusetts.[79] In other cases, the inclusion of part-timers has been made contingent on their teaching loads. The state labor board of Connecticut found that the appropriate unit at state technical colleges consisted of full-time faculty and those adjuncts who taught at least half time.[80] In still other cases, all part-timers have been brought within the bargaining unit. For example, in 1981, the Public Employment Relations Board in California placed all part-time lecturers in the same unit as the full-time faculty of the California State University and Colleges system.[81]

Bargaining on Their Own

Exclusion from a full-time unit does not automatically signal the end of collective bargaining for part-time faculty. The history of the unit of part-time and visiting lecturers at the Community College of Philadelphia (CCP) illustrates what is possible, even when confronting an intractable administration. Part-timers increased rapidly at this school, as they did at many community colleges during the 1970s, growing from 85 at the beginning of the decade to 600 in 1980, when they constituted two-thirds of the entire faculty. In addition, 45 visiting lecturers taught full-time on temporary contracts, many for several years in succession. Conditions for part-timers mirrored those of adjuncts at other two-year institutions. They earned about one-third as much as full-time faculty for teaching a course and lacked fringe benefits, sick leave, job security, and a grievance procedure. Visiting lecturers received the same salary as other full-time teachers but were denied benefits and job protection. As their job title indicated, they were considered short-term faculty members, regardless of their length of service.[82]

Part-timers and visiting lecturers began to organize during the mid-1970s and joined the full-time faculty union, AFT Local 2606 in 1975. Three years later, the Pennsylvania Labor Relations

Board ruled that, although these instructors could not be included in the same bargaining unit as tenure-track faculty, they did have the right to constitute a separate unit and bargain collectively. The administration fought for six years to overturn the certification of the part-time and visiting lecturer unit. It appealed first to the Court of Common Pleas. When this court affirmed the decision of the Labor Relations Board, the college appealed again. Nevertheless, the case could not be scheduled in the Commonwealth Court because the judge in the Court of Common Pleas delayed writing his decision. Convinced that the judge had been pressured by the college administration to postpone delivering his written opinion, the part-timers and visiting lecturers went on strike in March 1981, demanding both that their working conditions be improved and that the college cease stalling. As part of the strike settlement, the college agreed to use its good offices to convince the judge to write his opinion and to expedite proceedings at the next two levels. In June, the Commonwealth Court declared that the two groups of temporary faculty did constitute a legal bargaining unit. The case was then appealed to the State Supreme Court, which affirmed the decision below.[83]

The process of negotiating a contract was equally problematic. Bargaining began in March 1982, but, after four months, virtually no progress had been made. A mediator appointed in the summer declared the situation hopeless. Recognizing that negotiations were at an impasse, the Pennsylvania Labor Relations Board imposed "fact-finding" in September; according to state law, the fact-finder studies the issues in a labor dispute and then recommends terms for an agreement. When the fact-finder's report was issued in March 1983, the union accepted many of the recommendations; the college rejected the report in its entirety. Shortly afterwards, the union called for a strike. The college administration expressed a willingness to compromise after part-timers and visiting lecturers had virtually shut down the school for a week.[84]

This struggle is remarkable because a group of marginal teachers forced a college to negotiate with them, not because of the terms of the contract. The principal winners were the eighteen visiting lecturers who had taught at the college more than five years and were awarded tenure-track positions. Others were less fortunate. Part-timers and visiting lecturers employed more recently received a 16 percent pay increase, a few fringe benefits, and seniority rights, but they failed to secure their chief demand of job security.[85] Moreover, visiting lecturers who were not promoted to the tenure track felt even more exposed than before. Many feared they would be fired before they reached the five-year mark. Nevertheless, by the summer of 1983, it was clear that the part-timers and visiting lecturers at CCP were a force to be reckoned with.[86]

A number of factors may explain the ability of the union to wage a protracted struggle and to exact concessions from the administration. Most significantly, part-timers were not fighting alone. Because they were members of the same union as full-time faculty, they received not only secretarial and financial assistance but also important political support from their tenure-track colleagues. No matter how fearful the latter might have been of the consequences of a victory by adjuncts, they did not feel they could abandon their union brethren. The intransigence of the administration also may have heightened the willingness of the more secure teachers to come to the aid of the dispossessed. The refusal of the administration to accept any of the fact-finder's recommendations particularly outraged the full-timers. Moreover, it was clear that all faculty members at the college faced a common enemy. The full-timers, too, had never been able to negotiate a contract without a strike. Abiding by the no-strike clause in their contract, the full-timers refused to join the part-timers and visiting lecturers on the picket line. Most, however, remained away from school during the course of the strike.[87]

The role of the visiting lecturers also was critical. The struggle at CCP required people willing to sustain their commitment for more than seven years despite continuous discouragement. By 1983, several visiting lecturers had taught at the college between five and ten years and thus had an enormous stake in the outcome of the fight. Employed on a full-time basis, they tended to be more involved in campus affairs than part-timers; none had other sources of income or competing professional interests. A number of the most dedicated union leaders and loyal supporters were drawn from the ranks of the visiting lecturers. Finally, the union solicited, and received, assistance from the broader labor community. Local trade unions honored the picket lines and spoke to members of the city council on behalf of the part-timers and visiting lecturers.[88]

Although the victory at CCP has inspired groups of marginal academics throughout the country, it remains the exception. In most instances, part-time faculty excluded from bargaining units of full-time teachers have failed to pursue collective bargaining.

Depending on Full-timers

Nevertheless, even their inclusion in the regular faculty unit guarantees little to adjunct faculty. According to a study conducted by David W. Leslie and D. Jane Ikenberry, agreements negotiated by unions provide only incremental improvements. Although some contracts sampled by these authors instituted regularized procedures for both the hiring and firing of adjuncts, they did not provide true job security; virtually none entitled part-timers to apply for tenure or protected them from being bumped by tenure-track professors. A number of contracts did grant part-timers the right to grievance procedures, but Leslie and Ikenberry doubted this right was invoked with any frequency. As they pointed out, employees who lack job security tend to be reluctant to file grievances; moreover, unions often are reluctant to furnish grievance advisers to temporary workers. Those agreements that entitled adjuncts to any fringe benefits generally restricted the benefits for which they could apply or provided coverage only for that minority of part-timers who taught more than half time.[89]

It should be noted that the few victories won by part-time faculty are precisely the concessions tenure-track faculty could afford to grant. Neither seniority nor grievance rights undermined the privileged status of full-time teachers. At all campuses, part-timers continued to serve as the cushion between tenure-track professors and unemployment. Pro-rated salary and access to fringe benefits were the only provisions that could compromise the interests of full-timers. However, the great majority of adjuncts gained neither.

But the fact that the concessions to part-timers have been meager cannot be attributed solely to the antagonism of their full-time colleagues. Administrators may respond differently to the demands of part-time and tenure-track faculty. By improving the conditions of full-timers, administrators can enhance their loyalty and commitment. But there are few incentives for acceding to the demands of part-timers. If adjuncts obtained job security, pro-rata pay, and fringe benefits, their value to administrators would evaporate. Moreover, the low status and salaries of part-timers serve to promote the high rate of turnover many administrators wish to encourage. Finally, should part-timers succeed in equalizing the conditions of the two segments of the faculty, divisions between the groups might vanish and the potential for collective action might be heightened.

Nevertheless, the ambivalence of academic unions toward the demands of part-timers also may explain why most contracts have failed to raise their status. Leslie and Ikenberry concluded, "The union tends to see itself as the guardian of the vested interest of full-time faculty....The union may be willing to trade away [part-timers'] interests for more security, higher wages, and priority access to preferred assignments for full-timers."[90] Many part-timers suspect that, even when their concerns are included in the initial package of employee demands, they are treated as negotiable items.

The contract signed between the AFT College Guild and the Los Angeles Community College District in January 1978 illustrates these dynamics. The nine community colleges in Los Angeles constitute the largest community college district in the country.[91] In 1977, they enrolled 192,296 students and employed 7,046 faculty members.[92] Part-timers (known as "hourly instructors") were a majority of that faculty and were included in the bargaining unit. Thus, one might have expected them to attain many of their goals in contract negotiations. However, their actual achievements were minimal.[93]

Both the AFT College Guild and its rival, the Los Angeles Classroom Teachers Association, had focused their energies on full-time faculty prior to the election. Although both had accepted part-timers as members, they had refrained from involving and mobilizing them. Nevertheless, each devoted special efforts during the campaign to winning their allegiance. Hourly instructors, who previously had complained of being ignored by both unions, suddenly found themselves wooed by two organizations promising to get them equal pay, fringe benefits, professional status, and access to tenure.[94]

Because AFT won the election, it is important to concentrate on its campaign. A small group of part-timers coordinated the campaign mounted by AFT to attract hourly instructors. Despite their commitment to AFT, however, these activists doubted that any union dominated by full-time faculty could adequately represent the interests of part-timers. Their campaign strategy revealed their wariness. One of their first decisions was to phone each hourly teacher at home. Because the administration refused to release the telephone numbers of hourly instructors, this tactic required them to look up the numbers of over 3,000 individuals scattered throughout the entire Los Angeles basin. They undertook this arduous task for two reasons. First, the organizers realized that most adjuncts were convinced that the campaign was irrelevant to them; personal contact was necessary to convince them of their stake in the election. More significantly, the phone numbers would permit the creation of a caucus of part-time faculty within the union.

The actions of the leadership of the AFT College Guild following the election failed to allay the suspicions of these organizers. The day after the AFT victory was announced, they met with the executive secretary of the union to demand that four hourly instructors be included in the ten-person negotiating team. As they explained, such representation would be minimal recognition of their numerical strength in the bargaining unit and their role in determining the outcome of the election. True, a disproportionately small number of part-timers had voted at all, and a lower percentage of hourly instructors than of full-time faculty had cast their ballots for AFT. Nevertheless, the majority of part-timers had voted for AFT, and their support had been decisive.

The executive secretary refused their request. After expressing gratitude for the efforts of the part-timers during the campaign, she stated that the lower turnout of adjuncts at the polls demonstrated their relative indifference to collective bargaining. Moreover, she asserted, full-time faculty were sympathetic to the plight of their part-time colleagues and, on such issues as class size, the interests of the two groups were identical; thus, any faculty member could represent the concerns of the hourly instructors. Finally, union leaders had decided that the bargaining team should be representative of the different campuses, academic disciplines, genders, and ethnicities, not teaching loads. She told them that the team would include only one hourly instructor.

This decision strengthened the conviction of the part-timers that a caucus within the union was essential. One person could not defend the interests of the hourly instructors without the support of an ongoing organization. Unfortunately, however, most of the more active part-timers could not afford to invest further time in union work and thus failed to create such a group. A few weeks after the election, they did hold a series of open meetings to solicit input from other part-timers on contract demands. But they went no further. They neither kept hourly instructors informed of the progress of negotiations, nor did they provide them with a vehicle for influencing the outcome. Perhaps as a result, most members of the bargaining team felt free to disregard this sector of the teaching staff during negotiations.

The absence of an organized bloc of part-timers also exacerbates the problem of evaluating the final contract. The union hailed it as a victory for hourly instructors. Their major gain was a clause granting them rights to retention and security. As a result, hourly instructors no longer could be replaced by other part-timers or bumped by full-timers who preferred to teach that particular course. Whenever layoffs were necessary, hourly instructors were to be fired in order of least seniority. In short, the contract put an end to particularistic forms of control over hourly instructors and gave them a modicum of job security.

Nevertheless, the basic characteristics of part-time employment remained unchanged. Because hourly instructors did not organize, they could not easily disseminate their own response to the contract. However, it is highly likely that many would have wanted to challenge the official union position. The key demands of part-timers during the election had been pro-rata pay, fringe benefits, first class citizenship, and tenure. None was realized. Instead of parity pay, part-timers received an 8 percent cost of living increase, while the tenure-track faculty received 10 percent.[95] The contract failed to provide fringe benefits for hourly instructors or to address such status issues as access to secretarial assistance, office space, and the right to select textbooks. Furthermore, the retention and seniority rights were in no sense equivalent to tenure. Part-timers still would be fired first during any retrenchment.

The critical test for the contract came six months after it was signed. The passage of Proposition 13 in June 1978 affected community colleges throughout California almost immediately. About a third of their funding traditionally had been obtained from local property taxes, and, although state subsidies augmented their budgets, this did not prevent the cancellation of classes and the dismissal of instructors. The benefits of the seniority system were readily apparent. For the first time, the order of firing was determined by formal rules, not the decision of individual department chairs. Nevertheless, it was equally clear that the contract gave hourly instructors only minimal job protection. Although virtually all full-time faculty retained their jobs, large numbers of part-timers were fired. The surviving adjuncts also were not spared. Those who previously had taught two classes were assigned only one. Thus, many hourly instructors who had voted for the AFT College Guild in the hope of winning pro-rata pay either lost their jobs or received salary cuts of 50 percent.

Independent Adjunct Associations

Disenchanted with the unions on their campuses, some adjuncts have organized independent associations. Others have formed separate groups because they were denied membership in the existing unions or none was active at their schools. Occasionally these associations have survived for several years and secured significant benefits for their members.[96] But most separate associations of part-timers have been ephemeral. Without the protection and resources of major unions, they have succumbed to the difficulties of organizing marginal workers and bargaining with intransigent administrators. Moreover, instead of resolving tensions with tenure-track faculty, this strategy simply transfers them to a new arena. Although part-timers control their own group, they still must contend with the hostility of regular faculty. The most vivid example is provided by Nassau Community College, in New York, where part-time and full-time faculty have been organized in two separate AFT locals since the mid-1970s. The situation has been characterized by the leader of the adjunct association as "unrelenting war."[97] The two locals cross each other's picket lines and bargain competitively in contract negotiations.

During the mid-seventies, part-time teachers at the Peralta Community Colleges in Oakland, California attempted to counteract their sense of powerlessness by joining forces with adjuncts on other campuses and creating a statewide association. Founded in 1975, the California Association of Part-time Instructors (CAPI) boasted over four hundred dues-paying members two years later.[98] It lobbied for legislation to raise the pay and status of part-time community college teachers and cosponsored a suit against the Peralta Community College District, seeking tenure and pro-rata pay.[99] Although the association did manage to increase awareness throughout the state about the plight of part-time teachers, it also was short-lived. Some members grew discouraged because the lawsuit benefitted only a few part-timers. Others either changed careers or simply withdrew their energies from the association, having concluded that organizing part-time faculty inevitably was doomed to failure.[100]

Looking Ahead

In short, part-time faculty have secured only minimal benefits through unionization. Despite the diversity of faculty unions, virtually all are dominated by full-time professors and concerned primarily with safeguarding their interests. Most union contracts barely have touched the more pressing concerns of part-timers. Only a handful of independent associations of adjuncts have lasted more than a few years.

Can future organizing efforts be more successful? One possibility is that full-time faculty will begin to cast their lot with part-timers. Many realize that both groups of teachers might be strengthened if they waged a united fight. Moreover, the conditions of part-time employment are being extended throughout the academic profession. Full-timers earn far more than adjuncts, but the real income of tenure-track faculty has declined steadily during the past decade.[101] Another major concern of tenure-track professors is their diminishing autonomy. Although the *Yeshiva* decision[102] denied instructors in that university rights to collective bargaining by defining them as management, most faculty members believe their control over their schools is fading.[103] The job security of tenure-track faculty also is endangered. Since the mid-1970s, tenure has been awarded less frequently. Moreover, both government officials and university administrators have proposed new regulations to make tenure still harder to receive and easier to lose.[104] Particularly ominous are the increasingly common reports of the firing even of tenured professors in institutions throughout the country.[105] Finally, some full-time faculty share the fear of all part-timers that their skills are being debased. As the number of liberal arts majors continues to fall, full-timers in these disciplines are forced to teach outside their fields of specialization. Some are confined entirely to introductory courses. Others are compelled to devise new courses that may appeal to students but that bear little relation to their own areas of expertise. Still others are "retooling" in order to teach in other departments that are expanding.[106] Thus, the conditions of part-timers may be a harbinger of the future for all teachers in higher education. By protesting the inequities of part-time employment, tenure-track faculty may hope to resist the proletarianization of the entire profession. Nevertheless, most remain confident that the continued exploitation of adjuncts helps to insulate them against that process. Viewing retrenchment as inevitable, they seek to divert the brunt of the cuts from themselves onto others, not to resist them altogether.

Another possibility is that part-timers will begin to fight back more effectively. Declining expectations may heighten the potential for organization. Adjuncts who have relinquished the dream of promotion to full-time status may be more willing to invest time and energy in protest. But the contraction of higher education also has raised many of the obstacles to unionization. If deteriorating conditions propel some part-time faculty into political action, they encourage others to leave the field of teaching. The constant threat of layoffs imperils whatever tenuous hold part-timers have on their jobs and thus increases their timidity and docility. Moreover, the principal victims of retrenchment have been the part-timers most disposed to collective bargaining. Because enrollment is shifting from liberal arts to vocational subjects, adjuncts in the former field are the first to go. Finally, the enthusiasm even of dedicated organizers has been blunted by past disappointments; many now are convinced that unionization is not worth the effort. Thus, it is doubtful that part-timers, acting alone, will successfully launch a militant or effective union campaign.

CONCLUSION

Similar problems confronted both part-timers who sought to improve their status through unionization and women faculty who filed sex discrimination grievances to protest their denial of tenure or promotion. The major obstacle was the widespread adherence to the concept of meritocracy. Because many women faculty who had reached the top saw themselves as uniquely deserving, they refrained from rallying around the grievants. Defining part-time faculty as failures, full-timers felt justified in resisting their demands for first-class treatment. Although the two groups of faculty faced a common enemy, they failed to wage a united struggle.

But women grievants and part-time faculty also tended to be ambivalent about collective action. The overriding priority of a significant proportion of the women who pursued grievances was to rectify personal injustices and advance their own careers. True, the majority did hope to change fundamental patterns in the university. To further this goal, they sought the support of women's groups, tried to hire lawyers who would be willing to raise political issues, and publicized their cases widely. Nevertheless, even these women remained attached to the ideal of meritocracy. Displaced academics who worked part-time tended to be more supportive of unionization than other adjuncts, but most were unwilling to abandon individual action for cooperation. A residual hope of joining the academic establishment deterred many from challenging it. Others devoted their energy to finding new careers in other fields.

The very powerlessness both groups were protesting also impeded their efforts. Working in situations that fragmented and marginalized them, part-timers rarely could create permanent associations themselves or wield significant clout in the unions they joined. Sex discrimination grievants were engaged in legal battles against universities that commanded almost limitless resources. Additionally, these women lost control over the grievance process itself. Those who wanted to stress systematic patterns of discrimination were forced to couch their cases in individualistic terms, focusing on their own merits and achievements. University grievance committees restricted their purview to procedural matters and ignored larger issues of racism and sexism. Similarly, government agencies typically limited their investigations to the specifics of the case rather than look for patterns of institutional behavior.

But, though neither group succeeded in altering hierarchical relationships within institutions, both could claim credit for some achievements. A few sex discrimination grievants won back pay or promotions; most demystified university procedures and politicized other women on campus. Part-time faculty at some schools received salary increases, seniority rights, and the institution of grievance procedures. More significantly, both groups gained heightened self-respect and challenged prevailing stereotypes. The seeming willingness of part-timers to submit to demeaning conditions often intensified the perception by other faculty that adjuncts are unworthy of the full rewards of academic careers. By asserting their entitlement to higher status, part-timers refuted this assumption. In addition, they began to view themselves as members of an oppressed group, rather than as individuals who had been singled out for mistreatment. Many women grievants became convinced that they had been evaluated unfairly and, as they eloquently testified, several grew in self-confidence as a result of having fought back.

What possibilities exist for taking more effective action in the future? Above all, it is important for displaced academics to raise their sights and create alliances with other groups who share similar concerns. As a result of cutbacks in government funding, clerical and maintenance staff on campuses have witnessed the erosion of their wages, security, and working conditions. Educational opportunities also are diminishing. When financial aid programs are cut and public colleges raise tuition, fewer working-class children can attend. The proliferation of part-time slots impairs the quality of education of many students who do succeed in enrolling. Moreover, the situation of part-time faculty mirrors that of their students. Many are painfully aware that a B.A. no longer guarantees social mobility. Like hundreds of doctorates in the humanities and social sciences, a high proportion of recent college graduates have been forced to relinquish their aspirations and accept jobs that do not reflect their academic attainments.

Displaced academics could forge still a broader unity. Throughout the public sector, workers have suffered speed-ups, layoffs, and wage cuts. Consumers of social services are affected equally. As many poor and working-class people realize, the government's attack on human services represents a reversal of the victories they have won since the 1930s and 1940s.

The campaign launched by British academic unions against cuts in governmental spending for higher education helps to illuminate the direction all faculty members can take. Shortly after the election of the Conservative government in 1979, it began to reduce the money available for higher education. Because all British academic institutions rely heavily on governmental funding, they were extremely vulnerable to the Tory action. In March 1982 a Government White Paper warned that one out of every six academics would be out of work by 1984-85.[107]

One of the first responses of British academic unions was to form coalitions with unions representing manual and clerical staff. They created both a national organizing committee and joint union committees on individual campuses. Although close collaboration was rare, the unions did speak with a common voice against the cuts. The unions also appealed to the broader community for support, publicizing the impact of the cuts on educational opportunities as well as on jobs and exhorting the public to rally in defense of higher education. Finally, the unions worked closely with the consumers of their services. Many lent support to the campaign of the National Union of Students to resist the reduction in student loans. In turn, students on many campuses spearheaded drives to oppose governmental policies.

The actions of British academics do not provide an ideal model. The major goal of teaching unions was to preserve their members' relative advantages. Partly because the unions were unwilling to question the elitism of the institutions they were seeking to defend, they could not elicit widespread public support. Nevertheless, academics did form alliances with other groups and publicize the effects of cutbacks on all social services.[108]

The difficulties of following this strategy are even more formidable in the United States. This country lacks a strong trade-union tradition, and U.S. academics are far more reluctant to organize than their British counterparts. Moreover, they tend to cling even more tenaciously to professional identity and privileges. Because displaced academics find it unbearably degrading to apply for unemployment compensation, join faculty unions, or even accept entry-level positions in business, they are unlikely to embrace the suggestion that they join forces with students and other occupational groups. Nevertheless, the assault on all human services compels displaced academics to cross barriers of status and class in order to pursue broad-based political goals. Without the assistance of these groups, academics will fail to address the economic and political forces responsible for the collapse of the academic job market. With their support, they can work toward the creation of a society that provides full and rewarding employment for all of its members.

NOTES

1. One-half the women lived in California. Of the remainder two-thirds lived on the East Coast. The interviews were semistructured, lasting on an average of between one and two hours. They were tape recorded, except in the case of four women who voiced objections.

All the women had filed charges of sex discrimination against four-year colleges and universities in which they had held full-time appointments. In addition, two women alleged discrimination on the basis of national origin, one on the basis of religion, and three others on the basis of race.

I declined to evaluate the merit of the women's claims because it would have been impossible to assess the women's qualifications and to compare them to those of their male colleagues.

2. As amended by Executive Order 11375, effective October 1968.
3. Public Law 88-38, 1963.
4. Public Law 92-318, 1972.
5. Public Law 88-352, 1964. In May 1972, the Supreme Court ruled that Title IX applies to employment in education. (Cheryl M. Fields, "Supreme Court Rules Title IX Bars Sex Bias against College Workers as Well as Students," *Chronicle of Higher Education*, 26 May 1981, pp. 1, 14.)
6. Public Law 92-261, 1972; see Barbara Sinclair Deckard, *The Women's Movement: Political, Socioeconomic, and Psychological Issues*, 2nd ed. (New York: Harper & Row, 1979), p. 410; Mary Eastwood, "Legal Protection against Sex Discrimination," in *Working Women*, ed. Shirley

Harkess and Ann Stromberg (Palo Alto, Calif.: Mayfield Publishing Company, 1978), pp. 113-17; Jo Freeman, *The Politics of Women's Liberation* (New York: Longman, 1975), pp. 53, 188; Donald Allen Robinson, "Two Movements in Pursuit of Equal Opportunity," *Signs* 4 (Spring 1979):413-33.

7.   Bernice Sandler, "Sex Discrimination, Educational Institutions, and the Law: A New Issue on Campus," *Journal of Law and Education* 2 (1973):613. By 1974, 1,500 complaints against colleges and universities had been filed with EEOC. (Thomas M. Divine, "Women in the Academy: Sex Discrimination in University Faculty Hiring and Promotion," *Journal of Law and Education* 5 [1976]:434n.)

8.   Ruth B. Cowan, "Legal Barriers to Social Change: The Case of Higher Education," in *Impact ERA: Limitations and Possibilities,* ed. California Commission on the Status of Women (Millbrae, Calif.: Les Femmes, 1976), pp. 158-83; Arlene Kaplan Daniels, "A Survey of Research Concerns on Women's Issues" (Washington, D.C.: Association of American Colleges, 1975), pp. 4, 15; Sara Evans, *Personal Politics: The Roots of Women's Liberation in the Civil Rights Movement and the New Left* (New York: Alfred A. Knopf, 1979), pp. 212-32.

9.   Nancy Gertner, "The Illusion and the Courts," *Radical Teacher,* no. 19 (n.d.), pp. 26-28; Judith P. Vladeck and Margaret M. Young, "Sex Discrimination in Higher Education: It's Not Academic," *Women's Rights Law Reporter* 4 (1978):59-78. There have, however, been recent victories at Muhlenberg College, Keene State College, Georgia Southwestern College, and the University of Minnesota.

10.   Divine, "Women in the Academy," p. 431; Suzanne Howard, *But We Will Persist: A Comparative Research Report on the Status of Women in Academe* (Washington, D.C.: American Association of University Women, 1978).

11.   Studies that discuss the human impact of filing charges of sex discrimination against universities include Joan Abramson, *The Invisible Woman: Discrimination in the Academic Profession* (San Francisco: Jossey-Bass, 1975); Joan Abramson, *Old Boys, New Women* (New York: Praeger, 1979); Athena Theodore, "Academic Women in Protest," unpublished paper, January 1974.

12.   Howard, *But We Will Persist,* p. 8.

13.   Because most part-time faculty are ineligible for promotions and lack access to grievance procedures, the issues raised in this section do not pertain to them. Hence, none of the women grievants were employed solely on a part-time basis.

14.   Howard, *But We Will Persist,* p. 57.

15.   Ibid., p. 22.

16.   A number of studies of grievance behavior have concluded that Americans are inhibited about complaining because of the fear of appearing to have been "taken"—or even acknowledging it to oneself—in a society that prizes autonomy and competence. See, for example, Arthur Best and Alan R. Andreasen, "Consumer Response to Unsatisfactory Purchases: A Survey of Perceiving Defects, Voicing Complaints and Obtaining Redress," *Law and Society Review* 11 (1977):701-42; Barbara A. Curran, *The Legal Needs of the Public* (Chicago: American Bar Foundation, 1977); Carrie Menkel-Meadow, *The American Bar Association Legal Clinic Experiment: An Evaluation of the 19th Street Legal Clinic, Inc.* (Chicago: American Bar Association, 1979). We can assume that these fears are particularly pronounced for victims of discrimination because those who are discriminating invariably explain their behavior in terms of the inadequacies of the victim.

17.   For example, Marianne Githens and Jewel L. Prestage, "Introduction," in *A Portrait of Marginality: The Political Behavior of the American Woman*, ed. Githens and Prestage (New York: David McKay, 1977), pp. 6-9; Carolyn G. Heilbrun, *Reinventing Womanhood* (New York: W. W. Norton, 1979), pp. 37-70; Arlie Russell Hochschild, "Making It: Marginality and Obstacles to Minority Consciousness," in *Women and Success: The Anatomy of Achievement*, ed. Ruth B. Knudsin (New York: William Morrow, 1974), pp. 194-99; Dorothy Richardson Mandelbaum, "Women in Medicine," *Signs* 4 (Autumn 1978):138; Adrienne Rich, "Toward a Woman-Centered University," in *Women and the Power to Change*, ed. Florence Howe (New York: McGraw-Hill, 1975), p. 2; G. Staines, C. Tavris, and T. E. Jayaratne, "The Queen Bee Syndrome," *Psychology Today* 7 (1974):55-60.

18.   It was not possible to explain the women's political orientations by differences in individual background.

19.   See Curran, *Legal Needs*; Austin Sarat, "Studying American Legal Culture: An Assessment of Survey Evidence," *Law and Society Review* 11 (1977):427-88; Adam Podgorecki et al., *Knowledge and Opinion about Law* (London: Martin Robertson, 1973).

20.   See Best and Andreasen, "Consumer Response," pp. 701-42; H. Laurence Ross and Neil O. Littlefield, "Complaint Problem-Solving Mechanism," *Law and Society Review* 12 (1978): 199-216; Sarat, "Studying American," pp. 427-88; Patricia Ward Crowe, "Complainant Reactions to the Massachusetts Commission Against Discrimination," *Law and Society Review* 12 (1978):217-36.

21.   Nuala McGann Drescher, "Affirmative Action: Outlook Not Sunny at SUNY," *Universitas* 1 (1979):10; Florence Howe, "Introduction," in *Women and the Power to Change*, p. 9; Deborah S. Rosenfelt, "Affirmative Action: The Verdict Is Still Out," *Radical Teacher*, no. 11, p. 5.

22.   The exhaustion of internal remedies can be viewed as a means of "cooling out." Although most of the women interviewed for this study went on to file a charge with a government agency, large numbers of women grow discouraged after appealing to campus administrators and grievance committees and decide not to proceed with any further protest. (Cf. Laura Nader, "Complainer Beware," *Psychology Today* 13 [1979]:60.)

23.   In this section, I am discussing only the agencies that enforce Title VII because all of the women relied primarily on this law. Four women also brought charges under Executive Order 11246, which was administered by the Office for Civil Rights, Health, Education and Welfare until 1978. This agency also had authority to enforce Title IX. HEW has been particularly unresponsive to allegations of discrimination and, in 1974, a number of women's groups sued it for failure to enforce antidiscrimination laws. (*Women's Equity Action League et al. v. Califano, F. Ray Marshall, et al.*, United States District Court for the District of Columbia, filed Nov. 26, 1974; see also Abramson, *Invisible Woman*, pp. 169-85; Bernice Sandler, "Backlash in Academe," *Teachers College Record* 76 [February 1975]:407; Women's Equity Action League, "Facts about Women in Higher Education," p. 11.) Since the reorganization of civil rights agencies in 1978, all individual cases filed under the Executive Order are referred automatically to EEOC. Before 1978, the Equal Pay Act was enforced by the Wage and Hour Division of the Employment Standards Administration of the Department of Labor; one interviewee filed a complaint with this agency. In 1978, EEOC was given responsibility for administering the Equal Pay Act; administration of the Executive Order was transferred to the Office of Federal Contract Compliance Programs. What follows is an account of the experience of the women interviewed for this study, not an analysis of the actual operation of state and federal agencies.

24.   Joel F. Handler, "Public Interest Law and Employment Discrimination," in *Public Interest Law*, ed. Burton A. Weisbrod, Joel F. Handler, and Neil K. Komesar (Berkeley: University of California Press, 1978), p. 264; Cynthia Stoddard, *Sex Discrimination in Educational Employment: Legal Alternatives and Strategies* (Holmes Beach, Fla.: Learning Publications, 1981), pp. 14-18.

25.   Abramson, *Invisible Woman*, pp. 186-97; Cowan, "Legal Barriers," p. 171; New Jersey Advisory Commission on the Status of Women, "Report on Sex Discrimination Cases in Higher Education Filed with the New Jersey Division on Civil Rights" (1978); Norma K. Raffel, "The Enforcement of Federal Laws and Regulations, A Report and Recommendations for the U.S. National Commission on the Observance of International Women's Year" (Washington, D.C.: Women's Equity Action

League, 1975); see also U.S. Commission on Civil Rights, *The Federal Civil Rights Enforcement Effort—1974: Volume V: To Eliminate Employment Discrimination*, pp. 500-41.

26. Freeman, *Politics of Women's Liberation*, p. 35.

27. Deckard, *Women's Movement*, p. 411. After 1977, however, the backlog was substantially reduced, and cases were concluded more quickly than before (Barbara L. Schlei and Paul Grossman, *Employment Discrimination Law*, 2nd ed., [Washington, D.C.: Bureau of National Affairs, 1983], p. 938).

28. If EEOC intends to litigate the case, the agency may refuse to issue such a letter.

29. See Theodore, "Academic Women in Protest," p. 35; Leonore Weitzman, "Affirmative Action Plans for Eliminating Sex Discrimination in Academe," in *Academic Women on the Move*, ed. Alice S. Rossi and Ann Calderwood (New York: Russell Sage, 1973), p. 502; but see "Proceedings of the Symposium on Equal Employment Opportunity and Affirmative Action," Wellesley College, Mass., April 28-29, 1977, pp. 20-21; Raffel, "Employment," p. 10; cf. Leon H. Mayhew, *Law and Equal Opportunity: A Study of the Massachusetts Commission against Discrimination* (Cambridge, Mass.: Harvard University Press, 1968), pp. 234-35, 253-56. Legally, the EEOC is empowered to ask only for individual relief.

30. Even after an agreement is reached, many complainants remain dissatisfied. Unlike almost all other agencies, EEOC lacks the power to enforce its conciliation agreements except by initiating litigation.

31. Numerosity is a third requirement for class action suits: the plaintiff must demonstrate that the class she or he is representing is so large that it would be impossible for all members to join the suit. In some instances, academic women have been successful in claiming that they represent all past, present, and future women employees and applicants. (Vladeck and Young, "Sex Discrimination," pp. 68-69.) Nevertheless, the paucity of female professors has occasionally been used as grounds for refusing to certify the class of academic plaintiffs. In other words, women are penalized precisely because most academic departments are composed primarily of white men.

32. See Abramson, *Old Boys, New Women*, p. 91.

33. These conflicts have been analyzed in other substantive areas of legal practice, such as personal injury (Douglas E. Rosenthal, *Lawyer and Client: Who's in Charge?* [New York: Russell Sage Foundation, 1974]) and criminal defense (e.g., Abraham Blumberg, "The Practice of Law as a Confidence Game," *Law and Society Review* 1 [1967]:15. See generally "Plea Bargaining," *Law and Society Review* 13 [Special Issue—1979]).

34. See Rosenthal, *Lawyer and Client*, chap. 4.

35. Gerda Lerner, *The Majority Finds Its Past: Placing Women in History* (New York: Oxford University Press, 1979), p. xxxii.

36. On the importance of collective rather than individual action in litigation, see Marc Galanter, "Why the 'Haves' Come Out Ahead: Speculations on the Limits of Legal Change," *Law and Society Review* 9 (1973):95-160; Stuart A. Scheingold, *The Politics of Rights: Lawyers, Public Policy and Political Change* (New Haven: Yale University Press, 1974); Joel F. Handler, *Social Movements and the Legal System: A Theory of Law Reform and Social Change* (New York: Academic Press, 1978).

37. See Abramson, *Invisible Woman*, pp. 111-25; A. Leffler, D. L. Gillespie, and E. Lerner Ratner, "Academic Feminists and the Women's Movement," *Insurgent Sociologist* 4 (1973):45-56. One striking exception to the isolation of women grievants is the case of Estelle Freedman, who received an enormous outpouring of support from women faculty throughout the country when she challenged an adverse tenure decision at Stanford University in 1982.

38. See Women's Equity Action League, "What WEAL Fund Can Do" (Washington, D.C.: 1979).

39. The coordinator of a local chapter of the National Organization for Women, who had organized a "Title VII Hotline," noted that, of all the women she aided, academics were the most resistant to the strategy of filing charges of sex discrimination with other women: "Each woman wanted to believe that her case was worse than that of anyone else." Similarly, although I informed all of the interviewees that I was speaking to a large number of women in similar situations, many told me that their cases were "unbelievable" or "too incredible for words." Their determination to consider themselves unusual inhibited them from taking group action.

40. Abramson, *Invisible Woman*, pp. 105-8; Theodore, "Academic Women in Protest," p. 24.

41. Retaliation can be the source of a new complaint. One of the women in this study did file such a charge with the EEOC.

42. See, for example, Leigh Biene, Alicia Ostriker, and J. P. Ostriker, "Sex Discrimination in the Universities: Faculty Problems and No Solutions," *Women's Rights Law Reporter* 2 (1975):3-12; Cowan, "Legal Barriers," pp. 173-74.

43. A primary source of dissatisfaction among litigants is the endless delay they must endure, see Curran, *Legal Needs*; and Sarat, "Studying American," pp. 427-88.

44. See also H. Laurence Ross, *Settled Out of Court: The Social Process of Insurance Claims Adjustment* (Chicago: Aldine, 1970).

45. Many public institutions are primarily advantaged because they are not required to pay legal fees out of their institutional budgets. A study conducted in New Jersey discovered that, as a consequence, private colleges and universities settled sex discrimination cases sooner than did public institutions (New Jersey Advisory Commission on the Status of Women, p. 6).

46. Phyllis Z. Boring, "Filing a Faculty Grievance" (Washington, D.C.: Women's Equity Action League, 1978), p. 4.

47. The extraordinary difficulty of isolating the impact of law upon social change is revealed in many studies; see, for example, Theodore Becker and Malcolm Feeley, eds., *The Impact of Supreme Court Decisions*, 2nd ed. (New York: Oxford University Press, 1973); Stephen Wasby, *The Impact of the United States Supreme Court: Some Perspectives* (Homewood, Ill.: Dorsey Press, 1970).

48. However, because reforms occurred only as a by-product of legal action, they were often used to reinforce the belief that universities are dedicated to eradicating inequities. It is easy to understand why university officials would deny a causal relationship between protest and reform. By demonstrating that improvements in the status of women result solely from their own long-standing commitment to equal opportunity, officials can prove that both pressure from outside groups and intervention from the government are unnecessary. Even those women who gain indirectly from a Title VII case have a stake in ignoring the impact of the litigation on their campuses and attributing their promotions or salary increases to their individual merit and achievements. Thus, many groups on campus are intent on denying the impact of the sex discrimination suit. As long as the role of legal action remains invisible, however, the academic process is legitimized, and future protest is discouraged.

49. The classic statement of this position is Erik Olin Wright, "Intellectuals and the Class Structure of Capitalist Society," in *Between Labor and Capital*, ed. Pat Walker (Boston: South End Press, 1979), pp. 191-212.

50. See Dennis Chamot, "Professional Employees Turn to Unions," *Harvard Business Review* 54 (May-June 1976):119-27; Patrick Lacefield, "As Business of Health Grows, Doctors Start to Talk Union," *In These Times*, 9-15 April 1980, p. 19.

51. Verne A. Stadtman, *Academic Adaptations: Higher Education Prepares for the 1980s and 1990s* (San Francisco: Jossey-Bass, 1980), p. 69.

52. Lewis C. Solmon, Laura Kent, Nancy L. Ochsner, and Margo-Lea Hurwicz, *Underemployed Ph.D.'s* (Lexington, Mass.: Lexington, 1981), p. 52.

53. See Jack Magarrell, "Decline in Faculty Morale Laid to Government Role, Not Salary," *Chronicle of Higher Education*, 10 November 1982, p. 28.

54. Stadtman, *Academic Adaptations*, p. 69.

55. Alice Kessler-Harris has made a similar point about women in trade unions. ("'Where Are the Organized Women Workers?'" in *A Heritage of Her Own: Toward a New Social History of American Women*, ed. Nancy F. Cott and Elizabeth H. Pleck [New York: Simon and Schuster, 1979], pp. 343-66.)

56. See David W. Leslie, "Current Perspectives on Part-Time Faculty," *Research Currents*, November 1978, p. 4.

57. "Report of the N.E.A. Committee on Substitute, Part-Time and Paraprofessional Personnel" (Washington, D.C.: National Education Association, 1976), p. 106.

58. Quoted in Jack Magarrell, "Increasing Use of Part-Timers Condemned by Teachers' Union," *Chronicle of Higher Education*, 16 September 1977, p. 4.

59. In about half of all institutions, the division or department chairperson is responsible for hiring part-time teachers. (David W. Leslie, Samuel E. Kellams, and G. Manny Gunne, *Part-Time Faculty in American Higher Education* [New York: Praeger, 1982], p. 74.)

60. See Paul Lauter, "A Scandalous Misuse of Faculty," *Universitas* 1 (December 1978):12-15.

61. See Edna Bonacich, "Advanced Capitalism and Black/White Race Relations in the United States: A Split Labor Market Interpretation," *American Sociological Review* 41 (February 1976):34-51.

62. Elementary and secondary school teachers have expressed similar attitudes toward substitutes. (See *Ms.*, September 1981, p. 20.) For conflicts between part-time and full-time workers in the work force at large, see Jerry Flint, "Growing Part-Time Work Force Has Major Impact on Economy," *New York Times*, 12 April 1977, p. 56.

63. The issue of security is further complicated at many community colleges where full-time faculty teach one or two courses at part-time salary in addition to their full course loads. Although most part-timers argue that they should be assigned classes first, "overloading" instructors consider themselves entitled to priority consideration. Hence, they have additional impetus for resisting the efforts of adjuncts to gain security of employment.

64. "NEA Resolutions, 1981" (obtained from National Education Association, Washington, D.C.); American Federation of Teachers Advisory Commission on Higher Education, *Statement on Part-Time Employment* (Washington, D.C.: American Federation of Teachers, accepted by AFT Executive Council, April 7, 1979).

65. Unless otherwise noted, information about UPC is based on my own experiences as a member of the UPC Committee on Lecturers, 1980-82.

66. In 1980, the name was changed to Committee on Lecturers; the committee represented the interests of full-time temporary faculty as well as those of part-timers.

67. *Part-Time/Temporary Faculty Handbook: Surviving in the CSUC System* revised ed., (Sacramento: United Professors of California, 1981).

68. The UPC brief filed before the PERB Hearing Officer Stuart Wilson in the PERB Unit Determination Hearings for the Professional Employees of the California State University and Colleges, 1980.

69. According to a poll conducted by Louis Harris and Associates for UPC in March 1981, the number of nontenure-track faculty who supported UPC was almost six times as great as the number who favored the Congress of Faculty Associations, the opposing union. (Information from State Office, UPC.)

70. Although all temporary teachers constituted almost half of the teaching staff in CSUC in 1981, they accounted for only 20 percent of the union membership. (Figures obtained from the State Office, UPC.)

71. Ronald B. Head and David W. Leslie, "Bargaining Unit Status of Part-Time Faculty," *Journal of Law and Education* 8 (July 1979):361-62.

72. C. W. Post Center, 189 NLRB No. 79 (1971).

73. University of New Haven, 190 NLRB No. 102 (1971).

74. NYU 205 NLRB No. 16 (1973).

75. See, for example, Fairleigh Dickinson University, 205 NLRB No. 101 (1973); Point Park College, 209 NLRB No. 152 (1974); University of Miami, 213 NLRB No. 64 (1974); University of San Francisco, 207 NLRB No. 15 (1973); University of Vermont, 223 NLRB No. 46 (1976); Yeshiva University, 221 NLRB No. 169 (1975).

76. Faculty unions and administrations also have taken inconsistent positions on the issue of unit determination. The majority of administrations have sought broader, most inclusive units. (For example, University of Detroit, 193 NLRB No. 95 [1971]; University of New Haven, 190 NLRB No. 102 [1971]; University of San Francisco, 207 NLRB No. 15 [1973].) Others have staunchly resisted the inclusion of part-time faculty in full-time bargaining units. (For example, C. W. Post, 189 NLRB No. 79 [1971]; Los Rios Community College [1 PERB 185].) After the faculty at the University of Massachusetts voted in favor of unionization, the Board of Trustees refused to negotiate, partly because it disagreed with the ruling of the Massachusetts State Labor Relations Commission including in the bargaining unit those part-time faculty who taught less than half time. (Sheridan Care, "Reasons Why Faculty Members Accept or Reject

Unions in Higher Education: The University of Massachusetts Experience," *Journal of Law and Education* 7 [January 1978]:85.)

There is also no uniformity in the positions held by unions. Some have urged that part-timers be included in the bargaining unit. (For example, C. W. Post, 189 NLRB No. 79 [1971]; Fordham University, 193 NLRB No. 23 [1971].) Others, however, have taken the position that the appropriate unit should include only tenure-track faculty. (For example, University of Detroit, 193 NLRB No. 95 [1971]; University of New Haven, 190 NLRB No. 102 [1971].) In institutions where part-timers constitute over half of the faculty, full-time faculty often express fears that, should part-timers be included in the unit, they will dominate the negotiations. (See Head and Leslie, "Bargaining Unit Status," pp. 363, 373; see also Kenneth Kahn, "The NLRB and Higher Education: The Failure of Policymaking through Adjudication," *UCLA Law Review* 21 [1973]:111-12.

77.   David W. Leslie, "Part-Time Faculty in Unionized Colleges and Universities." Paper presented at the Annual Meeting of the National Center for the Study of Collective Bargaining in Higher Education, New York, April 1979, p. 5.

78.   1 *Public Employee Reporter for California* 185 (1977).

79.   *In the Matter of the Board of Trustees of University of Massachusetts*, Cases No. SCR 2079, SCR 2082, Labor Relations Commission, Commonwealth of Massachusetts (October 15, 1976).

80.   *In the Matter of Federation of Technical College Teachers and Board of Trustees of Connecticut State Technical Colleges*, Cases No. SEPP-3846, SPP-3887, SPP-3929; Decision No. 1567 (August 23, 1977).

81.   *In the Matter of Unit Determination for Employees of the California State University and Colleges Pursuant to Chapter 744 of the Statutes of 1978* (Higher Education Employer-Employee Relations Act), Cases No. LA-RR-1001, LA-RR-1001-1, LA-RR-1001-2, LA-RR-1001-3, LA-RR-1002, LA-PC-1002, LA-IP-2, PERB Decision No. 173-H (September 22, 1981). Although the primary issue at stake has been the similarity between the working conditions of the two segments of the faculty, both the NLRB and state boards have been forced to consider the issues debated at length about part-time faculty. Are most of them "moonlighters" or unemployed academics? Are they transient employees, or do they have ongoing interests in the affairs of the institutions at which they teach? A dissenting opinion in the case involving NYU in 1973 pointed out that some part-time faculty taught at that institution longer than did some of their full-time counterparts; all part-timers were compelled to devote many hours to class preparation. (205 NLRB No. 16.) Similarly, the brief of the United Professors of California, seeking to include part-time and full-time faculty in a single bargaining unit in CSUC, noted the similarity between the two segments of the faculty in

terms of educational background and professional aspirations. (UPC brief.) By contrast, the union that supported splitting the units asserted that the part-time faculty "are not necessarily University calibre." (Post-Hearing Brief on Behalf of the Congress of Faculty Associations, In the Matter of United Professors of California, Congress of Faculty Associations and California State University and Colleges, California Public Employment Relations Board, Case No. LA-RR-1001-1 [October 11, 1980], p. 93; see also Joseph N. Hankin, "Unit Determination: Basic Criteria in Federal and State Jurisdictions, Trends in Exclusion of Supervisory and Managerial Personnel, Faculty in Professional Schools, Multi-Campus Units, Support Professionals, Part-Time Personnel and Others," [paper delivered at the Annual Meeting of the National Center for the Study of Collective Bargaining in Higher Education, April 23, 1979], p. 10.)

82. Interview with Fay Beauchamp, Sherrie Ernst, and Carol Stein, members of the Faculty Federation of the Community College of Philadelphia, AFT Local 2026, Philadelphia, June 1981.

83. *On Campus*, February 1982, p. 3; interview with Beauchamp, Ernst, and Stein; Faculty Federation of the Community College of Philadelphia, "Newsletter," 22 July 1981; Linda A. Rabben, "On Strike at an Academic Sweatshop," *Radical Teacher* no. 20 (n.d.), pp. 30-31.

84. Interview with Carol Stein, June 1983.

85. Faculty Federation of the Community College of Philadelphia, "Newsletter," 13 June 1982.

86. Interview with Stein.

87. Ibid.

88. Ibid.

89. David W. Leslie and D. Jane Ikenberry, "Collective Bargaining and Part-Time Faculty: Contract Content," *The Journal of the College and University Personnel Association* 30 (Fall 1979):18-26.

90. Ibid., p. 24.

91. "Read On," Newsletter of AFT College Guild, 18 April 1977.

92. Figures obtained from the Office of the Los Angeles Community College District.

93. Unless otherwise noted, information about unionization in the Los Angeles Community College District is based on interviews with Pat Vines, Los Angeles, October 1981 and Alice Clement, Los Angeles, November 1981. Neither is responsible for the interpretation of the events in the text.

94. Campaign literature distributed by the AFT College Guild and the Los Angeles Classroom Teachers Association, 1977.

95. At this rate, one part-time teacher wryly noted, parity pay would not be achieved until the year 2050.

96. Adjunct associations that have negotiated their own contracts include the Cornell University Adjunct Association, representing part-timers at the New York City Branch of Cornell's School of Industrial and Labor Relations (*On Campus*, April 1982, p. 9), the Nassau Community College Adjunct Association (interview with John T. Meehan, president of the Nassau Community College Adjunct Association, New York, June 1981), Lane Community College Part-Time Teacher Association (*NEA Advocate*, September 1981, p. 6), and the English Language Institute Faculty Association of American University (Suzanne Perry, "A New Union Presses Its Case," *Chronicle of Higher Education*, 3 November 1982, p. 27).

97. Interview with Meehan.

98. Interview with Jeff Kerwin, former president of CAPI, December 1981.

99. Peralta Federation of Teachers, Local 1603 v. Peralta Community College District (1977). Although the suit was filed in the name of the AFT local at the Peralta Community Colleges, part-timers assumed they could retain control over it only if they raised half the money; CAPI did fulfill this goal. (Interview with Kerwin.)

100. Interview with Kerwin. Only 26 part-time faculty members won back pay and tenure. (*The California Teacher* October/November 1980, p. 3.)

101. In real dollars, faculty compensation declined 19 percent during the 1970s. (W. John Minter and Howard R. Brown, "Despite Economic Ills, Colleges Weathered the 70's with Larger Enrollments and Stronger Programs," *Chronicle of Higher Education*, 12 May 1982, p. 5.

102. *National Labor Relations Board v. Yeshiva University*, 444 U.S. 672 (1980).

103. According to a study conducted by the Institute of Higher Education at Teachers College, Columbia University, the proportion of faculty members who believed they shared authority with administrators fell from 64 percent in 1970 to 44 percent in 1980. (Magarrell, "Faculty Morale," p. 28.) A major issue in the faculty strike of 1979-80 at Boston University was the attempt by the administration to take responsibility for assigning textbooks. ("Radical Historians Newsletter," no. 29, May 1979, p. 1; "Radical Historians Newsletter," no. 31, February 1980, p. 1.) As we have seen, the proliferation of part-time slots also reduces faculty autonomy.

104. Charles S. Farrell, "Ill Will Remains at U. of Nevada After Tenure Truce," *Chronicle of Higher Education*, 15 June 1983, p. 5; Malcolm S. Scully, "Colleges, States Weigh Rules to Make Tenure Harder to Get, Easier to Lose, *Chronicle of Higher Education*, 8 December 1982, p. 1.

105. During the past few years, tenured professors have received layoff notices at the following institutions: Temple University, Michigan State University, the University of Michigan, the University of Washington, the University of Idaho, Lewis-Clark State College, Sonoma State University. (Jack Magarrell, "Budget Cuts in Some States Arouse Fears of New Layoffs of Professors," *Chronicle of Higher Education*, September 1981, pp. 1, 10, 11; Barry Mitzman, "Financial Emergency at Washington State Follows Similar Crisis at U. of Washington," *Chronicle of Higher Education*, 3 October 1981, p. 3; Malcolm G. Scully, "Cutting Back at Temple: The Hard Lessons of Retrenchment," *Chronicle of Higher Education*, 15 October 1979, p. 3; William Trombley, "Sonoma State to Lay Off Ten Percent of Its Tenured Faculty," *Los Angeles Times*, 6 May 1982, pp. 1, 22; Beverly Watkins, "Michigan States' Budget Cut $13.5 Million," *Chronicle of Higher Education*, 13 April 1981, p. 1.)

106. According to a contract negotiated by the Professional Staff Congress, CUNY faculty in departments threatened by retrenchment can be retrained in order to teach in departments that are likely to grow. (*On Campus*, April 1982, p. 3.)

107. *The Government's Expenditure Plans, 1982-83 to 1984-85* Cmnd. 8494 II (London: HMSO, 1982), p. 40.

108. Emily K. Abel, "The Union Campaign against Cutbacks in Higher Education in Britain," *Insurgent Sociologist* (forthcoming).

A NOTE ON METHODOLOGY

The interviews were tape recorded and semistructured, lasting between one and four hours. Although I approached the interviews with tentative hypotheses, the primary purpose was to generate hypotheses that could be useful for further study, not to test preexisting ones. Thus, most of the generalizations recorded in the book emerged from the interviews themselves.

Displaced academics were defined as Ph.D. recipients and Ph.D. candidates who either were unable to secure tenure-track academic appointments or had been fired from such positions at the stage of tenure or pretenure reviews. The demarcation between graduate students and professional academics is often indistinct; many graduate students begin their professional careers before finishing their dissertations. Thus, I interviewed doctoral candidates who had completed enough of their theses to be encouraged by their advisers to enter the job market and who were devoting most of their time to writing their dissertations. I did not include in the sample any people who had discontinued work on their theses or were still at an early stage in writing them.

The interviewees were located in various ways. The names of the great majority were referred by other academics or previous respondents. Some were selected from a list of Ph.D.s in a retraining program for doctorates and others from newspaper articles about unemployed academics. Six of the interviews were conducted at academic conferences.

Only one of the displaced academics whom I contacted refused to be interviewed. Most were happy to have an opportunity to discuss their employment situations. Many went out of their way to meet at hours or places that were convenient to me and several commented after the interview that it had enabled them to reflect on issues that were critical to their lives.

Academic labor markets seldom are restricted to one locale, and the search for a job often extends over national areas. Geographical diversity among respondents was achieved in two ways. First, respondents were selected and interviewed at various geographical locations in the United States. Second, many of those interviewed in one area had attended graduate school or taught in another.

As noted in the text, slightly over half the interviewees were women. In this respect, the members of the sample matched the population of displaced academics as a whole. (See explanation in the Introduction.) In general, however, it was impossible to establish the population of displaced academics in advance in order to pick a random sample. Although surveys have been conducted of Ph.D. recipients and of faculty members, none has attempted to define the demographic characteristics of academics who fail to secure regular faculty appointments. (My own survey of faculty with temporary academic jobs, reported in Chapter 3, does permit us to compare the members of the sample who taught on a temporary basis with other marginal academics.)

The ages of the respondents ranged from 27 to 50; the median age was 36. Twenty-three were married. All but two were white. Eleven either reported that they came from working-class backgrounds or noted that neither parent had attended college; the rest identified their family backgrounds as middle class. Two of the interviewees had attended Oxford and Cambridge; all but three of the remaining interviewees had attended universities defined by *The Gourman Report* as having the leading graduate programs in their fields.[1]

The interviewees were asked to discuss subjects that often were painful to them, and some spoke more freely than others. Hence, I had to rely on the respondents who were more forthcoming. I returned to reinterview those who had more to say or whose situations had changed since the first interview.

NOTE

1. Jack Gourman, *The Gourman Report: A Rating of Graduate and Professional Programs in American and International Universities* (Los Angeles: National Education Standards, 1981).

INDEX

ABOUT THE AUTHOR

EMILY K. ABEL received a Ph.D. in history from the University of London in 1969, and she has taught part-time at both two- and four-year institutions in the fields of history and women's studies. Her writings have appeared in *Feminist Studies, Insurgent Sociologist, Social Service Review, Socialist Review,* and *Teachers College Record.* She is the coeditor of *The Signs Reader: Women, Gender and Scholarship* (University of Chicago Press, 1983).

Like many of the displaced academics she interviewed, she recently has changed fields. She will receive a Master's Degree in Public Health from UCLA in June 1984.